D1519542

MENACHEM BEGIN
His Life and Legacy

By the same author:

In English:
Agnon: Encounter in Buczacz (New York: 1964)
The Festival of Joy (New York: 1965)
The Glory of the Jewish Holidays (New York: 1968)
History of a Movement and a Man (New York: 1969)
United Nations: Perfidy and Perversion (New York: 1982)

In Hebrew:
Yoman Ghetto Varsha (Tel Aviv: 1946)
Yeshivot b'Mizrach Europa (New York: 1960)
Ishim Shehikarti (Jerusalem: 1962)
Chazon Ish (New York: 1962)

In Yiddish:
Togbuch fun Warshaver Ghetto (Buenos Aires: 1947)
Di Sedra fun der Woch (New York: 1966)
Tsu der Geschichte fun der Warshaver Kehilla (New York: 1967)

In Polish:
The Oath According to Jewish Law (Warsaw: 1937)
Judaic Studies and Scholarship in Poland (Warsaw: 1937)
Answer and Rebuke to Anti-Semitic Attacks
   by Rev. Stanislaw Trzeciak (Warsaw: 1937)
Religious Revival of Jewish Women: Beth Jacob and Sara
   Shenirer (Lodz: 1938)
Taxes of the Jewish Community in Warsaw (Warsaw: 1938)
History of the Jews in Palestine (Warsaw: 1938)
The Jewish Religious School System (Warsaw: 1938)
The Dream of a Jewish State (Warsaw: 1939)
The Abolishment of the Kahal in Warsaw, 1820-1822 (Warsaw: 1939)

MENACHEM BEGIN
His Life and Legacy

by
Hillel Seidman
with
Mordecai Schreiber

Shengold Publishers, Inc.
New York

ISBN 0-88400-142-3
Library of Congress Catalog Card Number: 90-53262
Copyright © 1990 by Hillel Seidman

Published by Shengold Publishers, Inc.
New York, N.Y.

Printed in the United States of America

Contents

Acknowledgments

Heartiest thanks to Mr. Mordecai Schreiber. His dedicated work for this book started with his role as editor, and soon became an inspiration. He became a partner in fulfilling the task the book strives to achieve: to set the record on Menachem Begin straight. It became clear to me that for him, as for me, it was a labor of love. We were both motivated by the same goal, to tell the truth about the commander of the Irgun Tzvai Leumi, about his ideas and struggles which eventually, and inevitably, resulted in the birth of the Jewish state. Both of us have been motivated by the desire to serve the cause of truth, and to see to it that people do not fall prey to distortions and falsifications. For this, and for the cherished friendship which resulted, my deep gratitude.

Mr. Shragai Cohen, a longtime friend and admirer of Menachem Begin, merits special gratitude for his decisive, efficient help at every stage of this project. He was actively and efficiently instrumental in bringing this project to completion.

Rabbi Richard Yellin, spiritual leader of Congregation Mishkan Tefila of Chestnut Hill, Massachusetts was a most important supporter of the project. He was especially instrumental in bringing in Mr. and Mrs. Michael Cykier who made possible the publication.

Mr. Moshe Sheinbaum, the publisher, took a constant personal interest in all the phases of our work. He deserves cordial thanks for bringing together Mr. Schreiber and myself in this common endeavor.

Special heartiest thanks to Yechiel Kadishai, the closest man to Menachem Begin, besides the family, who accorded me invaluable guidance and advice, and who was, and is, my valuable link to the great leader. His wisdom and wit, his enormous knowledge and penetrating understanding, his encouragement and help made this book a reality.

My gratitude to the publisher–editor of the Jewish Press, Rabbi Sholom Klass for permission to reprint my articles that appeared in his paper.

My heart overflows with gratitude to my dearest, my wife Sara, and our family: Rabbi Meyer and Dr. Ruchama Fund, Dov S. and Miriam Schechter, Avraham-Moshe and Chasia Seidman, and Naomi Seidman. Also Gad and Naama Frenkel; and our grandchildren. They are the Sabbath of my life.

— H. S.

DEDICATION

Publication Made Possible by
Helen and Michael Cyker
In Memory of
SOPHIA CYKER
סאסיל בת מיכאל
LOUIS CYKER
אריה ליב בן משה
Sainted Mother and Father of
Helen and Michael Cyker
Jenny and Meyer Cyker

בחייהם ובמותם לא נפרדו
In life and in eternity
they were never parted
—2 Samuel 1:23

Introduction

One of the greatest surprises of recent times took place in late 1977, when the newly-elected prime minister of Israel, who for years had been described as an uncompromising ultranationalist fanatic whose main goal in life was to expand by war the borders of Israel, entered upon peace negotiations with Israel's most powerful enemy, Egypt, and paid an enormous price for peace. He subsequently relinquished Israel's largest territorial gain, namely, the Sinai Peninsula, in return for a peace treaty.

The signing of the Israeli-Egyptian peace treaty focused world attention on Menachem Begin, and resulted in more than a few biographies of the Israeli prime minister. Their authors—mainly journalists and political scientists—have approached their subject as one would approach the writing of a life of any world figure who has captured the world's attention and created a need for a book that tells the readers who the person is, where he or she came from, important accomplishments, and so on, not to mention trivial details about the celebrity, which are always of interest to the reader who is curious about the human face behind the public mask.

Most of those biographies of Begin are superficial or deliberately biased. Some are vicious slanders, full of distortions, falsifications, and defamation. Almost all of them are misleading. None seems to penetrate the many layers of misunderstanding and long-standing fabrications that have covered the person and work of Menachem Begin. Hence the need for this book.

Rather than repeat the dates and events of Menachem Begin's life, I have drawn upon decades of my own observation of his life and work, and of our close friendship, to present a personal account of Begin the man and the leader, and offer some evaluation of his historical role in the creation and development of the State of Israel.

Begin has made decisive and enduring contributions to our people in many ways and in different areas. Not only did he change the course of history, he also changed the course of our lives. The stamp of his personality and his life's work is indelibly imprinted on our generation, and will affect generations to come. We have only begun to appreciate the far-reaching consequences of his actions, and as time goes on their impact will be made more apparent.

From the day the young Menachem Begin challenged his fellow-Jews to break with Jewish passivity and submission and start the fight for Jewish liberation, this bespectacled, modest man became one of the most controversial leaders in the Jewish world. This was quite natural, given Begin's revolutionary approach to political reality and his rebellion against the ruling establishment. What seems less than natural is the fact that for many years Begin has been the butt of a vicious, unbridled campaign of defamation on the part of his political opponents. Even today, over fifty years later, the old retired prime minister of Israel is being maligned by an assortment of writers in Israel, the United States, and elsewhere, who refuse to look objectively at the record of contemporary history. They prefer to cling to half-truths and deliberate distortions as the defamation campaign continues, fed by old animosities and new misinterpretations.

Begin needs no apologies. His contribution to his people as freedom fighter and statesman is a matter of historical record. However, too many things have been said and written about him, and, no doubt, will be said and written in the future, which threatens to tarnish the image of this unique Jewish leader, who, in my opinion and in the opinion of others ranks as one of the great statesmen of the twentieth century. The purpose of this book, is to set the record straight.

What qualifies me to undertake such a task?

I have known Menachem Begin throughout my long journalistic, scholarly, and political career. Back in pre-World War Two Poland, I was active in the cultural and political life of the Jewish community of Warsaw, the largest Jewish community in Europe at that time, and the world center of Jewish life. While I did not belong to Begin's party, the Revisionist Zionists, or to its youth organization, Betar, which he headed in Poland—I was a member of Agudath Israel—I became friendly with some of the local Revisionist leaders, whose ideas and personal commitment I learned to respect and appreciate. I would mention especially

Yosef Klarman, Isaac Remba, Dr. Yosef Wdowinsky, N. Rothman and their associates and comrades.

When Begin's mentor, Ze'ev Jabotinsky, founder of the Zionist Revisionist party, argued in 1938 that Jewish life in Poland and in the rest of Europe was in grave danger, and proposed his plan of evacuating the Jews from Poland for settlement in Palestine, all the other Jewish parties denounced him as an alarmist and rejected his plan. I was one of the few outside his party who defended his ideas at that time. I did it on the pages of Agudath Israel's Yiddish-language daily, *Dos Yiddishe Togblatt.*

When the Germans occupied Warsaw in 1939, Begin fled to Vilna, where he was arrested by the Soviets and spent a year in a Soviet prison (he wrote about it in his book *White Nights*). He was released and allowed to join the Polish Army, and subsequently found his way to Palestine.

On September 1, 1945, I was freed from a German internment camp in Vittel (Vosges), France, where, as holder of a Paraguayan passport, I had been kept prisoner by the Germans to be exchanged for their nationals who had been imprisoned in South America. Following World War II, the indescribably cruel massacres committed by the German people against the Jews were becoming known to the world in all their enormity—the worst atrocities ever committed by man. As my sorely afflicted soul was grieving for the martyred millions, I was sure that our world was about to undergo a total transformation. I was sure that after we saw what the Germans did to us we would be completely changed in our way of thinking, acting, and living. I was sure that nothing was going to be the same. The change would be as deep as the abyss that had swallowed up our people throughout Europe.

In my despair following the destruction of my world, the world in which I had grown up and lived, and in which I interacted with the top echelons of Jewish leadership, I was expecting something that would affect every aspect of Jewish life, thought and action.

And yet I had to face an incomprehensible phenomenon which I completely failed to come to terms with. Nothing had changed! Nothing, that is, except for a "small" detail: Entire Jewish communities, some over a thousand years old, had disappeared, massacred by the Germans.

The few survivors, including their leaders who did not lead, behaved in quite the same way they did before the catastrophe. The same speeches and articles, the same debates and controversies, the same frivolous frictions and petty rivalries as in the pre-war era. If I were to sum up the situation that followed the worst defeat that befell a nation in human history, I would have to say—business as usual.

All the fibers of my tormented being cried out against this intolerable absurdity. I was waiting for something extraordinary to happen, something never heard or seen before. And yet, nothing of this sort happened.

Suddenly, out of these dark clouds, out of the abyss that had swallowed our people in Europe, a ray of light broke through: The *Irgun Tzvai Leumi*, the Jewish fighting organization in Palestine, under the command of a man named Menachem Begin, IZL had declared a revolt!

It was not only a revolt against the evil policies of Ernest Bevin, Great Britain's foreign minister, one of the most brutal and vulgar leaders of the post-war era, whose objective was to make Hitler's "Final Solution"—final. It was a revolt against all the inertia, complacency and paralysis that reigned in the Zionist and other establishments, and in the institutions of the *Yishuv* in the land of Israel.

It was this revolt that, after three years of heroic fighting, forced the British out of Palestine and resulted in the birth of the first independent Jewish state in two millennia.

I recall how the word about the revolt first reached me in a rather strange and peculiar way. Rabbinical bodies at the time were denouncing Begin and his IZL rebels, using biblical quotations to describe their "un-Jewish" actions. To me those denunciations sounded like hymns of praise to the great heroes of Israel. I was living in France at the time, and subsequently in the United States, and, to my regret, I could not join those fighting brave men in the land of Israel. But I did all I could to help them. My pen was put at their service. In Paris I also helped obtain legal documents for them, making use of my good connections with the authorities. I was in close touch with Dr. Yaakov Rubin, an IZL activist and later the editor of the *Herut* newspaper (whose correspondent I became in the U.S.); Dr. Paul Riebenfeld, who contacted me in London; and Shmuel Katz, the editor of the London Revisionist weekly *The Jewish Stand-*

ard, in which I resumed my journalist work as early as December 1945.

When the state came into being I met Begin for the first time, quite by accident. The editor of the New York Yiddish daily *Der Tog*, Mordecai Dantzis, a Revisionist, was visiting Israel, and a welcome reception in his honor was given by the Herut party at the Savoy Hotel in Tel Aviv. As the correspondent for *Der Tog*, I was invited by Dantzis to the reception. Begin showed up. I was not introduced to him, and I frankly doubted he knew of my existence, since my activities in France, England, and the United States on behalf of the IZL were "illegal" and, of course, clandestine.

I sat at a corner, far from Begin, who presided at the head of the table. To my surprise, as he was giving a speech welcoming the guest of honor, he suddenly stopped, pointed at me, and said: "You see the man sitting at corner of the table? He is an unassuming, modest person. He stood by our side during our days in the underground and did everything he could to help us. This is Dr. Hillel Seidman."

Later, in 1949, when my wife came to Israel and we were invited for the first time to Begin's home, Sara was greatly surprised by the kind of person she saw. She had read about the "tough, brutal, dangerous terrorist" who had savagely fought the British Empire, and here she saw an extremely polite, likable gentleman, with a chivalrous manner, who received us with genuine warmth and friendship. How different he was from the way so many people had pictured him!

During 1950 and 1951 I served as an official in the Israeli government's Ministry of Social Welfare. I had been living in New York, and I was invited to undertake that position by Israel's first Minister of Social Welfare, Rabbi Yitzhak Meir Levin, who before the war was the president of Agudath Israel in Poland while I served as its political secretary.

Despite the fact that I was serving under Prime Minister David Ben-Gurion, Begin's long-time bitter adversary, I remained an ardent adherent and admirer of Begin. This "double loyalty" was no secret. I was also the correspondent of the New York Yiddish daily *Der Tog* at that time, and editor of the organ of Agudath Israel, *Hamodia*. How I managed to perform all those conflicting and unrelated tasks at one and the same time is another story. Suffice it to mention here that in

1951 Begin, as opposition leader in the Knesset, the Israeli parliament, entered into a very serious conflict with the Ben-Gurion government over the question of reparations from the West German government. While I was serving the government which denounced Begin as dangerous to the state and as an enemy of democracy, who harbored "fascist designs" to overthrow the government, I published articles in *Der Tog* strongly defending Begin and supporting his position. (See his letter to me on these articles.)

Back in New York after my short service as a government official in Israel, I remained a close adherent of Begin, and I continued to publish articles in Hebrew, Yiddish and English, both in the United States and Israel, explaining Begin's ideas and actions first as opposition leader, later as member of the Unity Government prior to and following the Six Day War, and eventually as prime minister. During all those years we continued to correspond, our families became close, and it became my personal custom to call Begin on the eve of every holiday and on Israeli historical dates.

Now that Begin has retired from political life, I still call him regularly before every holiday and I maintain a correspondence with him. I continue, of course, to write articles about his ideas, policies, and accomplishments which outlast his retirement.

The purpose of this book is to attempt to draw an accurate and true picture of Begin, based on my personal friendship with him and on my years of study and observation of this great leader from a historical perspective. It is important that Begin's contribution to Jewish life be realistically and accurately assessed and properly understood.

• • •

Objectivity is a qualification appreciated in a writer who depicts a person of public interest. But I cannot say that I am objective on the subject of Menachem Begin. Very few who have written about him are. Begin evokes either ardent admiration or strong antagonism. Everyone who approaches him is forced to take a stand.

As for myself—how can I be objective about a man who has deeply influenced my way of thinking and living—as he has influenced so many, particularly, survivors of the German mass-murder of our people?

If the reader detects in this work some noble feelings, some deep emotions, some sublime elevation—it is because these, and much more, radiated from the subject of this book. His personality shone onto the people who were privileged to be in his orbit.

When I began to write about Begin, I was advised to recount my personal relations with him. That wasn't easy for me. I am used to keeping my person in the background of the events that I describe.

But on the other hand, I do not wish to disregard the opinion of sensitive people familiar with the subject I am writing about.

I decided to follow the path of S. J. Agnon, with whom I had spent some time, and to whose talks I had listened carefully. Speaking about a subject of his, Yoseph Chaim Brenner, the great Hebrew writer, Agnon remarked:

"It would be good to tell about Brenner and not push myself into the middle of things. However, this is the habit of all the authors of memoirs, and I am not innocent of this. Thus, whenever possible, I'll skip myself; but where it is impossible, it is impossible." (*Me on Myself*, by S.J. Agnon, Schocken Publications, Jerusalem, 1976, p. 112.)

Chapter One

What Brought Me
to Menachem Begin?

I studied a great deal, both Judaic studies and secular. But the "university" that taught me most was my experience in the ghetto and camp under the Germans. In these five years, I learned more than all the years until then—and since.

Many of my notions, ideas, opinions and values were influenced by this experience. My entire thinking was transformed and shaped anew.

I was and am deeply convinced that after what happened to us—the most horrendous and cruel defeat that befell any people in the history of mankind—nothing remained the same. Nothing should remain the same.

And nothing in the Jewish people, in Jewish history, was as different, so dissimilar—in fact, so unique— as Menachem Begin's IZL revolt.

Rabbinical bodies—the Chief Rabbinate of Palestine and its most bitter antagonist, the Rabbinate of Neturei Karta, Agudath Israel and others—were right when, in their condemnations in rare unity of the IZL "terror," they castigated it as something "unheard of." Indeed, when did we hear of Jews fighting back, of Jews revolting against their oppressors, persecutors, mortal enemies and monstrous ideas?

These vituperations, peppered with fragments of pious irrelevant quotations, sounded to me like poems in praise of glorious and heroic fighters for our people and land. Ironically, it was these proclamations which first brought me the message of the IZL (and LEHI) Revolt, and of its leader, Menachem Begin.

They lifted me from the depth of despair to the sublime heights of a new beginning.

While all the many offices and officers of the establishment busied themselves in their strenuous efforts to "return to normalcy," I saw in these activities nefarious attempts to go back to abnormalcy—back to the monstrosity of the "Jewish situation" of disaster, destruction, devastation and despair, back to the abyss of powerlessness and leaderlessness that had swallowed the Jewish people in Europe. Begin's struggle was not only a revolt against the British, who were intent on making the Final Solution final. It was a revolt against the whole thinking and acting hitherto dominating the Jewish masses.

This was a war of liberation not only from the British occupation but also from the mentality of the eternally weak victim—a victim who submitted passively to his oppressor, begging for mercy with the plea that he may be useful to the aims and whims, the causes and interests, of other peoples and their rulers, mostly inimical and cruel.

Ze'ev Jabotinsky's slogan, "for ruling we are chosen," was to be implemented by the greatest of his followers, Menachem Begin.

The German mortal onslaught against the Jews gave Jabotinsky's perception an extremely different meaning. This wasn't political principle—the choice wasn't between being rulers or being ruled. The German murder of the Jews taught us that the alternative to assuming the role of ruling our own country, of deciding our own destiny, was our total annihilation.

Some Orthodox adversaries of a Jewish state repeat that "not like all peoples is the House of Israel." True. Other peoples are able to afford the luxury of living without their own state. They may strive for their own sovereignty, like some peoples in the Soviet Union presently making noises or attempts for independence. But they are not threatened with annihilation. Not so the Jews—as we learned under the German monsters. For Jews, the alternative to statehood is not statelessness but mass massacre.

This was what Begin taught—not by declarations and statements, but by acts; not by words, but by deeds. Ideas are weapons, we are told. No one among the Jewish wordsmiths formulated ideas so lucidly and convincingly as did Begin. But his words were not intended to replace weapons. They instead transformed ideologies and theories, sacred causes and lofty aims, into the reality of the Jewish State.

Chapter Two

Revelation of the Meaning of A State

I had the privilege of personally and tangibly experiencing the revelation of the meaning of a state—of its essence, force and value in the life of the individual and of a people.

In the summer of 1942, it became known in Poland that there was a way to be saved from the German onslaught by obtaining passports of foreign countries. It was also rumored that such passports could be obtained from certain Latin American consulates in neutral countries, especially Switzerland. A few people started making efforts in that direction through their relatives or other connections in those countries.

Recha and Isaac Sternbuch in St. Galen, Switzerland, were especially active and inventive. A number of well-connected Jews managed to get these passports. I was one of them.

When, in the summer of 1942, it became known that the Germans planned to deport the Jews—even though it was not known that this was only a euphemism for murder—Jews intensified their desperate efforts to get these Latin American passports. Would these passports be the savior?

It soon became clear that the answer was Yes. The Germans recognized the possessors of these passports as citizens of the states that issued them, and treated them accordingly.

The German authorities weren't deluded that we, born in Poland, were authentic citizens of the respective countries. But they wanted to be deceived in their own interests.

They maintained a vast network of agents and spies in Latin American countries. A number of them had been detained by the authorities in those countries and, as a result, negotiations had been initiated between the German government and the governments of those countries.

The Germans held few bargaining chips—in other words,

hostages. There was a dearth of citizens of Paraguay, Uruguay, Peru, and so on in Poland. People of these regions seldom ventured into Poland, which was a poor country, a country of emigration rather than immigration.

Thus, these new Latin American citizens suddenly appearing in Poland were a blessing for the German endeavor to free their detained spies. All of a sudden, the Germans came into possession of hitherto scarce exchange commodity.

They issued an order commanding all the new foreign citizens to register at the special foreign agency, "Ausslandstelle"—which the Jews, of course, did.

The Germans detained some of us in the infamous and dreadful Pawiak prison in Warsaw. But rather than put us in cells, they put us in rooms in an administrative building in the prison compound. They treated us reasonably well as valuable exchange material. From here, they took us through northern Poland, and then through Germany, from east to west, until we arrived at the internment camp in Vittel (Vosges Department), France. Vittel is one of the most luxurious resorts in Europe—with mineral waters, known as Vitelois water, with large luxury hotels and with a wonderful park. The internment camp was surrounded by barbed wire. There the Germans interned foreign diplomats and other citizens from the British Commonwealth, the United States, Canada, and South America, who had been caught in occupied Europe. Conditions equalled those of the most sumptuous resorts, with all kinds of comforts, including enough food (those observing kashruth exchanged their non-kosher food with other internees). We were treated like diplomats, since the Germans had their own diplomats interned in Allied hands.

Once we were settled in the hotel, which could compete with the Waldorf Astoria, we went out to see the magnificent park. We were overwhelmed by the extraordinary transformation from dismal bunkers and imminent extermination to treatment with respect and service—from the abysmal depths to the loftiest heights.

I was there with my friend, Chaim Leibush Berglass, a brilliant student of the Yeshiva of Lublin, a man of great intellect and knowledge. I told him:

> This is what is meant by having one's own state! We are a people
> of sixteen million, the people of the book, a people of *gaonim*,

geniuses, Nobel Prize Laureates; a valuable people—refined, talented, with enormously creative powers in every field of human endeavor and achievement—and see what we are: led like sheep to slaughter. This is our "Jewish situation." But should a banana republic with a population of two million and no visible contributions to mankind, declare that so-and-so is its citizen—see how we are treated!

This is the difference that a state makes!

The contrast between the Warsaw Ghetto and Vittel was total. In Vittel, the Germans treated us like human beings. They even permitted us to have a school to teach the children Torah. I was the teacher. I was a *melamed*, an elementary school teacher; when I came to America, I discovered that I had been a "rosh yeshiva." Four of my students reside in Borough Park; both they and their children are Torah scholars.

Because we were "Paraguayans," we regained our human value.

During the heated debates of 1946–1947 within Agudist circles over the Partition Plan—i.e., a Jewish State—we were fiery advocates of the state. I was accused of being a turncoat, of siding with the "Zionists."

At that point, I said, and wrote in many papers:

> I had a revelation of what a state means. Now you will ask: How can a simple Jew be worthy of a revelation? Still, our Sages tell us that during the splitting of the Red Sea, a maid-servant saw what even the Prophet Ezekiel couldn't attain—Ezekiel, who said, "The heavens opened, and I saw visions of the Almighty." How could that be? The answer is: She just happened to be there.
>
> Similarly, by Divine Providence, I happened to be there. . .

I heard an inner voice: Learn from the revelation you experienced! Shout aloud this lesson that you have learned! A state is neither a theological nor an ideological notion. A state is a necessity for existence. A state spells the difference between Treblinka and Vittel, between Auschwitz and Entebbe, between life and death.

Chapter Three

At the Turning Point

One of the most remarkable phenomena of our time is the fact that somewhere between 1943 and 1948 the Jewish people underwent a change which is probably without precedent in human history. During the previous five years, some six million Jews throughout Europe were degraded and dehumanized, debased and tortured, and finally systematically murdered by the Germans. By 1948, the the Jewish remnants gathered in Israel, including thousands of survivors of the German slaughterhouse, took up arms against the combined forces of seven Arab nations, and prevailed. After 1948, the Jewish people will never be the same. For the next forty-two years, Jews will win wars, rescue fellow-Jews held hostage in the heart of Africa, and act to force the Soviet Union to let out hundreds of thousands of their fellow-Jews. In short, do things totally out of character when we consider the past 2000 years of Jewish passivity, typified by the Jewish policy of *Shtadlanut*, a Hebrew word which describes the activities of Jewish leaders in the Diaspora, consisting of verbal persuasion, begging, bribery, and the like, in their interceding with the authorities on behalf of the Jewish community in the hope of eliciting a measure of political and economic tolerance toward the Jews in an often hostile environment. In 1948, with the birth of the first Jewish state in two millennia, the Jewish people were transformed from a passive object of history to an active subject. They took their destiny into their own hands, and, putting their faith in Divine Providence, they found the courage and the inspiration to face great odds and prevail.

How and why did such a radical change occur? To answer this question, one would have to undertake a lengthy study, and even then the question may not be fully answered. One thing, however, is clear. As often happens in history, there are certain remarkable individuals who help change the course of events, by affecting the thoughts and actions of their contemporaries. Such a person is Menachem Begin.

During the critical period of *the German murdering of the Jews* and the fight for the state, Begin played a decisive role in providing the leadership, the inspiration, and the tools for the armed struggle that forced the British out of Palestine and resulted in the creation of the State of Israel.

Jabotinsky's words "Almighty, you have created us to rule," were deliberately misinterpreted by his adversaries to mean that he was power hungry. Worse yet, he was accused by the socialist Zionists, who, under the leadership of David Ben-Gurion came to dominate the Zionist movement, of being a fascist, a man who glorified power and sought to promote dictatorship and hero-worship cult associated with European fascism. This was the beginning of the great conflict in contemporary Zionism, which was transferred to Menachem Begin.

In actual fact, Jabotinsky was a political liberal and a great believer in the democratic process. By "ruling" Jabotinsky meant that Jews were not meant to be ruled by others. He considered the condition of the Jews in the Diaspora to be unnatural, hence all the oppression and persecution. Jews were meant to be masters to their own destiny, have their own state, and, like all other free nations, have their own means of self-defense and security. Looking back now, fifty years later, try to imagine a free state of Israel existing for one day without strong means of self-defense against implacable enemies bent on its annihilation.

When Begin arrived in Palestine in 1943, reports of the mass killings of Jews in Europe were reaching the outside world. In 1939 the Germans were still willing to let Jews out of Germany, as part of their goal of making Europe *Judenrein* (free of Jews). But Jews had nowhere to go. The United States would not let in Jewish refugees. The British Mandate in Palestine kept the gates of the Jewish "national home" tightly shut. Other countries followed suit. Some boats with Jewish refugees roamed the seven seas, unable to find a haven anywhere. It became clear that a Jewish state was not only a cherished goal, but a matter of life or death. The question was not statehood or statelessness, but state or annihilation.

Samuel Pisar, a prominent international lawyer and an Auschwitz survivor, wrote in his book *Of Blood and Hope* (Little Brown & Co., Boston, 1987):

> The transformation [of the Jewish national character] had been

made inevitable by the martyrdom of the ghettos and [death] camps. After that to lay one's head defenselessly on the chopping block of history and hope that some foreign power will come mercifully to the rescue would have been criminal folly, a form of deafness and blindness to the obvious lesson of the past. (Page 278)

This lesson was not ignored by the rulers of the Zionist establishment. The difference between them and Begin was that while they continued to believe that they could reach the objective of establishing a Jewish state through persuasion and negotiations, by protests and proclamations about the just cause or by means of political maneuvers and pressure, Begin did not trust the British rulers, and did not believe in the old methods. He realized that the only way to force the British to leave Palestine was through an armed confrontation.

In order to broaden the base of the armed struggle, initiated by Begin in the land of Israel with a mere 300 followers during the height of the German massacre of the Jews, it was necessary to start educating the Jewish community and inspire Jewish youth to resist the foreign occupant. Historically, the Jews in exile, deprived of a state and of armed forces, living for the most part under hostile rulers, had to rely by necessity on words alone. In their relations with the rulers of the lands they inhabited, their only instrument of defense was persuasion, pleading, reasoning, begging—words, words, words. These were the sole "weapons" of an unarmed people. We have seen how effective such means of defense have been. . .

In the inner life of the Diaspora, the word, both spoken and written, was a tool of sages and scholars, of teachers and leaders. Often these two would be combined in one person—for expounding the Torah, exploring the Law, and for issuing rules and guidelines. Thus the far-reaching power of the word became a cohesive force which kept the dispersed people together and cemented a religious community which cultivated a distinct national identify.

In modern times, Jewish leaders, in particular rabbinical ones and the heads of the Zionist movement, often made masterly use of speech for the propagation of ideas and ideologies and also in negotiations, mostly with foreign rulers. Dr. Theodor Herzl, Max Nordau, Nahum Sokoloff, Prof. Chaim Weitzmann, Ze'ev Jabotinsky, Dr. Shemaryahu Levin, are some of the outstanding examples. All of them, incidentally, were also gifted writers. Hence one can appreciate the paramount importance of the word, both written and spoken.

Menachem Begin caused a fundamental departure in this area, which ultimately led to the revolutionary change of the Jewish destiny. He used the word not *instead* of the sword, but *as* a sword. His was a call to arms. (Not unlike the call to arms of Rouget de Lisle in the *Marseillaise*-Aux armes citoyens!) Thus was the word transformed into the sword. Begin's proclamations, exhortations, orders and calls transmitted through underground posters and leaflets which were distributed or pasted at night on the walls of Tel Aviv, Jerusalem and Haifa by young boys and girls at the risk of their lives,* sounded like a clarion-call to battle. This sound, initially both unfamiliar and strange, first startled, then awoke the Yishuv. Gradually, Begin's battle cry reverberated through the hearts and penetrated the minds—even minds frozen in routine, and hearts which had been previously hermetically sealed against it. The meek became rebellious, the tamed—courageous, the obedient—disobedient, and the submissive—subversive. The initially dissonant voice evoked a resonance far beyond the confines of the Irgun Tzvai Leumi.

Thus Begin's call also reached those who were opposed to him and his ideas. It had an impact, both direct and oblique, on the Haganah, the defense force of the *Yishuv*. As a result, Begin's inimical antagonists were sometimes forced to harden their posture and intensify their campaign against the Mandate government.

Soon Begin's alarm was ringing not only among the Jewish population of Palestine but even in distant Jewish communities throughout the world, from South Africa to South America, and from Western Europe to North America. Few remained unconcerned and unmoved. No one could remain indifferent. To be sure, there were many adversaries, including some formidable ones, who were determined to put an end to this "unauthorized" rebellion by the "separatists," as the Jewish establishment labelled the underground fighters. Yet no one could possibly remain untouched.

During the five years of the revolt, Begin went into what he later described in his memoirs as an "open underground." He changed his identity, but continued to live in the open in a small apartment in the Tel Aviv area, posing as an Orthodox rabbi named Yisroel Sassover,

---

* Indeed some did lose their lives in the process, like the sixteen-year-old Rubinovich who was killed by a British Agent.

whom neither the British, their legendary intelligence services notwithstanding, nor the Zionist establishment, with its many arms, were
able to discover.

He became, in effect, a one-man propaganda department of the
Irgun. In addition to commanding the revolt against the foreign ruler,
he spent most of his time writing the underground's wall posters and
leaflets. His message was read by thousands. It explained the cause of
the Irgun, the need for an armed struggle, the right of the Jews to their
own ancestral home, and the fact that the British had become cruel
occupiers of the land of the Jews. He issued warnings prior to Irgun
attacks (which were often unheeded, as in the case of the bombing of
the British headquarters at the King David Hotel, which resulted in
unnecessary loss of life because of the unwillingness of the British
authorities to take the Irgun's warning seriously). He explained the
operations after they took place, and continued to publicize the
demands of the *Yishuv* for free immigration and an independent state.

In retrospect, the revolt also changed the psychology of the main
defense force of the *Yishuv*, namely, the Haganah, which later became
the basis of the Israel Defense Force, one of the finest defense forces
in the world today, as well as a force for social integration of the
many ethnic groups in present-day Israel.

It put an end to the myth that Jews are cowards. It proved that Jews
are ready to give up their life for freedom, as was shown by such
Irgun fighters as Dov Gruner, who could have asked for clemency
from the British throne (which might have been granted), but refused
to recognize the foreign rule and was hanged while singing *Hatikvah*.

Begin's revolt changed the attitude of the Jewish people as a
whole. When Begin arrived in Palestine in 1943, in the middle of
World War Two, as a soldier in a Soviet-sponsored Polish Anders'
army, the Revisionists were in disarray. The first commander of the
Irgun, David Raziel, had been killed in 1941 on an anti-German mission in Iraq (where, ironically, he had been sent by the British). The
commander of the Irgun's splinter group, the LEHI, Abraham (Yair)
Stern, was murdered by the British in 1942. As soon as Begin was
discharged from the Polish army, he assumed the leadership of the
Irgun, even though there were others, with more seniority, who could
have assumed that position. It was an act of Divine Providence.

Leading a few hundred young men and women, Begin had the

courage to defy the British Empire and sustain his revolt in the face of a continuous man-hunt, which at one point (known as the "Season," or "Saison") was exacerbated by the collaboration of the Haganah. He sustained it for five violent years, culminating with the Haganah joining forces with the Irgun—unfortunately only for a short time—in the fight against the British, who were battling the Jewish survivors of the death camps preventing them from entering their homeland. By late 1947 and early 1948, the idea of Jews taking their fate into their own hands and fighting for their freedom took root in the hearts and minds of Jews everywhere, enabling the new Jewish state win its War of Independence.

Looking back upon those harrowing yet heroic years, Begin, the much-maligned "terrorist," does emerge as the most far-sighted of all the so-called Jewish leaders of that time.

Chapter Four

The Early Years

Brest Litovsk, where Menachem Begin was born in July 1913, was part of eastern Poland which at that time belonged to Czarist Russia and today to the Soviet Union. Jews had first settled there in the fourteenth century by permission of the Grand Duke Kiejstut. Menachem grew up in Brisk, as the city was called in Yiddish, at a time when Jews comprised about seventy percent of the population.

Brisk's rabbis, the great Talmudic dynasty of the Soloveichiks, were recognized as religious authorities throughout the Jewish world. The orthodox Jews were a prominent presence, but the majority of the city's Jews were in effect secularist. Of those, only a small part were anti-religious leftists and Bundists (Jewish socialists). This was a vibrant community, abounding in religious, cultural and political activities. The town had Jewish deputy mayors, such as Abraham Levinson of Poale Zion, a former Jewish member of the Polish parliament. This vibrant environment was to have profound influence on Begin.

Menachem was the youngest of the three children of Dov Zeev and Hasia Begin. Zeev Dov was a lumber exporter and a communal activist, who served at times as secretary of Brisk's Jewish Community Council. He was a scholarly man, well-versed in the Talmud and the Bible, and religiously devout. Under his influence, the Sabbath and holidays in the Begin household were imbued with the Jewish spirit.

"Reb Berl," as Menachem's father was known, was not afraid of taking an unpopular stand. He was an early Zionist at a time when only two other persons in the city emulated him. One was N. Shainerman, whose grandson would become Israel's legendary and controversial General Ariel Sharon (see Chapter Forty-Six), and the other was N. Neumark, the local Hebrew teacher. Others later joined the group, but it remained relatively small and isolated in a city where many Jews were non-committal or even antagonistic towards the Zionist movement.

When Dr. Theodor Herzl died on July 3, 1904, Brisk's Zionists announced a memorial service for the founder of modern Zionism at the main synagogue of the community. The renowned Rabbi Chaim Soloveichik, who like most other rabbis was strongly opposed to Zionism, ordered that the synagogue be closed. Zeev Dov was an admirer and friend of the great rabbi of Brisk, but he did not waver. He and his friends forced open the synagogue gate and the house was soon filled with the mourning throng.

The elder Begin also served as a string corespondent of the Warsaw Yiddish daily *Haint*, in whose columns he strongly voiced Zionist ideals.

Like her husband, Hasia Begin was a vigorous personality. Member of a prominent rabbinical family, she counted among her forebears the noted Talmudic scholars Rabbi Yekele and Rabbi Yosef Leib of Rovno, Wolyn, in Russian-occupied Poland, who were revered as saintly men; on the anniversary of their deaths, pious Jews lit candles at their graves. Hasia managed the household, stretching a meager income to cover the family's daily needs.

The first child born to Zeev Dov and Hasia was Rachel, now Mrs. Halpern, a warm and gracious woman who lives in Tel Aviv. Herzl came next, named after the founder of Zionism (Zeev Dov's plan to call the first-born daughter Herzliah yielded to Hasia's wish to name her after her own mother). Their third child was born in July, 1913, on the eve of Shabbat Nachamu, the Sabbath of Consolation, on which the words of Isaiah, "Nachamu nachamu ami" ("Be consoled, be consoled, my people") are read in the synagogue. The Begins called their son Menachem (Consoler), a name that would later become a symbol to many. At a meeting in Tel-Aviv with Rabbi Meyer Fund, his sister, Rachel, described in vivid language the childhood and adolescence of her younger brother in the environment of Brisk. Begin told us that Chief Rabbi Isaac Herzog once wrote to him during the underground fight, referring to him as "Menachem [Consoler of] Zion."

Menachem was two years old during World War One when the Russians, who suspected the Jews of being sympathetic to the enemy, expelled them from the occupied regions in anticipation of the advancing German troops. The Begins fled to Rovno, where Hasia still had relatives.

At war's end, in 1918, the Begins returned to Brisk and Menachem was enrolled in the public school. For religious instruction, he was placed in the Mizrachi (religious Zionist) Tachkemoni School. While there, he heard a speech by the visiting Rabbi Yehuda Leib Fishman (later Maimon), who later became the leader of the Mizrachi movement, and the first minister of religion of Israel.

Menachem's kindergarten teacher, Mrs. Pitlik, now residing in Philadelphia, Pennsylvania, still recalls the precocious, serious five-year-old Menachem and his insatiable curiosity about the world.

One area in which he experienced difficulty was speech. The boy who was destined to become a fiery orator and spell-binder was afflicted with shyness and handicapped by difficulty in pronouncing the sounds of the Hebrew letters gimmel and kaf. His older sister helped him overcome his handicap. She encouraged and supported him in a way that he never forgot. He mentioned it during a celebration of her seventieth birthday, when he remarked that if anyone referred to Rachel as merely "Begin's sister," he would be sharply rebuked.

Rachel recalled how later a less shy Menachem at age ten climbed on the table and delivered an impromptu speech. It was a great success, leading to frequent demands for more which he gladly accepted, as she mentioned decades later in a conversation with Rabbi Meyer Fund of New York.

The Begin family was warm and close-knit. The family's income was barely sufficient for daily needs, but Menachem's parents were happy with their lot and taught their children to be content with what they had, which they heeded throughout the years. The household was religious, but the parents' outlook was modern, especially with regard to education. Zeev Dov and Hasia made sure their children studied both Jewish and secular subjects. The Sabbath and Jewish holidays were marked at home by traditional meals accompanied by singing and festivities.

Outside the home was a city which offered a stimulating educational environment. Menachem first joined the Hashomer Hatzair, the dominant leftist youth movement, and then became an active member of Betar, the youth movement of the Zionist Revisionist organization, where his organizational talent and his devotion to the idea of a

Jewish state soon became apparent. He exhibited a strong commitment to Jewish tradition and the Jewish faith, and displayed a superior intellect and an exceptional capacity for organizational work. In 1938, at age 25, he became the head of Betar in Poland.

He assumed his post while studying law at the Josef Pilsudski University of Warsaw. (I happened to attend the same university at the same time, but I did not know my fellow-student, the future prime minister of Israel). Jewish students were intensely involved in politics, in Jewish political parties and in the various factions of the Zionist movement. A critical moment during that period was the ideological clash in 1938 between Begin and his revered leader and teacher Ze'ev Jabotinsky (see Chapter Twenty-Eight). It marked the turning point in Betar's history. The position the young Begin's took, which prevailed, would affect the course of the Jewish struggle for liberation and statehood.

At the time I was living at the university's Jewish Academic House, or student dormitory, in the Praga suburb of Warsaw. I happened to hear that Jabotinsky was in town and in the auditorium of the Academic House and was going to give a speech, and so I went to hear him. To my regret, I missed Begin's speech.

Chapter Five

My Visit to Brisk Before the Destruction

In 1937 I visited Brisk. The reason for my visit was an attack on the local Jewish population, which was reported on the front page of the Warsaw Polish afternoon paper *Wieczo'r Warszawksi* with a screaming headline—"Pogrom in Brest [Brisk]." I was at that time the secretary of the club of Jewish members of the Polish parliament (the Sejm and the Senate). I decided to travel to Brisk and find out what happened.

To me Brisk meant the home of the Brisker Rav. After travelling all night by train I arrived in Brisk on the morning following the "pogrom." I am putting the word pogrom in quotation marks because as an eyewitness I got a more accurate report of what had happened than the one I had read in the paper.

A Jewish butcher had bribed a Polish policeman not to report the full number of livestock slaughtered for his store so as to avoid paying the full amount of the tax due. The policeman took the bribe and then came to the butcher's shop to confiscate the illegal meat. A violent quarrel broke out, and the butcher stabbed the policeman with a knife. When the news of the event got out, a mob of Poles started a riot. Jews were beaten, stores looted, houses attacked, windows broken. But fortunately no Jews were seriously injured or required hospitalization.

I went straight from the railway station to the residence of Reb Yitzhak Ze'ev (Reb Velvel) Soloveichik, the famous rabbi of the community. I remember the distressful sight of his residence. The windows were broken, the home desolate, all around there were debris and destruction, and the atmosphere was tense. I recall very clearly how humble the rabbi's residence was, but rather than describe it myself I would let Brisk's most illustrious Jewish son describe it. In a Hebrew greeting sent at my suggestion by Menachem Begin to Rabbi Aaron Soloveichik the head of Chicago's Brisker Yeshivah on February 10, 1982, the then Prime Minister of Israel reminisced:

> There once was on the road between Warsaw and Moscow a city with a great Jewish community. It had thousands of Jews, splendid yeshivot, and great Torah scholars, headed by Rabbi Chaim Soloveichik of blessed memory. He was adored and revered by the Jews of that city of Brisk de Lita.
>
> From the standpoint of the Jewish people, Brisk no longer exists. But the memory of the old, small, poor, warm house, resplendent with love of Jews and love of Zion, still lives in our hearts.

I spoke with the Rav in Brisk and with his children and followers, and then I visited the Jewish deputy mayor of Brisk, Hilary Mastbaum, a friend of mine from Warsaw who had served there as Jewish affairs adviser to Prime Minister Walery Slawek.

He gave me a true picture of the disturbances. He assured me that the situation was under control, as the city authorities had taken the necessary steps to restore order and ensure the security of the Jews. Subsequently, at my suggestion, the Jewish senators Rabbi Moshe Schorr and Jacob Trockenheim came over from Warsaw. Rabbi Soloveichik hardly said a word during my visit with him. Later on I asked Rabbis Yeruchem Gorelik and Avram Abba Zions, now a Talmud professor at Yeshivah University, in New York, both of whom had been present at that time at the rabbi's house, whether he had made any comment about my visit. Both told me he had said the following: "This fellow Hillel is a strange person. People run away from a pogrom; he comes running to one."

When I was in Israel in August 1982 I visited the illustrious head of the Brisker Yeshivah in Jerusalem, Rabbi David Soloveichik. He received me warmly and recalled my "strange" visit to Brisk.

I cherish to this day the remark of the great Brisker Rav, as the highest praise.

Chapter Six

Harmony in Contrasts

Who is Menachem Begin? How can we separate the man from the myth? What would be an objective assessment of his person and his contribution as a Jewish leader?

Several traits in Begin seem to contradict each other. Their existence in one person seems to be a paradox. But the real paradox is not only the fact that they coexist in one person, but rather that they complement each other in perfect harmony. No split personality here. His traits add up to a harmonious whole, a finely tuned character, a highly analytical mind and a warm and compassionate heart.

Let us look at some of his traits which may at first seem contradictory, but when seen in their real context complement each other and help us see him as he really is. This kind of in-depth observation is indispensable in his case, since there are few personalities whose image as formed in the minds of outside shallow observers is so different from reality as in this case.

There are several reasons for these errors and deceptions. Some of these were created with the intent of defaming him, falsifying his intentions, misrepresenting his goals, and distorting the facts.

Since Menachem Begin broke with traditional moulds, and did things which were "unacceptable" (to the establishment), defying leaders who ruled almost unopposed for decades and controlled the powerful institutions of the *Yishuv*, it was only natural for those autocrats to attack the man who questioned their authority and rebelled against their inaction.

Before they started using other means to liquidate the danger they saw embodied in him and the organization under his command, the IZL, they launched a propaganda campaign in order to degrade their opponent, turn the public against him, and justify their all-out war against him, which otherwise might have backfired by causing anger and resentment among the Jewish public.

This campaign lasted from the beginning of the Jabotinsky revolt to the Begin revolt. But it did not stop with the establishment of the State of Israel, despite the fact that the commander of the Irgun dissolved his organization and put it under the command of the IDF (Israel Defense Force), as he proceeded to integrate himself and his followers in the democratic political life of the new state.

Years later, when Begin was elected Israel's prime minister, the enemies of Israel, both overt and covert, launched a campaign of defamation against him which they thought would elicit a sympathetic response from world opinion, considering the fact that Begin had been the butt of scurrilous attacks for so many years. Their intention was not only to harm the new prime minister, but also the country that had chosen him as its leader.

But the strident tone of this hysterical attack proved counterproductive. Any thinking person with a modicum of decency realized that there was little truth in those attacks. The nefarious intent of certain attackers to harm the State of Israel was so transparent, that the citizenry of Israel, including many belonging to the opposition parties, perceived the danger to the state in that onslaught, and came to the defense of their new prime minister.

Gradually, the horizon cleared. The human and political profile of Menachem Begin began to emerge from the fog of deliberate distortions.

One cannot help but ask the question, how was it possible to err so gravely in assessing Begin?

Aside from the deliberate falsifications, open or latent, one of the reasons for this campaign is the fact that there are some components in Begin's character which seem contradictory or superficially exclusive, especially at a quick glance. When one is predisposed to dwell on Begin's negative traits, it does not take much to come up with an uncomplimentary portrait of this man.

Let us examine some of those contradictions and try to find out how they are actually reflected in his thinking and behavior.

Hard as steel and soft as a reed

Begin has been known to be hard as steel. He is not made of clay one could easily mould. When this trait is described in negative terms, the result is an unbending, unfeeling, obstinate and inflexible person, a person who does not know the art of give and take.

And yet he has also been known to be kind, possessed of noble sentiments and delicate feelings, a gentleman who always treats people with respect and consideration.

His detractors have emphasized that his rigidity was his dominant quality. They have dismissed the opposite traits as a veneer, a pretense, a mask covering up his true nature.

In reality the opposite is true. The Begin I have known has been a man of noble spirit and deep feelings, and it is precisely these qualities that have resulted in his iron will and his legendary courage. He managed to escape from the clutches of the Germans, survived a year in a Soviet prison, and witnessed the beginning of the catastrophe in Europe in which his entire family was murdered by the Germans. It was not cruelty and heartlessness that impelled him to lead the revolt against the British. On the contrary. it was his deep love for his persecuted and martyred people. He absorbed all their pain and suffering. Like Dante, he descended into the depths of the abyss of that monumental tragedy, the like of which no people and no nation ever experienced. He came back from the valley of death carrying in his soul the boundless suffering of the martyred nation. And this suffering kindled his will and his strength.

Feels the pain of the catastrophe like no one else

Few if any Jewish leaders have suffered the pain of their people like Begin. Not only did he feel in the depths of his soul the martyrdom of the entire nation; he felt the suffering of every single child, of every single person who was humiliated, tortured, killed. He was loath to use the tired expression "the six millions." He felt the agony of every Jew in the massacre, as if every individual were the entire universe.

This compassion released in him a tremendous power which impelled him to lead the revolt. Not only against the British who turned against the persecuted Jews of Europe and later the survivors of the catastrophe, but also against the acquiescence of many Jews to this evil rule, and their willingness to submit to it and be abused by it.

The source of his power was his compassion for his people.

A modern man and a traditional Jew

Begin grew up as a modern Jew in his behavior, appearance, speech and culture. He spoke several European languages, was at home in world literature, had a law degree from the University of Warsaw, in short, had all the ingredients of the "acculturated" Jew. At the same time, he was deeply imbued with Jewish faith, tradition, and learning.

While he mastered European culture, European culture did not master him. He adapted that culture to his own spirit and ideas, to his origins, to his soul. He used it as a tool to express his Jewish inspirations and aspirations. This was so because he was perfectly at home with the Jewish patrimony. In this respect, he stood out among the non-religious, thoroughly secular Zionist leaders, especially in contrast to the Socialist Zionists. While many of them regarded Western culture as an object of emulation, Begin considered the principles of Judaism the center of his spiritual life, and Western culture merely a periphery.

He absorbed those principles at his father's house, in the town of Brisk, a major Jewish spiritual center before the war. He further absorbed them as a young man in Warsaw, at that time the largest Jewish community in Europe, and the world center of Jewish culture. His deep Jewish roots and his religious faith have been a natural part of his being.

Whenever someone would threaten the spiritual foundations of the Jewish faith, Begin would rise to the full height of his spiritual stature and would defend his patrimony—the secret of the Jewish national existence—with the same fervor he had shown in defending his people and his homeland. None of the secular Zionist leaders has been closer to the leading rabbinical authorities of his generation, despite the fact that several of those secular leaders came from religious homes, and some even studied in a *Yeshivah* in their youth.

In his meetings with rabbinical scholars, Hasidic leaders, or heads of Talmudic academies, he would never enter into any polemics. He would invariably engage in a friendly discussion, as if he were a close ally of his interlocutor. Similarly, in his political negotiations with the leaders of the Orthodox parties in Israel, such as the Mizrachi (National Religious Party), Agudath Israel, and Poale Agudath Israel, he would not argue over religious matters, but would seek to find a practical solution to the problems of state and religion.

His respect for religious leaders (which cannot always be said about other non-religious Jewish leaders) has not been politically expedient but wholly sincere. It stemmed from his personal views and from his background.

His hometown, Brisk, gave rise to famous rabbis. The last three rabbis of Brisk—Joseph Dov, Haim, and Yitzhak Zeev, all of the house of Soloveichik, introduced a new method of studying the Torah, and left their imprint on the world of the Yeshivot with their original methods and style which at times was considered revolutionary. Their descendants have continued in their footsteps as heads of Yeshivot in Israel and in the United States, and have perpetuated the "Brisk mode" of Talmud study (the best known of their descendants being Rabbi Joseph Dov Soloveichik of Boston, the former head of Yeshivah University's Rabbinical Seminary).

Begin's father, Dov Zeev Begin, was a frequent guest at the home of the famous rabbi of Brisk, Reb Haim Soloveichik, despite the fact that the latter was a staunch anti-Zionist, while the senior Begin was an ardent Zionist. The young Begin, while following in his father's footsteps, nevertheless was influenced by his father's great respect and admiration for the rabbinic dynasty of his town.

It was another rabbi, however, who had a decisive influence on Begin, greatly deepening his respect for traditional Judaism, namely, Rabbi Aryeh Levin, known as the Tzaddik of Jerusalem. It would be hard to find two personalities more different than Begin and Levin. Rabbi Levin was a member of the old Jewish community of Jerusalem, a teacher at the Yeshivah Eitz Haim. His entire life revolved around teaching Torah and performing acts of *chesed*, charity, and he was quite removed from Begin's armed struggle. He was a quiet, self-effacing man. He never sought a position of authority, and was only interested in alleviating the suffering of others. And yet, something happened which certainly seemed strange to those who did not understand Begin's true essence. Begin and Levin became close friends, deeply admiring each other, bound together by a deep spiritual bond.

Begin's relation to Reb Aryeh was not unlike the relation of a hasid to his revered rebbe, yet the same relation existed on the part of the

Rabbi towards Begin. It was more than the affection of a rebbe to his hasid, because it was characterized by self-effacing before the greatness this particular admirer.

The Tzaddik of Jerusalem loved and admired every underground fighter. He considered it a great privilege to be associated with those who offered their life for their people and their land, who, in his words, "sanctified the Holy Name." Kiddush Hashem. And so, when he stood in the presence of their commander, or when he spoke about him, he was always moved by *Herdat kodesh*, or holy tremble. I recall how, in August 1967, after the Six Day War, while visiting Rabbi Aryeh in Jerusalem, we mentioned Mr. Begin in our conversation. The old Tzaddik said: "He is going through great suffering right now. Someone in his family is seriously ill. He needs the help of heaven, and we all must pray for him, for he is one of the greatest Jews of our generation. . ." And he burst into tears.

This unusual relationship did not seem unnatural to those who really knew the two of them. What tied them together was a boundless love for their people, for every single soul in Israel. Both felt the pain of the nation and suffered along with it. Both were willing to sacrifice their lives for the people and its land. Both lived their entire life with no other thought than the welfare of the Jewish people.

(An aside: When I expressed my admiration for Benny Begin's remarkable family—his wife Ruthie and their six children, Dr. Begin—now a member of the Knesset and a rising leader in the Likud—remarked: "Is it any wonder? Reb Aryeh officiated at our wedding. . . .")

Begin has been depicted by his adversaries as a cold, heartless person, devoid of sentiments. The opposite is true. Here again reality is altogether different from the image his critics have tried to create. Here was a man of refined and noble feelings, whose heart worked as a seismograph, responding to every vibration in other people's hearts and recording every tremor in the soul of the nation. Without relinquishing the rule of the mind or the application of cold logic, he remained a sentimental and emotional person, possessed of deep and noble feelings. He conveyed empathy.

I had the privilege of interacting with him personally and I was aware of those qualities at all times. Begin was the rare kind of a leader who did not have to draw a line between himself and others in order to assert his authority. He was always unassuming, down to earth, accessible, a fatherly or an avuncular figure, a friend, "one of the people." He thought nothing of lecturing U.S. presidents when he disagreed with them, and at the same time would hold the door for the cleaning woman, whose very existence in a room full of politicians and "big shots" was generally ignored by everyone else. It is ironic to think that other Jewish leaders, priding themselves on being "socialists," seemed to be devoid of such feelings towards the common people, while Begin the "right wing nationalist" was always tuned in to the least and lowliest of God's children.

The man who represented the elite of Jewry was very far from, and opposed to, the elitism prevailing among some Israeli party leaders. His relation with people was vivid and cordial. He restrained his material authority to be close to people as an equal.

Man of mind and heart.

Chapter Seven

If Not for Menachem Begin in 1981 . . .

> *"Thus hath said the L-rd of hosts. Every one of the*
> *broad walls of Babylon shall be utterly over-*
> *thrown, and her high gates shall be burnt with fire;*
> *so that nations shall have labored in vain, and the*
> *people for the fire, and so shall they have wearied*
> *themselves."*   *(Jeremiah LI: 58)*

If not for Menachem Begin in 1981 . . .

If not for his decision to destroy on June 7, 1981, Iraq's nuclear bomb reactor Osirak in Baghdad, Saddam Hussein would, in August 1990, be in possession of nuclear weapons. According to experts it would take Iraq 5 to 6 years to produce the deadly Damocles sword which would hang over the world today.

Then we thought that Begin saved Israel. Today we know—he saved the world. All these governments who then condemned Israel owe her an apology.

Commander Randy "Duke" Cunningham, Commanding Officer, U.S. Navy Squadron, First ACE, writes:

> With the world situation as it is, would you as a U.S. citizen want . . . Iraq to have a nuclear bomb capability? What if they were our neighbors sworn to our destruction? *Bullseye—One Reactor* is a historical and dramatic account of Israel's reaction to the above questions. (Foreword to *Bullseye—One Reactor* by Dan McKinnon, naval aviator, San Diego, CA 92115, 1987.)

The same book terms the Osirak destruction as the greatest surgical bombing attack in aviation history. "It was the riskiest mission in the history of the Israeli Air Force." An example of why the Israeli Air Force has become legendary." (*Ibid.*)

Two thousand years and—two minutes. . .

On the eve of Shavuos 5741, which fell then on June 7, 1981, Israel's air force swiftly and totally destroyed Iraq's nuclear reactor, Osirak, near Baghdad, destined to produce atom bombs for the annihilation of the Jewish State and its people.

Here, an American news report on this action: "Like a bolt out of the Bible, they hurled at Baghdad out of the setting sun. Eight F-16 Israeli fighter-bombers roared down on the concrete dome of the Osirak nuclear reactor. In a single series of lighting passes they dropped many bombs.

Within two minutes they disappeared clearly into the gathering darkness, leaving behind a fearsome new turn in the dangerous nuclear game." (Newsweek, June 22, 1981)

Thus we were privileged to live the fulfillment of the above Jeremiah prophecy in our own time. It is, therefore, proper, no, obligatory, to remember in gratitude to the Almighty this momentous event that happened to us *Erev Shavuos* nine years ago.

For the first time in two thousand years of extreme helplessness Jews were able to repulse a deadly threat to their very survival. In two minutes "G-d's help comes in the twinkling of the eye." Two thousand years and—two minutes. . .

Saddam Hussein, who plotted through murders his ascendency to the presidency of Iraq, a dangerous dictator, uninhibited by any moral principles, was bound to achieve nuclear arms capacity aimed at Israel. Anwar Sadat, the Egyptian president told Menachem Begin that Saddam Hussein is worse that the Libyan strongman Qaddafi.

His air force perpetuated the missile attack on the American frigate Stark, killing 37 American marines. His spokesman termed the deadly assault as "inadvertent." But coming from such a murderous tyrant we may have our doubts. . .

In 1981 Saddam Hussein moved inexorably and feverishly toward producing nuclear arms. What was even more astonishing and revolting was that West European democratic governments, notably France and Italy, accorded to Iraq scientific, technical and physical help in that deadly enterprise.

Already the Labor government of Israel tried very hard to dissuade these governments from helping Iraq in this disastrous build up. To no avail.

It was Menachem Begin who took up the challenge. He, too, made the most strenuous diplomatic efforts to get Paris and Rome to cease their support of the Osirak reactor. To no avail.

Then Begin came out again in the strength of his character and his decision-making capability that he demonstrated in many other fateful moments of crisis. His leadership overcame the hesitancy of some members of his Cabinet and of other factors.

As in his struggles against the British during the Revolt he didn't put his trust—and the fate of the Jewish people—in the hands of foreign statesmen.

In spite of Begin's strong protests the then French president Giscard d'Estang, and the then Italian Prime Minister Emilio Colombo continued to support the construction of Osirak, while trying to quiet down the Israelis as to the intentions of the Iraqi dictator. The most ardent promoter of the Iraqi nuclear reactor was the then (and present) French Prime Minister Jacques Chirac, as Menachem Begin described him (Tamuz BeLahavoth by Shlomo Nakdimon, Jerusalem, 1986).

Labor opposed the bombing of Osirak, on the ground, among others that the socialist leader François Mitterand, who was supposed to win the forthcoming elections for president, will prevent the nuclear collaboration with Iraq. (In fact he, too, didn't stop this criminal collaboration.)

Shimon Peres, the leader of the Opposition, warned Begin on May 10, 1981 against the bombardment of Osirak.

There were other opposing views. Some were afraid of the reaction of the world, particularly of U.S.A. But Begin was adamant. "There will be no other Holocaust," he said, and the fateful decision was made. And victoriously implemented.

The accuracy and precision of the bombing without the slightest hitch was astonishing. All bombs were direct hits. This accomplishment was without precedent.

On the day of the deed Begin convoked the members of the government in deep secret, 3:30 the eve of Shavuoth, each thinking that he was the only one invited and was astonished to find there all the others. When the call came from the Chief-of-Staff: "Mission accomplished," they all were in a highly emotional shock. Some laughed, some wept, some just stared blankly into space. The action had to be still kept secret. Begin wanted the Arabs to reveal it first.

When Jordan announced what happened, immediately an orgy of condemnation swept the media. The Israeli people, without distinction, and Jews everywhere were overwhelmed with joy.

Soon a flood of vituperations broke out. Begin branded them what they were: abysmal, hypocritical and shameful. While Begin was deeply outraged by these outbursts, he took them in stride, weighing them against the lethal danger.

He said: "Better condemnation without the Iraqi reactor that the Iraqi atomic bombs without condemnation. . ."

It was one of his finest hours. It was one of his many historical achievements which deserve the eternal gratitude of the Jewish people.

These accomplishments should not be ignored or forgotten, or as many endeavors, distorted and falsified.

The Talmud says: "How one doesn't feel and doesn't realize when the Almighty help him" (Tractate Yoma, 22a).

We have a duty to recall and be thankful for G-d's help, and to remember the ones who were the instruments of the Divine Providence.

Thus let us recall the glory of this act of Menachem Begin which changed the course of history.

After two thousand years—and two minutes. . .

Chapter Eight

Fighting and Forebearance

Begin's written and spoken word can be discussed on several levels. Let us look at some of the more contradictory ones.

His eloquence was powerful. He did not mince words. He always said what he thought, and he said it with amazing lucidity and uncommon force. He did not hesitate to criticize, whether with his pen or with his tongue, and at times his criticism would cut like a scalpel. He was quick to repel an attack, and equally quick in counterattacking.

He has been widely perceived as a contentious man, yet he has always been extremely careful with the dignity of his opponent, and always took pains not to offend anyone, keeping his words free of defamation.

No other contemporary Jewish leader or party has suffered more indignities, has been subjected to more insults and even physical threats, than Menachem Begin and his movement. What would have been more natural for its members, who by nature were far from faint-hearted or docile, than to be quick to seek retribution? Obviously, Begin had to have an enormous amount of courage and strength to restrain his colleagues and followers whose natural instinct prompted them on many occasions to exact an eye for an eye. He used his considerable persuasion powers and the full measure of his authority as Betar chief and commander of the Irgun to prevent his movement from stooping to their adversaries' level, and made superhuman efforts to keep the confrontations at the ideological level and avoid a civil war.

For indeed, long before the "Saison" and the Altalena affair, his adversaries resorted to uninhibited, vicious incitement against him, using all means to this end, including character assassination. Yet, despite the fact that when one continues to sling mud, some may stick, he was immune to these attacks. Even his extreme opponents eventually were forced to admit that Begin was a man of unquestionable honesty and integrity.

Even his most scathing reactions show a sense of regret at being forced to resort to such a response, than satisfaction at having given an effective rebuke. He did not enjoy attacking his adversaries. His action was always defensive in nature.

I have had the occasion over the years to discuss with him various matters and persons, including those who acted unfairly and caused great harm to his movement and its unselfish objectives, and even to the vital interests of the nation and the state. He would always listen with sadness in his eyes and react with subdued sorrow.

I can attest to it from personal experience that I have never felt any rancor in his voice towards his enemies or even those who sought to physically liquidate him.

In my public activities, even back in Warsaw before World War II and for decades thereafter, I have met many statesmen and communal leaders of every ideological persuasion, with long lists of accomplishments, and I can safely say that very few ever came close to Begin in their attitude towards their opponents and detractors.

This was due to two factors. The first was his upbringing and the environment in which he grew up. The second was Jabotinsky, his mentor and model. Begin was a constant target for his adversaries' barbs, often poisoned ones. He could have easily made mincemeat out of them, availing himself of his great mastery of the spoken and written word and of his biting sarcasm, yet he never—not even during the most violent disputes—descended to his opponents' level. At the same time he demanded of his aides and associates to show great restraint and not pay their detractors back with the same currency.

He always used Jabotinsky's example as support. In a letter dated July 12, 1930 which he sent from Paris to the editor of his own paper in Jerusalem, *Doar Hayom*, Jabotinsky wrote: "For God's sake, forbid our contributors all brands of hysteria. Strong words are hysteria; uncontrolled accusations are hysteria." (*Fighter and Prophet*, Schechtman, p. 96).

An example of Begin's extreme care not to offend others can be seen in the elections to the Ninth Knesset, when the fate of his movement and his leadership were at stake. At that time the Labor party was embarrassed by some public disclosures concerning corruption involving one of its leaders (Asher Yadlin), and the suicide of another leader (Avraham Ofer). What could have been more natural than to use those disclosures to settle scores with old adversaries?

Yet, throughout the election campaign it was clear that Begin was determined not to exploit those discoveries for political gain. This restraint was the result of the political education of the leader of Herut, which in some instances even compelled him to intervene personally in order to prevent excesses on the part of others.

Although at times the election propaganda seemed rowdy, in the final analysis one can conclude that with rare exceptions on the part of tiny leftist parties and the Independent Liberals, whose fear of failure made them go to extremes, the campaign was generally conducted with decency and along the lines of a legitimate ideological contest, in no small measure thanks to the leader of the Likud.

I recall a visit to Begin's official residence on Balfour Street in Jerusalem on a Sabbath afternoon in July 1980. Present were also Ben Millner, Herut leader from Montreal, Harry Horovitz, the Prime Minister's aide, and others. During the conversation, the recently published autobiography of Yitzhak Rabin came up. The Herut leaders were not unhappy with some of the unflattering remarks Rabin made in the book about Shimon Peres, the leader of the opposition to Begin's government. Begin made a sour face, and murmured something like, "I don't like such things. . ."

He knew quite well that Rabin's criticism of Peres might be used in the upcoming election campaign, but his sense of fairness did not allow him to approve of an attack by one leader on another.

Begin, known for his phenomenal memory, his constant dwelling on the events of the past, and his determination to perpetuate the memory of the German massacres of the Jews, chose to forget one set of events in the struggle of the underground before the creation of the state. At the height of the underground fight against the British, the latter persuaded the Jewish Agency to collaborate and help turn in the members of the Irgun. This collaboration was given the cynical name of "Saison," or Season, which meant open season on Irgun fighters and supporters. Many of them were arrested and sent to detention camps, some were tortured, and a few died. From our present perspective, in light of what has happened since, and after additional facts have come to light, these actions look even more astounding and shameful than they were at the time they took place.

Yet Begin, the dauntless and persistent fighter against the inaction of the establishment, against acquiescence to foreign oppression, did not retaliate against his fellow Jews during the Saison, and to this day has made it his policy not to bring it up.

The most apparent reason is his great concern for Jewish unity, which he pursued with equal consistency and single-mindedness during the pre-state years, during his parliamentary opposition, and at the helm of power. As mentioned before, he always put the good of the nation above partisan interests, and when something did not reflect well on the nation, he preferred to relegate it to the archives of history.

This shows that this man, in spite of everything, never became embittered, never lost his faith and confidence in his people. It takes greatness of character not to become vengeful considering all that Begin had to endure. Ultimately, his love for the Jewish people overcame justified bitterness. It was not only the result of his analytical thinking, according to which, to paraphrase the great Hebrew poet Uri Zvi Greenberg, "Although we Jews are guilty, yet we are not the most guilty of nations. . ." It also stemmed from his particular inner life, of being able to forgive those who have wronged him.

Some Israeli journalists had denounced his friendly attitude towards opposition leaders, which was not in keeping with the "tradition," and which blunted the effectiveness of the opposition, whose role, in their opinion, is to always disagree with the government. Some have even suggested that it was a clever maneuver on the part of the prime minister. Thus, for example, his embracing of Shimon Peres was reported in a negative light. As one who witnessed that embrace, I can testify that it was done spontaneously and sincerely. It was typical of his positive feelings towards political adversaries whom he respected, and for some of whom even felt affection.

One such example dates back to the time when he was a member of the National Unity Government, after the Six Day War. In a conversation with him I mentioned the Allon Plan (concerning the future of the West Bank, in which the former Deputy Prime Minister offered to divide the West Bank between Israel and the Palestinians). I fully expected him to react sharply against the plan and its author. I was astounded when, after critically analyzing the plan, he praised its author, stressing his military achievements and personal friendship with him. I must confess that I have dealt with heads of parties who were not nearly so far apart in their views as Menachem Begin and Yigal Allon, yet seldom heard such kind words from one about the other.

Immediately after he became prime minister, Begin sought to introduce the American style of politics into Israeli political life. He publicly "waited" for the blessing of the head of the Labor party, Shimon Peres. When his expectations were not fulfilled, he solicited the blessing, and wondered out loud why it was not forthcoming. When Peres reminded him that in the past, when Labor won the election, Mr. Begin did not hasten to offer his blessing either, the latter reacted: How can you compare? In those days your slogan was "Without the communists and Herut."

Why did he go to such an extreme? Did Mr. Begin need Mr. Peres's blessing, as if Peres were the Lubavitcher Rebbe? . . . Of course, one should not underestimate any Jew's blessing, particularly a Jew with a record as illustrious as Peres's. But it appears that Begin wanted to start the new era of good will, in a new, good spirit, a new style in the relations between the government and the opposition.

Begin is European, and therefore closer to the European political culture than to the American. But he preferred to learn from the United States and follow its example when it came to the relations between the two main parties. He liked the American style, as I could tell from my conversations with him and from his actions. He did not consider the American custom of "conceding defeat" to be degrading, but rather to be proof of being a "good sport." It suited his character and his views, for, in effect, it meant accepting the will of the people as expressed in free elections, and showing willingness to cooperate with the person who was given the responsibility and the burden of running the country.

If this was true in relatively normal times, it was certainly true in times of crisis. When Israel faced pressures and danger, it was necessary that the government's policy, which mostly expresses a national consensus, be given bipartisan or even multipartisan support. This is what the national interest required, and the new prime minister was intent on introducing such a style.

Chapter Nine

Leadership and Camaraderie

The Begin I knew was above all endowed with boundless devotion to his people and to their spiritual and cultural heritage. He dedicated his entire life to them. His thoughts and yearnings at every moment, twenty-four hours a day, were imbued with love and concern for his people and their land.

He was blessed with intuition, imagination, faith, courage, and, above all, vision. Those qualities were nurtured by his father's house, by his hometown, his teachers, and particularly his mentor, Ze'ev Jabotinsky.

The master and his disciple had many things in common. Both had a burning faith in their mission and in its success. Jabotinsky was for Begin the example of a statesman, not of a politician.

Begin knew well how to distinguish between the goal and the many pitfalls along the way to the goal. For him the dream of a sovereign Jewish state was not merely a sublime idea but an elementary condition of existence, and at the same time a supreme historical imperative. Begin believed strongly that no one hands a people freedom and sovereignty on a silver platter. He knew that in order to gain those cherished goals one must go against the current, learn to fight, be ready and willing to offer the highest sacrifice.

He learned to walk tall, hold his head high, pay attention to outside appearance, and project confidence and trust. Begin's opponents saw in this attitude a theatrical appearance. They couldn't have been more wrong! Begin was anything but theatrical. He loathed imitations. He never pretended to be anything he was not. His honesty was absolute, both in private, in everyday life, and in public, on a podium and before the cameras.

His outward gentlemanly manner was a reflection of his nobility of character. His courteousness was the result of ethical principles, of his kindness, which is the hallmark of the Jewish character (according to the Jewish sages of blessed memory, Jews are compassionate, humble, and charitable).

He was always ready to protect the weak, help the persecuted, fight for justice. As prime minister, when he found out about a ship carrying Vietnamese refugees who had nowhere to go, he ordered the gates of Israel open to them, and several of those Vietnamese families have since been living in Israel.

As leader of the underground, Begin radiated faith and inspiration. The fighters of the IZL were totally selfless, absolutely committed to their people and their land. During the Revolt they struck fear in the heart of the British ruler. When imprisoned they stood before the British military court as proud soldiers defending their people and their homeland. They went to the gallows singing *Hatikvah*. They sanctified the Holy Name. Rabbi Aryeh Levin, the Tzaddik of Jerusalem, said to me: "The great in Israel had no idea how great those young people were!"

One such young man, Raphael Kirsch, a survivor of the German hell who came to Israel on the Altalena in 1948 (see Chapter Thirty-Three), and later fell in the battle for the Negev, wrote the following poem after the Altalena was fired at because of what turned out to be a tragic mistake on Ben-Gurion's part:

> We sailed to suffer and to fight for you,
> We brought the revolt and the munitions boat for your freedom.
> For years we toiled ceaselessly in Europe, and we brought
> Altalena, the fruit of our labor, to you, our land.
> God, how you received us! We shall never forget.
> We dreamed of our comrades-in-arms, but we were fired at instead.
> And although Altalena was sunk, lift up your heads, soldiers!
> We shall always be loyal to undivided Eretz Yisrael.
>> (Quoted from *Altalena* by Shlomo Nakdimon,
>> in Hebrew, Idanim, Tel Aviv, page 4).

Menachem Begin, spiritually rooted in timeless Israel, was a man of his time, immersed in the reality of the present, often a cruel and bitter reality. But he was always mindful of the past, of his people's glorious history and spiritual greatness, and its terrible suffering. At the same time his mind focused on the future, on the vision of the free and sovereign nation. Thus, as a true leader, he lived in the present, past and future.

In this age of wide-spread disrespect for one's patrimony, Begin's person and leadership remain a beacon of light to us all.

Chapter Ten

"Separatist" As Unifier

Begin and his organization were denounced during the revolt as
porshim, "dissidents" (at that time it was a pejorative notion) or
"separatists," who caused a split in the community and undermined
Jewish unity. It is true that Begin did not accept the absolute authority
of the establishment. He rebelled against its course of action, or rather
inaction. He parted ways with the majority, which followed it
obediently. He represented a small minority in the *Yishuv* and in the
Jewish world, as is usual with revolutionary forces.

He gained the image of an extremely partisan leader, one who put
his own party ahead of everything else, ahead of the good of the nation. This argument was repeated endlessly, until it started to
dominate the minds of many, and was accepted by the innocent and
the not-so-innocent alike as an indisputable fact.

Nothing is farther from the truth! The truth is that few Jewish
leaders have been as little concerned with partisan politics as
Menachem Begin. His outlook and his approach have been national
and not partisan. He thought, dreamed and fought for the entire nation
and its ideals and interests. He was always guided by the question,
what is best for the people as a whole? It is hard to find a person less
concerned with sectarian interests, or more dedicated to the overall
interest of *Klal Yisrael*, the totality of the Jewish people.

There is ample proof to back this up. During the entire period of
the "separation" he did not spare any effort to bridge the gap and
find a common denominator between the Irgun and the Haganah,
to reach an understanding and find a way to cooperate. The fact
that such cooperation was reached for a short time was due to his
tireless efforts, particularly to his concessions, which at times were
far-reaching.

Courage in fighting and the courage to prevent a fratricidal war

He showed great courage in fighting the foreign occupier, yet he showed equally great courage in preventing a war between brothers. The man who raised an iron fist against the British Empire at the peak of its power, and who avenged Jewish blood, that same man received blows and insults, endured betrayal by fellow-Jews (the "Saison"), and yet saw to it that a fratricidal war was prevented at all cost.

Was it only because of a sense of national responsibility, a desire to prevent a disaster resulting from such a war? This was certainly a major reason. Yet his seemingly acquiescent posture in this instance, compared to his uncompromising attitude toward the foreign enenmy, stemmed from his view that love of the people as a whole was the ultimate factor.

When the State of Israel came into being he joined the parliamentary system and acted according to the principles of democracy more assiduously than many other leaders who often paid lip service to democratic slogans. As a leader of the opposition for nearly thirty years, his attitude towards the government was animated by the need for national unity. He never once criticized the government of Israel while travelling abroad. He rejected any opportunity to do so with one consistent answer: I criticize my government in my country, in the Knesset, not abroad. He would stress the words *my* government with a convincing tone.

Yet, even in Israel he would criticize the government with restraint. He would always stay within the bounds of courtesy and good taste, and would stick to the point, always careful not to stoop to the level of personal attacks. I recall once when I visited him at his home in Tel Aviv with my son in law, Rabbi Meir Fund and my daughter Dr. Ruhama, his wife. We talked about some controversy that took place at the time between the government and the religious community, and Rabbi Fund criticized the prime minister, who happened to be Golda Meir. Mr. Begin, who in principle agreed with the argument of the Orthodox Jews, forcefully and persuasively defended his prime minister (he was in the opposition at the time).

Jews, unfortunately, are known to engage in a great deal of infighting and petty sectarianism. And yet Begin did not hesitate during one of the most critical moments in Israel's short history to suggest that the man who tried to physically liquidate him, (during the attack on the ship Altalena), the man who declared "No coalition with the communists and Heruth!" the man who for years maligned and damned him, be appointed Israel's prime minister. Begin did not spare any effort trying to make it a reality. This unprecedented and unbelievable episode occurred in late May 1967, on the eve of the Six Day War.

Would this be the approach of a separatist? Was there ever a precedent to such behavior in any other country?

The climax of this paradox named Menachem Begin occurred in more recent years when Begin visited Washington as Israel's prime minister on July 18–19, 1977. The man who had been tainted as a separatist, as a divisive influence, became the rallying point for American Jewry, with all its factions, movements and currents. He became a unifying factor for all Jews in the largest Jewish community in the world!

All the attempts to play up differences of opinion, to emphasize political contrasts in regard to the newly elected Israeli prime minister, evaporated and disappeared in the face of the spirit of unity shown by the masses of Jews in America and throughout the diaspora, as the Jewish people stood united in its support of the Jewish state and its determination to ward off any threat to its security and existence.

Furthermore, no sooner was Begin invited to form a government, than he turned to the main opposition party with an offer to form a national unity government, which meant sharing power after 29 years of "wandering in the desert of the opposition," as the Israeli expression goes.

When this offer was rejected, he appointed one of the leaders of the opposition, Moshe Dayan, as his foreign minister, and offered a key state mission to another member of the opposition. His party members complained that he was giving his opponents key positions, leaving few for his friends. They felt slighted, and circulated the joke that Begin was fulfilling Ben-Gurion's slogan, ". . . without the communists and Herut" (in the government!)

Their complaint was well founded. They were finding out, however, that Begin, as prime minister, acted as the leader of the state, not of a party.

Chapter Eleven

Warrior as Peace Maker

One of the happiest moments in Israel's existence was the arrival of Egyptian President Anwar Sadat in Ben-Gurion Airport in November 1977.

The irony of history, it seems, is boundless. The "infamous terrorist" accomplished what the peace-loving socialist-Zionist leaders were not able to achieve in all their years in power—peace with the largest neighboring Arab state. Begin the "maximalist" gave up the entire Sinai Peninsula—a territory larger than Israel—in return for a peace treaty. For once, Begin's most irrational critics were nonplused. Seeking some "method to the madness," they pointed to such parallels as Charles De Gaulle, the French superpatriotic president, giving up Algeria. They argued that the Israeli Left, meaning Labor, was afraid the Right might have started a civil war if the left dared give up the Sinai. The Right, the argument went, certainly did not have to fear the left, and therefore could act on a broad national consensus.

As of this writing, the peace with Egypt, signed in 1979, has just celebrated its tenth anniversary. Articles have been written in the Israeli and world press, assessing the meaning and effectiveness of the Treaty. There may still be some difficult years ahead before the problems of the Palestinian Arabs, of Lebanon, Iraq and Iran, and a whole host of others are solved. But the peace between the two most powerful nations in the region is well in place, and there are good reasons to believe that it is indeed the beginning of a new era, of a comprehensive settlement of the Arab-Israeli conflict, even as there are difficulties.

Historical events are like high mountain peaks. As long as we stand close to them and dwell under their shadows, we cannot grasp their tremendous height. Only from a distance are we able to perceive their true greatness. Thus, ten years after the signing of the peace treaty, we are beginning to understand the enormous significance of this historical turn in the course of events.

There have been disillusionments and deceptions. The treaty and its addenda talk a great deal about "normalization" of relations, but there has been less than complete normalization. Many hopes have not come to fruition. Economic relations, two-way tourism, cooperation in many areas, have not yet become a reality.

However, there is one outstanding fact which overshadows all the other. During the past ten years, not a single Israeli soldier has fallen on the Israeli-Egyptian border.

Knowing Menachem Begin's deep sensitivity to human life, aware as I am of his overriding concern during his fight against the British oppressors for the safety of his fighters and his efforts to avoid unnecessary casualties on the British side as well, I am sure that this factor plays a decisive role in his assessment of the importance of the peace treaty.

During these ten years there have been clashes, bloodshed and skirmishes between Israel and its other Arab neighbors. In the north, there was the Lebanon war. Imangine what would have happened if at the same time there had been an outbreak of hostilities on all fronts, in particular on Israel's southern border, with its biggest and most powerful neighbor, Egypt.

On September 17, 1988, the tenth anniversary of the Camp David accords, I called Menachem Begin and congratulated him on is achievement. "This was," I said, "one of your finest hours."

Usually in my calls to Begin I avoid political remarks. I respect his self-imposed "reserve." But this time I took the liberty of sharing with him a thought on the subject. What gave me the courage to take this liberty? The great Jewish commentator Rashi. The Torah says: "Many [of the Jews] may die [if they approach Mount Sinai] (Exodus XIX: 23)." Rashi comments, "The Almighty said, even if one dies, I consider it like many."

Accordingly, Begin's sensitivity to life and his ardent efforts to avoid bloodshed, as evidenced by his role in the Camp David accords, made it one of his greatest achievements.

Partisan historians and journalists have tried to diminish and to distort Begin's role in the peace process. They have attributed the main role to Anwar Sadat, and have portrayed Begin as a reluctant partner to the process. A recent example is Amos Perlmutter's book, *The Life and Times of Menachem Begin* (Doubleday, New York 1987). Perlmutter, a political scientist at American University in Washington, did a great deal of research for his book, and spoke to many of the principals in the peace process, including Israeli, Egyptian and American leaders. His painstaking scholarship is certainly impressive, but there is one problem with his conclusions. They are based on what is basically a biased and distorted picture of Begin. Perlmutter describes Begin as wandering by accident, as it were, into the peace process, getting involved in it in all the wrong ways, making all the wrong moves, and through some great good fortune a peace treaty did emerge in the end, not because of Menachem Begin, but in spite of him.

Perlmutter is not alone in his assessment. It reminds one of the fact that Moses is not mentioned even once in the Passover Haggadah. The entire saga of Passover is centered around the towering figure of Moses, yet the great liberator and law-giver is totally absent from the recounting of the Exodus. The traditional Jewish explanation to this strange fact is that the authors of the Haggadah did not want Moses to be worshipped by future generations, but rather make the point that the Exodus was a divine act, in which Moses was only a conduit. So be it. Begin, no doubt, would agree to the premise that everything he ever accomplished for his people was a divine act of which he was only an instrument and a conduit.

But taking a closer look at this event, perhaps a little objective chronology could help clear it up. One good source is a book by *Ha'aretz*'s political correspondent, Uzi Benziman, *Prime Minister Under Siege* (in Hebrew, Dvir, Jerusalem 1981). Neither Benziman nor *Ha'aretz* can be suspected of being particularly biased in Begin's favor. Benziman covered the peace negotiations and wrote the book right after the signing of the peace treaty, and although he does not appear to be an admirer of Begin, he must be given credit for a fair and objective coverage of the subject.

The important facts, as reported by Benziman and in many other sources, are the following:

When, rather unexpectedly, Begin became Israel's prime minister on May 17, 1977, the President of the United States at that time, Jimmy Carter, was engaged in finding a peaceful solution to the Middle East conflict. Carter's peace plan, which sought to establish a comprehensive peace in the Middle East through an international conference which would include the Soviet Union, did not take into account many facts of life in the Middle East, and was doomed to fail.

The real beginning of the process that did lead to a peace treaty took place at the residence of the U.S. Ambassador to Israel, Samuel Lewis, on the 4th of July, American Independence Day. The main player was the new Prime Minister, Menachem Begin, who participated in the celebration of the American national holiday at the U. S. Embassy. The broker was Jan Kuvac, the Rumanian Ambassador to Israel. Begin took the Rumanian ambassador aside and told him: "I would like you to know that if President Ceausescu invites me to Rumania, I shall accept the invitation." The answer arrived a few days later, letting Begin know of an invitation from the Rumanian president to come to his country on a state visit. Begin observed with satisfaction that his move was successful. He wished to make direct contact with the Rumanian president in order to have the latter relay his message to Egypt (Benziman, page 12).

This was the beginning of the peace process, and not, as many people have been misled to believe, Sadat's trip to Jerusalem. Sadat's visit was, no doubt, a most courageous act. It was clearly the turning point, the epoch-making move. It showed the world that an Arab leader can be a great statesman indeed. Sadat deserves the accolades he has received. And, for that matter, Jimmy Carter deserves a great deal of credit for his role in the Camp David negotiations, which—as Benziman and others report—were by no means simple or easy, and needed an enormous amount of effort, which Carter provided. The same applies to other players, such as Moshe Dayan, Ezer Weizman, Aharon Barak, Meir Rosenne, Elyakim Rubinstein, Yechiel Kadishai, Naftali Lavie and others. But that difficult man, that overly "legalistic" leader, that man of many contradictions, Menachem Begin, was the key player, without whom there would have been no peace treaty, simply because none of the other players, for all sorts of reasons, could not have pulled it off. It took precisely an "oddball" like Begin to do it. For many years to come people like Perlmutter and Benizman and many others will try to analyze, or psychoanalyze, or in any other way attempt to understand why Begin, the ultranationalist, the "terrorist" achieved what no one else was able to accomplish.

But to me it is all very clear: Begin wanted peace for his people more than anything else in the world. He longed for it all his years in the underground struggle, and it was his stated policy when he first came to power in May 1977. And he meant it, because throughout his life Begin always meant what he said. He later sent the IDF to Lebanon because he wanted to put an end to the PLO threat emanating from that country and make peace in the north as well, but, unfortunately, that did not work out. Certainly, we cannot blame him for trying.

Israel learned quite early in its existence that, to paraphrase the expression, "He who wants peace must be prepared for war." This is the unfortunate reality, and it is particularly true in the Middle East. Israel fought more than its fair share of defensive wars, invariably because war was imposed on her by her neighbors, either through a direct attack, as in 1948, or through hostilities in 1956, or through other wars and acts of aggression, the worst being the surprise attack on Yom Kippur in 1973.

The average Israeli, while excelling on the battlefield, dislikes war more than anything else in the world. Every Israeli mother dreads the day her son becomes a soldier, because every Israeli mother knows mothers who have lost sons on the battlefield, and she knows that their pain never goes away. The same, of course, also hold true for every Israeli father.

And Begin has known all of this as well if not better than anyone else. To this day he mourns his family and fellow Jews murdered by the Germans, and he mourns every member of the Irgun who died in the battle against the British. His beloved wife, Aliza Begin, is buried on Mount Olive in Jerusalem next to the two underground fighters who blew themselves up in a British jail after they were sentenced to die by hanging.

The main conclusion one may derive from Begin's peace treaty with Egypt is this: Begin's life's work is far from completed. But he certainly caused the breakthrough for peace; he paved the way. The goal is peace. Peace on all fronts, and peaceful coexistence with all of Israel's neighbors. It is certainly a goal that, as Begin has shown, can be achieved.

One of the best ways to understand Begin's attitude towards peace is to read the text of his acceptance speech at the Nobel Peace Prize ceremony in Stockholm Sweden.

Chapter Twelve

"Fascist" as Stalwart of Democracy

One of the most pejorative political terms of the twentieth century is the appellation "fascist." It has been used most often by leftist regimes to denigrate their enemies. In Palestine of the 1920's, as Mussolini rose to power in Italy, and as the socialist wing of the Zionist movement became dominant in the *Yishuv*, Jabotinsky and his Zionist Revisionist party were labeled by the Zionist establishment as fascists. Among other things, this was due to the fact that the left considered the Revisionists too nationalistic for their own liking, at a time when they strongly believed in the solidarity of the workers of all nations, and in a world of social justice and peace waiting around the corner. Clearly, as we know today because of hindsight, the Revisionists had a more accurate vision of the future than the Marxists.

The assault of the left against the Revisionists reached a climax in the attacks on Begin and his underground organization, the Irgun, and later on his political party, the Herut.

In 1989 a book was published in Israel by a history professor at Tel Aviv Unversity, named Yonathan Shapiro (*Chosen to Command*, published by the prestigious Laborite press Am Oved), in which the amazingly ignorant "scholar" promotes a thesis according to which Begin borrowed his political philosophy from the pre-world war Polish party, the National Democrats, or Endeks. I lived in Poland at that time ans I participated in its political life as secretary of the Jewish members of the Sejm and Senate (Polish parliament). I can only shake my head in sorrow at the complete ignorance of this professor in regard to Polish history between the world wars.

The overreaction of the Zionist left against Jabotinsky during the pre-state days could perhaps be explained away in light of the great ideological fervor that typified that era. But why is it that even today, in what is generally considered a post-ideological age, we still witness an avalanche of books and articles perpetrating old canards and even creating some new ones?

One possible answer is the fact that the socialism that dominated the Zionist movement and ruled the State of Israel during the first thirty years of its existence has reached the point of ideological decline, a fact attested to in a recent book by the highly respected socialist Israeli historian, Professor Anita Shapira. It is only natural for leftist-oriented writers and scholars to try to cover up their ideological bankcruptcy by defaming the Israeli right.

When the Zionist left strove to establish a national home for the Jewish people in its historical homeland, it had another equally important goal in mind, namely, to establish social justice and to change the socio-economic structure of Jewish society, particularly to convert the Jewish masses of Eastern Europe from small merchants and artisans into workers. They planned to transform the Jewish immigrants from what they called "non-productive" elements, to farmers who cultivated the soil.

The socialist theories of A. D. Gordon, Ber Borochov and Berl Katzenelson had a decisive influence on the developent of the Zionist leftist movements. They provided the impetus for their war against the Revisionists and against the Irgun under the command of Menachem Begin. They went so far as to distort the nature of the German mass-murders of the Jews.

According to the socialist Zionist ideologues, the greatest crime of the German murderers was "fascism." A mistaken impression was created as though the war was fought between democracy and "fascism," in which the Jews were part of the democratic front, which included the socialist movement. The victory of the latter over the the "fascists" would solve the "Jewish problem."

The Zionist left put its trust in the European left and in democracy. Even when the Western democracies completely ignored the massacres of European Jewry caught in the clutches of the Germans, and closed their gates to Jews about to be systematically exterminated, the aforementioned illusions did not evaporate.

This perception was mistaken from the start. While totalitarianism did enable the Germans to embark upon a plan of total annihilation of the Jews, the mass murder was not done solely by orders from above, by a dictator and a ruling upperclass, but through the participation and cooperation of the entire nation, of all its segments, parties, classes, and circles. One might even say it was done "democratically." Clearly, the mass murder was the expression of the unanimous will and resolve of all the German people. German civilians and soldiers murdered Jews they encountered not waiting for orders from above.

Hitler, after all, was elected in democratic elections, with only a certain degree of pressure. The pressure did not prevent tens of thousands of Germans from voting for other parties. But the overwhelming majority of the German masses—about 90 percent—voted for the National Socialists of their own will and even with frenzied enthusiasm.

Secondly, the fascist regime in its country of origin, Italy, under the leadership of its founder, Benito Mussolini, did not persecute the Jews until Italy joined the Axis, and even then only under German pressure. The fact is that Italian cooperation with the Germans in this area was less than the cooperation of the French, who often took the initiative under German occupation to round up and deport the Jews to Auschwitz even before the Germans ordered it. Unlike the French, the Italians did not expel the Jews and send them to their death. On the contrary, under most adverse conditions and despite German pressure they made many efforts to save Jews. In detention camps like ours, in the south of France, which were under Italian Army occupation, the Italian officers more than once alerted the detained Jews of the danger on the part of the Germans, and some Italian soldiers even used force to prevent the deportation of Jews from those camps.

All of this took place under the fascist regime of Mussolini (despite the fact, one might add, that the Pope at that time, Pius XII, acquiesced to and by his pregnant silence aided the annihilation of the Jews). It may sound like a paradox, but it is a fact based on documentation and research. Of all the nations of Europe, the Italians (under fascism!) extended more help to persecuted Jews than any other people, including the democracies!...

Surely I cannot be accused of having shown any love for fascist regimes. I was always pro-socialist, and in Poland before the war I voted for socialist parties. I belonged to the religious workers' party, Poale Agudath Israel. The socialists had my heart, and I condemned fascism. But the trouble is that the socialist Zionist doctrine was frozen in a position that became obsolete during the years of the catastrophe, and proved to be a complet failure.

Ironically, the movement for the "Entire Land of Israel," which came into being after the Six Day War, was led by—among others—some of the oldest and best established leaders of the Israeli left, such as Tabenkin, Nathan Alterman, the poet, and Moshe Shamir, the novelist.

Today, the question is no longer one of labels. It is rather what political moves by the present Israeli leadership will yield the best long-term results. Begin's actions from the time he asserted himself as Betar head in Poland to the time he signed the peace treaty with Egypt, as history proved, were in the best interest of the Jewish people.

Chapter Thirteen

Avalanche of Defamation

Unlike the Zionist establishement, Menachem Begin was fully aware of the consequences of Jews publicly fighting Jews. Not only did Begin sternly warn against brotherly war, he scrupulously kept his polemics within proper limits, avoiding verbal violence. He realized that every assault, exposure and derogatory speech would be used by the British, who were the common enemy.

This difference between Begin and his adversaries persisted after the emergence of the State of Israel. As leader of the opposition, Begin fulfilled this role to the best of his ability. But whenever he appeared abroad he avoided criticism of the government. I remember that even when pressured by newspapermen at press conferences his standard reply was: "I have full opportunity to criticize my government (will emphasis on "my") at home. I don't have to do it abroad."

The leftist Zionist parties were not inhibited by similar considerations. Their attacks against the IZL, often vituperous and vicious, were conducted both inside and outside Israel without regard for eventual repercussions against Zionism in general.

When Menachem Begin was elected in 1977 to become head of the government, these attacks continued unabashedly, and in some cases became even more outrageous.

Many important newspapers were biased against Begin, influenced by decades of condemnations by the British and by his Zionist adversaries. When he came to power, government officials in the United States and other leaders were eager to gather evaluations and opinions on the new leader of Israel. Their inquiries were directed, of course, to Zionist spokesmen. Many of them issued their routine criticism of Begin as obstinate, inflexible, a warrior, and so on.

Some came out with yet sharper attacks against the new Israeli Prime Minister. Some organized special groups for this purpose.

During the years following May 17, 1977, various opponents of

Menachem Begin continued their endeavors to impugn his policies and prestige, distort his role and intentions, and weaken his government.

A special effort in this direction was made by Dr. Leonard Fein, a leftist with a particular antagonism toward Begin. Dr. Fein, a professor at Brandies University, gathered a number of liberal Jewish intellectuals in June 1980 with the sole aim of denouncing Begin's policy and leadership.

The New York Times accorded their statement front-page treatment. The erroneous impression created was that this group represented important segments of the Jewish community—perhaps even a majority of American Jews. In fact, this was a small and insignificant coterie of mostly frustrated individuals without any influence, who were never elected to any office, and who played no visible public role.

The only person with some following in this group was Rabbi Alexander Schindler, the President of the (Reform) Union of American Jewish Congregations.

Being friendly with Rabbi Schindler, and recalling our common endeavor to make Begin's leadership palatable to the American Jewish public, I sent the Rabbi a telegram of one sentence:"Et tu, Brute?"

It is interesting that Begin sent him a letter with the same Latin quotation. However, Begin added some warm words, expressing the conviction that it must have been a misunderstanding, and that Schindler must have been misled. (Schindler later showed me Begin's letter, a nice way of reproaching me why I didn't have the same attitude.)

Rabbi Schindler then publicly denounced Dr. Fein's attack, emphasizing his opposition to it.

The harsh attack by that group against the new Israeli Prime Minister evoked disgust and outrage among the Jewish public. I felt that something had to be done. Together with Mr. Shragai Cohen, a religious Zionist leader who assumed the active role of host and chairman, and Mr. Hagi Lev, then Secretary General of Herut in the United States, we called a meeting of representatives of various Jewish organizations at Young Israel headquarters in New York.

The meeting was well-attended. Major Jewish organizations, such as the Zionist Organization of America, Mizrachi, the Union of Orthodox Jewish Congregations, Young Israel, and, of course, Herut, participated.

We issued a strong statement of solidarity with, and support of, the new Israeli government with Menachem Begin as its head.

I covered this event at length in the press, and I reported it personally to Menachem Begin. I must say that he wasn't unhappy with this event.

This only confirmed the true feeling of a large number of American Jews of every type. This attitude toward Begin was confirmed whenever he appeared in America.

I recall his first appearance here, in 1977. I was, at the airport. It was a Friday, before Tisha B'Av, which fell on the following Sunday. There were representatives of many Jewish organizations, among them Julius Berman, then president of the Conference of Major Jewish Organizations. I saw Begin's happiness when I introduced Mr. Berman, whom he hadn't met before, as a remarkable Talmudic scholar, with ordination from Rabbi Joseph Dov Soloveitchik.

When Begin noticed me and embraced me, Yechiel Kadishai reminded me to say the Shehechiyanu blessing, which I did with tears in my eyes. . .

Chapter Fourteen

Misleading Misconceptions and Misnomers

In describing the struggle of the Irgun Zvai Leumi, many writers of articles and books produced an unusual number of misleading misconceptions and misnomers. Some of them are the result of misunderstandings, of failing to grasp the true character, significance and spirit of the IZL struggle. Others are the outcome of an intentionally hostile, biased approach and of planned distortions and even falsification. For decades, a well-oiled propaganda apparatus of the leftist Zionist establishment was busy doing this job, first against the Revisionists and then against the IZL.

Let us start with the last word in the above title—Misnomers.

The fight of the IZL was labeled "terrorism" by its adversaries and enemies, and "underground war" by its participants and sympathizers.

The struggle of the Hagana and then in 1948 of the Israeli army— is called the War of Liberation. This name is generally, and thoughtlessly, accepted.

It is not easy to fight established non-truths weaved into the fabric of the political scene, or try to change longtime rooted falsehoods. But we will dare to try anyway.

Liberation means to free a territory, a country, a nation, a people, of the yoke of a foreign occupier, of a tyrannical ruler.

Does this apply to the Jewish defense against neighboring Arab armies and gangs? Did they rule the people of the country?

Certainly not. This was the role played exclusively by the British. The Balfour Declaration of November 2, 1917, the San Remo resolution and the decision of the League of Nations of constituted the international legal basis of the British Mandate over Palestine. These resolutions entrusted the British government with the rule of Palestine in order to fulfill a specific task, to create a Jewish national home.

The moment the British Mandate administration issued the infamous White Paper of 1939, and mercilessly executed this unilateral and unjust edict to close the gates of the country before the Jews escaping from the German slaughter—this mandate government not only betrayed the trust of the international community, not only became guilty of breaking its international legal obligations and solemn promises, but utterly destroyed the very foundations on which its Mandate rested.

From a trusted executor of an internationally established mandate, this government became a malevolent and brutal occupier of a country to which it had no historical or legal claim whatsoever.

The mandate government became derelict to its duties and obligations, betraying the confidence put in it by the Jewish people. It degenerated gradually into a despotic oppressive regime exercising ruthless tyrannical power for its selfish ends, to the detriment of the people whose national homeland it was obliged to further.

Begin's revolt against this despotic rule was the war of liberation, preceding the defensive war of 1948. Any other term is a gross misnomer.

This War of Liberation was waged by the Irgun Zvai Leumi

The war against Arab armies and guerillas conducted by the Hagana and the Palmach and, since May 15, 1948 by the regular Israeli army, was a war of defense against *outside* aggressors, but cannot be termed in any way a "war of liberation." Israel's army is named the Israel Defense Forces. The war it fought was a war of defense against outside enemies.

True, there were instances of resistance by the Hagana and the Palmach against the mandate government, but those were isolated incidents of sabotage, responses to the more outrageous acts of the British against Jewish refugees. They caused some trouble to the foreign ruler, but in no way can they be dubbed war and certainly not a war of liberation.

During all those years, from the publishing of the White Book in 1939 up to the proclamation of the State on May 15, 1948, there were disputes, conflicts, protests and demonstrations against the Mandate government. But all this were probings—now we know illusionary ones—of possibilities or probabilities, of an eventual agreement and mutual accommodation.

Was this a war of liberation? The answer is no. The real life and death war, proclaimed with the stated aims of expelling the British occupier, was fought by Irgun Zvai Leumi. Their's was the War of Liberation.

We said before that normal civilized relations between the Jewish Agency and the British were maintained. These "relations" were one-sided, observed only by the Jewish side. The British, for their part, were conducting at the same time a cruel war against the homeless remnants of the German slaughter, who were trying to reach their historic homeland.

This was a one-sided and merciless war. The extreme inequality and overwhelming imbalance of power between the British Empire on the one hand and the Jewish refugees on the other, resulted in a cruel and barbarous war.

On one side the whole might of the British army and all the powers of the Empire, on the other—poor, weak, homeless broken people just escaped from the hell of bottomless pain and suffering devised by the Germans.

Looking back at this black page in British history, we are astonished at this unfamiliar face of the English, usually admired for their human values and civilized behavior.

But this was the face of Ernest Bevin. From testimonies and documents presently available he emerges as a savage anti-Semite of the worst kind. He was a man obsessed with pathological hatred toward Jews. He had the full support of the mediocre Clement Atlee, the then Prime Minister. (The chapter of the rule of these two Labor leaders doesn't belong to the glorious feats of Socialism. . .)

It is misunderstanding and misleading to speak of the period of 1945-1948 in terms of the white Paper, of mandate policy, etc.

It was war, all-out war by the British against the Jewish survivors of the German mass-murders.

The London government wasn't choosy in the ways of conducting this war. If diplomacy is war by other means, the British used every diplomatic trick to pursue their objective.

They found and used powerful allies especially in the State Department in Washington. Despite the humanitarian appeals by President

Harry S. Truman to let 100,000 Jewish refugees from the DP (Displaced Persons) camps in Germany into Palestine. the anti-Semitic Bevin found kindred souls in the State Department who covertly sabotaged the President's policy. Both found common ground in terming the President's stand as motivated by domestic politics i.e. the desire to get Jewish votes.

Both used the scurrilous and utterly false accusation that the Jewish refugees were infiltrated by communist agents.

As Peter Grose establishes in his thoroughly documented book, *Israel and the American Mind,* not a single Soviet communist was among the tens of thousands of the Jewish refugees.

The British tried to enlist the help of the Americans for the blockade of Palestine against the Jews. Their allies in the State Department were sympathetic to this outrageous demand. Only the watchfulness of Clark Clifford, the President's assistant, prevented this outrage and the shame.

The Zionist establishment refused to recognize the war as war. They were continuing official relations, "negotiations" which were in fact efforts of persuasion. What is more, the Zionist establishment, which titled itself "The Yishuv" (the Community) fought the IZL in alliance with the British. It went so far as to capture IZL fighters, tortured some and rendered them to the government during the infamous Season. The collaboration between Hagana and IZL was a glorious chapter of unity in the war against the British oppressor, but was short-lived. The Hagana leadership would later denounce the bombing of the King David Hotel which housed the General Secretariat of the Mandate government, despite the fact that it took part in the planning.

The War of Liberation was the one declared and fought against overwhelming odds by Irgun Zvai Leumi under Menachem Begin as Commander-in-Chief, culminating in the liberation of the Jewish homeland from the British rule.

No war was more just! It was conducted under self-imposed high human standards. There were many instances where the IZL under strict orders from Menachem Begin risked the life of its fighters in order to avoid civilian casualties.

If there were lapses they were rare, unintended, resulting from special circumstances, and deeply regretted (they will be treated later separately).

The label "terrorists"applied to the IZL belonged to the British. The terrorists were the government leaders in Whitehall, the High Commissioner's Office in Jerusalem, and the commands who pursued and persecuted the Jewish remnants seeking a home. The terrorists were the ones who illegally imprisoned the "illegal" immigrants. The Arch-terrorist was not Menachem Begin, but the brutal, union boss Ernest Bevin.

The terrorists were the ones who imprisoned Jewish refugees in Cyprus, who exiled Jewish leaders to Eritrea in Africa, who forced back refugee ships to Germany (Exodus 1947), who hanged captured Jewish soldiers, violating international conventions of warfare. The British, not the IZL, were the real terrorists.

Verbal War

But why are labels so important? What difference does it make how we call certain people and acts? Isn't the essential thing the actual events, the occurrence itself, no matter how you term it?

The answer is this:

Ideas are weapons, and so are words expressing them. In the war of the British against the Jewish survivors, against the Jewish homeland, semantics were used as arms. Semantic tricks, clever manipulations of words, false definitions, shameful distortions, erroneous and deceiving terms, defaming labels, all this verbal onslaught on the Jews striving to find a home in their homeland, served a well calculated purpose: to present the just cause and its defenders in the blackest colors; to create an image of savage gangs posing a danger to Western democracy and to the stability of the post-war world.

This verbal war's first objective was to deprive the Jewish fighters of the sympathy of civilized people and to silence protest against outrage. The second objective was to create a motive for the pitiless persecution and oppression; to justify a most unjust war of the British against the Jewish survivors.

It is sad to say that a similar method was used by the propaganda apparatus of the leftist Zionist establishment dominating the Jewish political scene, against the IZL and its Commander-in-Chief, Menachem Begin. This defamation continued against Herut and its leader even after the emergence of the State.

In this case the misnomers were also used to justify the many wrongs committed against IZL and its members. Like the blatant and outrageous injustice of discriminating against the veterans, invalids, widows and orphans of IZL fighters, depriving them of the pensions and benefits owed to them.

I cannot forget the shock and pain that I experienced listening in 1949 to the Knesset speech by Menachem Begin on the subject.

"Against whom are you waging war? You are fighting invalids, widows, orphans of the heroic war for Liberation of Israel!" cried out Begin.

This misnomer was also used in political battles, defaming the successor of the IZL, Herut, long after it became clear to neutral students and observers that it was IZL whose War of Liberation was the decisive force that put an end to the British occupation and made a Jewish State possible.

Therefore, on the question "what is in a name," the answer is: very much. Sometimes names not only define things, facts, events; they influence them, shape them, make them happen.

Thus, it is imperative to set the record straight for the sake of historical truth. More important, in order to cope with the present and plan for the future, we have to have a clear view of the past.

To understand the struggle for Jewish independence, one cannot rely on biased writers, some of whom are fanatical haters of the IZL and its commander.

The true mirror of this struggle can be found in the clandestine broadcasts of the IZL and LEHI, (Geulah Cohen being the leading voice), the posters, leaflets, communiques, and other pronouncements of the spokespersons of these fighters. A particularly revealing source are the statements of IZL and LEHI defendants at the trials before the British courts. (We have to include the statements of the defendants at the trial of Eliyahu Ben-Chakim and the executioners of Lord Moyne, before the Egyptian court in Cairo.)

From these, and not from the propaganda press releases and speeches by partisan politicians and just propagandists you'll learn the truth of what really happened in these dramatic times and how and why. You'll also learn which was the decisive factor in the expulsion of the British from Palestine. The truth of these sources is confirmed by documents of the British Foreign Office, and by publications of some of the English actors in this drama.

As for the term "underground" which was used by the IZL itself. Even this term is only partly correct. Of course, in face of the enormous disparity in the power between the two sides, the IZL on one side and the Mandate government on the other, with an army of 100,000 soldiers and police forces, with the Zionist establishment fighting the IZL in collusion with the British, on the other, it was necessary to go underground.

But the IZL conducted an open and declared war, which was constantly and consistently fought on many fronts, and the IZL command publicly took responsibility for every action.

On the contrary, the sporadic attacks by the Hagana were not surprisingly clandestine, and what clearly distinguishes them from those of the IZL, they were never admitted after the fact; responsibility was never recognized by the official leadership.

And don't forget that they occurred simultaneously with negotiations being conducted and official relations on all levels being maintained.

Paradoxically, these covert acts rather deserve the label, or the badge of honor, "underground fight," while the Begin underground was in truth War of Liberation.

This chapter of misleading misconceptions which cause misnomers, deserves the titles of two most edifying books of the great thinker, Dr. Max Nordau, who was, by the way, one of the ideological forecasters of the Revisionism. Their titles: "The Conventional Lies" and "Paradoxes."

The misapplication of the terms "terrorism" and "War of Liberation" are but the most glaring examples of the many misnomers used in the war of words against Begin and his movement, a war which, regrettably, is not yet over.

Chapter Fifteen

"Holocaust Syndrome"

Menachem Begin often spoke about the massacres of the Jews by the Germans during World War Two, commonly known as the "Holocaust." His seemingly excessive referring to this catastrophe was seen by his antagonists and critics as an obsession, a sort of paranoia, which some of them have diagnosed as a "Holocaust Syndrome." For me, a survivor of these massacres, nothing could be more normal. For a Jew to suppress the memory of such horrendous crimes committed against his entire people, to play down their significance, forget and forgive, is nothing short of sickness of the mind.

There is also a practical reason for remembering. If we put aside the greatest catastrophe that has ever befallen any people and minimize its consequences, we may jeopardize the Jewish future. Yasser Arafat and his cohorts, and all the Saddams, Husseins, Hommeinis and Qaddafis bent on destroying Israel, are certainly prone to think that if such atrocities and mass killings committed by the Germans against the Jews are forgotten and forgiven, who would call them to account for any repetition of the same?

Forgetfulness in an individual may only be a shortcoming. National forgetfulness is national disaster. When it comes to Jewish disasters, the world seems to have an amazing capacity to forget.

Examples: In February 1988, the Norwegian Ambassador to Israel, Torleiv Anda, had the temerity of telling reporters that "the Nazi occupation was actually more enlightened than the Israeli one in the West Bank and Gaza" (*From Beirut to Jerusalem*, Thomas L. Friedman, Farrar Straus Giroux, New York 1989, page 435).

In September 1989, the *Washington Post* quoted the head of the Catholic Church in Poland, Cardinal Jozef Glemp, as saying that he did not realize Auschwitz meant so much to Jews (in conjunction with his refusal to remove a convent from the grounds were millions of Jews were gassed and killed).

In addition, every once in a while some university professor somewhere in the world proclaims the thesis that the Holocaust never happened.

What is even worse and more painful is the fact that many Jews, including Jewish leaders, particularly those who have ascribed to Begin a "Holocaust syndrome," fail to understand the centrality of the European catastrophe in the Jewish experience not only in this century but throughout history, and its implications for Jewish existence today and in time to come.

I firmly believe that the German diabolic mass murder was not just another tragic episode in history. It was a turning point. Its repercussions and consequences have not yet been fully grasped. In the long run, it is bound to alter not only Judaism and Jews—which to some degree it already has—but also the entire Western civilization and the entire world.

Not to erase from one's mind the most traumatic event of one's life is the most natural thing in the world. A father or a mother who lose a child will think of that child every day of their life.

Menachem Begin lost his entire family (except for his sister, Rachel), among the millions of Jews slaughtered by the Germans, including one and half million children. Each one of those persons, every child and adult, was his personal loss. Other Jewish leaders may have also felt the pain of the massacre, but none like Begin.

The Jews never forgot the destruction of the Holy Temple. They have focused on this tragic event in their daily prayers. They mourn it in a day of fast called Tisha b'Av, which commemorates this event of nearly two thousand years ago as if it happened yesterday. How, then, are we to forget this recent destruction, which was even worse than *Hurban Ha'bayit*, the destruction of the Temple? Of the Temple it is written: "He vented his anger on wood and stones." How deeper should the present destruction be engraved on our souls and minds!

Recently we have had some shocking revelations about the general attitude of the Zionist and the general Jewish establishment toward the mass murders of Jews in Europe. It was an attitude of terrible apathy and even—what a shame to admit!—a calculated passivity on the part of the heads and apparatus of the Jewish Agency, the World Zionist Organization, and the various parties and their leaders.

These accusations have been made until now by some Orthodox

circles who oppose Zionism and the State of Israel. Their purpose was to accuse the Zionist movement and its institutions, and to justify and strengthen their opposition to the establishment and existence of the state.

This tendentiousness weakened those critics' arguments and made them lose their credibility. The conclusions they have drawn from the shameful behavior of those Zionist leaders are utterly false. They argue that it negates the justification for the state. The logical conclusion is just the opposite. The catastrophe proved beyond any doubt that Jewish existence is not possible without a sovereign Jewish state, without an army and a government that can protect the people from their enemies. The fact is that the same kind of leaders who conducted themselves so disastrously during World War Two, once they became part of a sovereign state showed responsibility, courage, and self-sacrifice, particular during periods of crisis and war.

The accusations against the Zionist establishment are based on scrupulous research in the archives of the Jewish Agency and the World Zionist Organization. The authors, scholars and professors of the Hebrew University who conducted this research are sympathetic to the Zionist leftist establishment. They have tried to soften their criticism by pointing to the weak condition of American Jewry and the *Yishuv* in Palestine at the time. They conclude that there was not much of an opportunity to save anyone.

But the facts refute this argument. First, in the face of the terrible catastrophe it was imperative to make at least an attempt to save lives, even if the chance of success was small. Such an attempt was not made. And even when an opportunity presented itself it was wasted.

The failure of the Jewish leadership in Palestine, in the United States, and in other parts of the world to do anything significant to rescue Jews will forever remain a dark stain on those leaders. This has direct bearing on Begin. I would refer the reader to Robert Morse's book, *When Six Million Died*, Ben Hecht's *Child of the Century*, and, more recently, Dina Porath's *Entangled Leadership* (*Hayishuv B'Milkud*, in Hebrew, Am Oved, Tel Aviv, 1986). These books deal with the issue at great length. I will only touch here on a few points, and try to show this grim picture from which emerged the phenomenon of the IZL and its commander.

The overall picture in the Jewish world during World War Two consisted of two separate realities—the reality of Jews under German occupation, and the reality of the rest of the Jewish world. Jews under German occupation were all, without a single exception, sentenced to death. One is reminded of a line in American novelist John Hersey's famous novel about the Warsaw Ghetto, *The Wall*, in which a Jewish father in the ghetto writes in his diary: "Today my wife gave birth to a son. Another Jew is going to die."

Jews in the rest of the world, including Palestine, North America, Great Britain, the USSR, and so on, were safe (the degree of safety varied greatly from, say, England to the United States, and for a while the *Yishuv* in Palestine came under the threat of invasion by Rommel's Africa Corps, which threat thank goodness did not materialize). It became the duty of Jews in the free world to make every effort imaginable to move heaven and earth to save their brothers and sisters (quite literally, for almost every Jew outside the war zone had relatives inside it).

The most sorrowful fact is that no serious rescue effort was made. It is only in recent years that the full extent of this shameful debacle is being made known, most notably by the exhaustive study undertaken by the aforementioned Dina Porath and others.

What was the situation?

First, the Jews of Palestine. In 1939 there were less than half a million Jews in Palestine. Yet this small community was split into numerous parties and factions, and suffered from an excess of "leaders," all of whom seemed to be forever arguing and battling with one another. In her book, Porath quotes Professor Ben Zion Dinur, later education minister in Ben-Gurion's government, as saying:

> Try to put in parallel columns, with exact dates, the news about the extermination of thousands of Jewish communities. . . and the news about splits and debates in parties and factions, and you will see the horror of these facts in relation to our entire future. . . We forget that future generations will consider it and will recount it, and will record every action which we undertake these days. . . and I am very afraid, that the sentence which the coming generations will pass on us , the sentence of our sons, will be quite severe.

Porath goes on to say:

> Indeed, as we look back on all the conflicts, the internal splits and the debates that took place at that time among our people and in the Zionist movement, then—without taking into account the question

of the rescue possibilities, the Germans, and the Allies—we agree
with every word he said, and our heart is terribly bitter (page 474).

These are the words of a scholar belonging to the Labor camp,
who probably did not realize when she first undertook this study how
far it was going to take her, and was deeply affected by what she
found out.

Factionalism and partisan politics did not only paralyze the *Yishuv*
and prevent it from putting forth any significant rescue effort, but went a
step further. Since the main voice for action on behalf of the persecuted
Jews of Europe was the Revisionists', and since the Revisionists could
not possibly be up to any good according to their antagonists, the
socialist Zionist leadership, instead of looking for ways to collaborate
with the Revisionists on rescue efforts, did exactly the opposite.

On the eve of World War Two, in 1939, the Revisionists were
engaged in bringing "illegal" immigrants to Palestine, while the
Jewish Agency was still unwilling to antagonize the British. These
immigrants went through hell before arriving in the promised land,
and many never made it. In June 1939, Moshe Shertok (later Sharett),
writing on behalf of the Jewish Agency, complained to Lord Josiah C.
Wedgewood, a British friend of the Zionist movement, that the
Revisionists were treating the immigrants on the boat "Af-Al-Pi" [in
spite of everything] "inhumanely" and "bestially." Wedgewood
responded on June 22, 1939 with barely contained anger:

> My Dear Shertok:
> Yours of 14th June received today about illegal immigration. I do
> wish you had not sent me this. It makes me think that you want to
> stop illegal immigration, except in your own boats. I gather that
> some 15,000 have got into Palestine in the last year, of which half
> must be yours. All over Europe ten times this number are dying of
> starvation because they can't get in.
> Don't put obstacles in their way because they are being saved
> less agreeably than are the lucky ones whom you rescue.
> For heaven's sake get together and improve conditions and ef-
> ficacy—if you really want to get more Jews into Palestine.
>
> Yours
> Josiah C. Wedgewood

(Quoted from Prof. Yosef Nedava, *Who Caused the British to
Leave Eretz Israel*, in Hebrew, Jerusalem 1987, page 24).

It took an Englishman to tell the Zionist establishment to get its act together and start saving Jews in earnest. How terribly sad!

Things did not improve in this respect even after the mass massacres were in full swing. Porath writes:

> In the second half of 1943 [one and a half years after the start of the mass killings, which were then reaching their peak!] relations deteriorated. . . between the organized *Yishuv* and the Revisionists. The administration [the Jewish Agency] was concerned that the "provocative elements," the "law-breakers among us"—namely, the Revisionists—are trying to take control of the public, whose disenchantment with the British has been growing, causing the leaders of the Agency to lose control of the situation and of the public. . . "of course we have to do everything [!] but we must not be influenced by the shouting, behind which there is nothing," said Kaplan [treasurer of the Jewish Agency, later finance minister under Ben-Gurion] (page 97).

The "shouting behind which there is nothing" were precisely the anguished cries of Begin and his comrades, described as "lawbreakers," "hysterical" people who could not be taken seriously. Begin and his followers were the Jeremiahs of that generation. They shouted, they pleaded, they cried bitterly about the *Hurban*, about the destruction of the Jewish people of East and Central Europe, of whom we today are but a pitiful remnant, a leftover.

On occasions, Begin was asked, what did you do to rescue the Jews in Europe? He explained that while he was in the underground in Palestine, there was very little he could do about sending people to Europe for rescue operations. He had even lost contact with the Revisionists in Europe and the United States who were engaged at the time in demanding of the Allies to bring about a rescue effort. But the hard cold fact remains that the official Zionist leadership, which had the ear of Churchill and Roosevelt, did nothing.

Begin at least tried, and was rebuffed by the establishment. That in itself makes a difference. Jeremiah did not save Jerusalem from destruction either. But he did cry, he did warn, he did plead with his people. Begin acted in this prophetic tradition. His stature keeps growing as the years roll by, and as the stature of others keeps diminishing.

Another reason why Begin understood the enormity of the

catastrophe even before and while it happened, whereas most of the Zionist left did not, is because he was rooted in Jewish history, tradition and values, while the Left was captive of the socialist and Marxist philosophies which, as of this writing, have become bankrupt. Porath writes:

> The main thing is that the Left in Palestine and in the world considered the Soviet Union the great fighter, physically and ideologically, against fascism in all its forms. It followed with admiration the fight of the Soviet population and the Red Army against the Nazis, and hoped, despite many disappointments, that the socialist ideology will provide the philosophical and human answer to the Right and all it stood for at that time (page 474).

In the face of the Final Solution, these Jewish leaders fell victim to the Final Delusion: they put their trust in the Western democracies, namely Great Britain and the United States. Dr. Chaim Weizmann continued to believe in Great Britain's good intentions all throughout the war. It was not until the war was over, and after Churchill's cabinet was replaced by a Labor government headed by the mediocre prime minister named Clement Attlee, and by a vulgar, mean-spirited, anti-Semitic foreign minister named Ernest Bevin, that Weizmann at long last woke up from his long nirvana and wrote in his memoirs:

> Mr. Bevin, as the new foreign minister, declared this policy [of restricting immigration of Holocaust survivors to the land of Israel] in the name of the Labor Government. . . In a talk with journalists immediately after the announcement, Bevin said, apparently in answer to our demand to implement the Balfour Declaration and the promises of the Labor Party: "If the Jews, with all their suffering, will try to get to the head of the line, there is a danger of a renewed anti-Semitic reaction everywhere.

Weizmann adds: "I found this comment unnecessarily brutal, even vulgar, but I cannot say it surprised me." (*Trial and Error*, Memoirs of Israel's President, in Hebrew, Schocken, Jerusalem 1949, page 428).

In spite of this not only Weizmann but also Ben-Gurion, head of the Jewish Agency, and Moshe Sharett, Israel's future foreign minister and Ben-Gurion's successor as prime minister, continued to put their trust and hope in Great Britain. As late as 1947, Ben-Gurion was still looking for an accommodation with the British

Labor government, as seen in the following letter to Bevin:

The Jewish Agency for Palestine

February 11, 1947

The Right Hon. Ernest Bevin, P.C., M.P.
Foreign Office,
S. W. 1.

Dear Mr. Bevin,
I may have to leave for Palestine very soon, and am wondering whether you could spare me an hour for a private talk—informal but business—at which we might see if it is really so impossible to find some common ground, to get over some of your and our difficulties, or even to reconcile our interests?
I am at your disposal during this week as regards time and place, and a message will always reach me.

Yours,
[signed]
D. Ben-Gurion

The overall conclusion derived from Porath's exhaustive study on the subject is that the Zionist leadership failed to act and make a real difference during the darkest chapter in Jewish history.

A shocking example of this ineptitude—or worse—was the mission of Yoel Brand to save Hungarian Jews in 1944 in return for trucks. Moshe Sharett, who headed the Political Department of the Jewish Agency at the time, conducted the negotiations in Istambul in a most peculiar way. Even if we dismiss the suspicion that a deliberate attempt was made to abort the mission, the amazing facts still remain.

Professor Chaim Weizmann, then president of the Jewish Agency, postponed the meeting with Brand for several weeks because he was "too busy." Quite clearly, the rescue of Jews in Europe was not a top priority with any of the establishment leaders at that time. They did not devote time and energy to this problem. When they did raise the question of the catastrophe, their main concern was to see to it that it did not harm the Zionist cause in the land of Israel. Yitzhak Gruenbaum, a Zionist leader who was a member of the Polish Sejm before World War Two, and left Poland in 1933, rejected the demand to use some of the Jewish Agency's budget to rescue Jews.

The representatives of the Jewish Agency in Geneva, Switzerland, Nathan Levita and Dr. Adolf Silberstein (also a former Sejm member), members of Poale Zion (socialist Zionists), were consistently, and I may say criminally, passive towards any demand for help for Jews under German occupation. I myself had such an experience when I wrote to them from the internment camp in Vittel, France, asking for help to save certain persons.

Poale Zion leader and ideologue Chaim Greenberg, one of the heads of the Zionist Labor movement in the United States, castigated the leadership in written and printed exhortations. He cried and wrote: "For whom are you building the state of Israel, for dead Jews? . . ."

The behavior of American Jewry at the time was by no means the "finest hour" of the largest Jewish diaspora in the world. Roosevelt's total refusal (although camouflaged in hypocritical statements) to do anything whatsoever during the entire war to save any Jewish lives is a dark chapter of his otherwise glorious career, and this in spite of the ardent support given him by American Jews. If American Jewry after 1948, and even more so after the Six Day War in 1967 changed its character from a complacent and acquiescent, "Uncle Tom"-type Jewry, to a politically-conscious and militant community, it is in no small measure due to the fact that Jews no longer are, to quote a nineteenth century English poet, "A homeless race, a hopeless faith," but rather a sovereign people who have taken their destiny into their own hands.

When the systematic slaughter of Polish Jewry was becoming total in early 1943, and after the Bermuda Conference in mid-April 1943 made it clear that Great Britain and the United States acquiesced to the fate of the doomed Jews in Europe and would not lift a finger to rescue even a small number of Jews, an Emergency Committee was organized in the United States, parallel to Begin's revolt and through Begin's influence. It was headed by Hillel Kook (alias Peter Bergson) and Shmuel Merlin, and enlisted the participation of such American public figures as Ben Hecht. The committee proceeded to mobilize American public opinion against the mass murder of the Jews. It employed protest methods such as full-page ads in leading newspapers and mass rallies. It was able to win over such personalities as Eleanor Roosevelt, Bernard Baruch (Roosevelt's advisor), and several senators and members of Congress.

And who, of all people, proved to be the committee's greatest enemy? The Zionist establishment in the United States, headed by Rabbi Stephen Wise! They denigrated the Jewish rescue activists. Meanwhile, Ben-Gurion lambasted the committee and called it "A gang of lawless Irgunists who defile the good name of Israel among the nations" (Porath, op. cit., page 97).

At the very moment when the so-called enlightened world, including the Western democracies, acquiesced to the total killing by the Germans of the Jews in Europe; at the time when Britain and the United States shut every door in the face of Jews who were being led like sheep to the slaughter—the members of the Jewish Agency were concerned about not defiling the "good name" of Israel among the nations through efforts by Peter Bergson's committee to rescue Jews from the German murderers!

Stephen Wise and other Jewish friends of President Roosevelt, who delivered the Jewish vote to the great Democratic leader, such as Judge Samuel Rosenman, his speech writer, helped to harden the President's already stiff and cruel posture against the doomed Jews of Europe, who were now being slaughtered by the millions.

One shocking fact is attested to by one of Roosevelt's associates, William D. Hassett, in his book *Off the Record with FDR, 1942-1945* (Rutgers, New Brunswick 1958):

> October 6, Wednesday [1943]. A full and varied day's program was behind the President when he left for Hyde Park tonight. A delegation of several hundred Jewish rabbis [sic] sought to present him a petition to deliver the Jews from persecution in Europe, and to open Palestine and all the United Nations to them. The President told us in his bedroom this morning he would not see their delegation; told McIntyre to receive it. McIntyre said he would see four only—out of five hundred. Judge Rosenman, who with Pa Watson also was in the bedroom, said the group behind this petition not representative of the most thoughtful elements in Jewry. Judge Rosenman said he had tried—admittedly without success—to keep the horde [!] from storming Washington. Said the leading Jews of his acquaintance opposed this march on the Capitol.

> The President and Sam spoke of the possibility of settling the
> Palestine question by letting the Jews in to the limit that the
> country will support them—with a barbed-wire fence around the
> Holy Land. Sam thought this would work if the fence was a two-
> way one to keep the Jews in and the Arabs out (page 209).

I note the date. It was the eve of Yom Kippur, and I was then in the
Warsaw Ghetto. It was in the middle of the deportation. Some Jews in
Warsaw said: If only American Jews knew. . .

This entry in a White House official's diary reveals the shocking
crime of the so-called Jewish leaders in America during the German
killings of the Jews. Let no one tell us that American Jewry at that
time was completely helpless, without any influence, with no access
whatsoever to the administration. The truth is that even if American
Jews did not have so much influence as they have now, they still did
have many contacts with Roosevelt and a good deal of influence. But
these Jewish leaders helped suppress the information about the mass
murders of the Jews which Yitzhak Sternbuch and his wife Recha
transferred from Switzerland to the United States. They muffled the
cries of their tortured and dying kin in Europe.

When the rabbinical organization headed by Rabbi Eliezer Silver
organized a march on Washington, attended by hundreds of rabbis
and religious leaders, in order to plead with the President to do something to save their people, the Jew who delivered the Jewish vote to
the President, Samuel Rosenman, counselled him to disregard the
"horde," assuring him that "the more thoughtful" elements in
American Jewry did not support them. . .

The above testimony by one of the White House staff members
also reveals the cruelty and cynicism of Roosevelt, who was praised
by Jews as a "lover of Israel" and as one of the "righteous of the nations." As Jewish blood was flowing in occupied Europe, and the cry
of the martyrs even reached Washington, Roosevelt joked with
Rosenman at their expense, making fun of the Jews "behind barbed
wire fences," who at that very moment were being gassed and
cremated.

The lessons of Jewish failure to act, on all levels, in all places, and
of the free world's apathy, including the cruel behavior of so-called
"friends of the Jews" like President Roosevelt, are so painfully glaring, that even if Begin were to have done nothing except spend his

entire life lecturing the Jewish people and the world about these lessons, he would be fulfilling a sacred and vital task.

But Begin did much more. He played a decisive role in helping the Jewish people establish a free sovereign state, and he set a personal example for Jewish unity and renewal, as will be seen in the following chapters.

Some of the authors of articles and books on Menachem Begin are applying to him amateurish "psycho-analysis" in this regard. Having never met him, or only perfunctorily, they ascribe his motives, indeed the inner driving force of his acts, to the influence of the Holocaust. They are defining this influence in a derogatory way, as an obsession, trauma, syndrome. They look at him as a man haunted by morbid fixation, by ghost-ridden complexes which impede his rational thinking and prevent him from using sober reason.

The truth is that Begin never forgot what happened to his family, relatives, friends and nation. But the lesson he had learned fdrom the German massacre of the Jews and the conclusions he drew from the experience are dictated by soundest logic.

There are forces in the world today which, given the opportunity, would complete the job started by the Germans. One notable example is the present ruler of Iraq, Saddam Hussein, who recently threatened to burn "half of Israel" with chemical weapons. Clearly, Begin, who has constantly reminded us of the Holocaust, was not fixated on the past, but rather deeply concerned about the present and the future. It appears that some leaders and intellectuals never fully learn the lessons of the past, and therefore accuse those who do of certain "syndromes,"

Begin has done much more. He played a decisive role in helping the Jews establish a sovereign state, and he opened the door for comprehensive peace in the Middle East thanks to Israel's ability to negotiate with its neighbors from a position of strength.

Chapter Sixteen

Partisanship and National Unity

One of the many false labels affixed to Menachem Begin by his adversaries describes him a fanatical partisan, a narrow minded and parochial politician, an obstinate doctrinaire. The name the Zionist establishment, dominated by the left wing partly Mapai, gave the Irgun Tzvai Leumi (IZL) was Porshim, Hebrew for separatists, those disrupting national unity and damaging the national interest. It creates the image of a group, or "a band" whose actions, whose very existence was detrimental to the Jewish struggle for statehood.

The facts prove just the opposite.

The attacks by the leftists against IZL conducted by vicious ferocity reached their peak in the so called "Season." The word was taken from the vocabulary of the hunting sport, meaning free hunting of animals without restrictions.

Members of the Hagana chased members of IZL, caught some, sometimes tortured them, and surrendered them to the British authorities.

In spite of the clear orders of the Jewish Agency—Zionist organization, there was strong opposition in these bodies, notably by the Mizrachi, under Rabbi Meir Berlin, Rabbi I. L. Maimon, Moshe Shapira and also by Izchak Gruenbaum.

This was such an outrageous act that many members of the Hagana refused to participate. It was then decided to implement it on a voluntary basis. The Palmach, the heroic fighting division of Hagana, under Yigal Allon, refused to collaborate in this enterprise.

The Season was a severe blow to the IZL. Top leaders of the Irgun, like Eiyahu Lankin, Dov Meridor and others were caught by Hagana members and turned over to the British, who deported them to Eritrea, one of Great Britain's colonies in Africa.

As a result, the IZL was depleted of many of its commanders, which prevented the organization from launching major attacks against the British.

The reports of the torturing of captured IZL fighters outraged their comrades, who demanded action. The question of survival of the IZL was in the balance, as Mapai decided to liquidate it through any means.

Here Menachem Begin appeared in his true character. He staunchly opposed any retaliation against the Irgun's attackers and tormentors. Eitan Livni, one of the IZL commanders and one of the closest aides of Begin, recounts the following in his book, *Maamad* (Yedioth Achronoth, Tel-Aviv, 1987):

"Begin was adamant in his resolve not to react and not to retaliate against the Hagana. This was a most difficult decision which caused no little opposition and revulsion.

"It occurred to me that if we seized a few of those responsible for the "Season," Ben-Gurion and his comrades may have second thoughts. I brought the proposal before Begin assuming that this may result in the cessation of the Season.

"We put tracing men around the home of Moshe Sharett, who was the head of the Political Department of the Jewish Agency. I said clearly that I didn't intend to cause violence or bloodshed. All I wanted was to seize hostages and thus put an end to the Season by the Secret Service of the Hagana.

"The head leadership of the IZL consisted of five commanders. My main argument was that it would be hard for us to prevent our people from acting.

"The commander, Menachem Begin, was adamant and didn't budge one inch from his stand. He repeated his arguments which he spelled as early as November 1944, at the beginning of the Season:

" 'There will not be a fratricidal war. Perhaps our blood will be shed—but we will not shed the blood of others.'

"In general the discussions of the command were concluded with the decision of the Chief. But at this meeting it was decided after a difficult discussion to put the question to a vote. David Grusbard sided with me, while Chaim Landau and Bezalel Amizur sided with Begin. The majority decided against retaliation.

"Begin's order was followed scrupulously. It stopped the spying on Sharett. The IZL was restrained from retaliating until the last day of the Season. And we paid the price" (*Maamad*—Actions and Under-ground, By Eitan Livni, Idanim, Yedioth Achronoth, Tel-Aviv, 1983).

It should be remembered that usually Jewish informers on Jews to the authorities (there were no instances of physically surrendering of fellow Jews to the authorities) called "Mossrim" were condemned and despised by the Jewish community, as the most abominable in-dividuals. The pressure by the IZL to retaliate was almost unbearable.

But Begin consistently and strictly forbade any form of retaliation.

The man who harshly condemned the restraint ("Havlaga") toward the attacks of the Arab murderers, and who fiercely fought the British Mandate forces, used all his authority to avoid a fratricidal war, even in the face of the unscrupulous onslaught aimed at the liquidation of the Jewish fighting forces.

Begin's consciousness of the exigencies of national unity, his ab-solute fidelity to Klal Yisrael, and his sense of responsibility for the fate of the Jewish people, prevailed over any other considerations. Without the slightest hesitation he always put the national interest over those of his party.

One may say that is as it should be. But in view of the opposite at-titudes of his adversaries, it is necessary to underscore this point.

Chapter Seventeen

Myth of Polish Imitation

When Begin came to power after thirty years of Labor rule, he brought with him a leadership style that seemed to anger and frustrate the Israeli Left. Unlike his predecessor, Yitzhak Rabin, who was the first native-born Israeli to head the government, Begin reminded people of the European-born Jew with his immigrant generation habits, which Labor had toiled for years to overcome and change. He was not the gruff, informal Israeli-born type, who has little patience for formalities and rituals, and approaches matters directly, abruptly and pragmatically. Rather, he would examine things analytically, raise questions, and choose his words carefully, making frequent references to historical examples. In addition, he would indulge in un-Israeli manners, such as kissing the hand of a lady introduced to him on official functions.

Such outward manifestations, coupled with old anti-Begin prejudices, led critics and commentators to conclude that Begin was not an authentic part of the Israeli political scene, but rather a foreign transplant from Poland, his native country, a product of the Polish political system of the period between the world wars. In other words, Begin, according to those commentators, was a Jewish imitation of a Polish politician.

Preposterous and false as this thesis may sound, it actually became the subject of the aforementioned so-called scholarly book *Chosen to Command*, by Professor Yonathan Shapiro of Tel Aviv University. The professor uses a broad brush to paint Begin and the entire Herut party as imitators of Polish political culture.

As someone who was part of the political scene in Warsaw during the thirties, it is hard for me to decide whether the author of the anti-Begin book speaks out of ignorance or malice. Perhaps both. But it seems that when a worthy person is being suspected of something, it is often of the thing he is least guilty of. Thus, for example, Moses, who we are told was "the humblest of all men," was accused by Korach of showing "arrogance of power" ("Why are you so overbearing?" was the reproach). One should not take the trouble to dignify this misbegotten book with a rebuttal, except for the fact that it reflects the misconceptions of many, and purports to be the result of thorough and painstaking scholarship.

The main theses of the book are:

1. The political ideology of Jabotinsky was nothing but an imitation of the chauvinism of the radical right in Europe.

2. Begin's personality, thinking and aspirations were shaped by the influence of political developments and ideas in Poland. There is nothing original about Begin. All he is is an imitation of the military commander, Jozef Pilsudski, Poland's ruler before World War Two, whose manners and ideas, as well as the struggle and aspirations of the Polish people, were adopted by Begin.

3. The driving force of the Irgun and Herut has been mythology which has little to do with reality.

4. The leadership and the rank and file of Herut have been also driven by a need for "status." This need stemmed from the fact that they were for a long time on the outside of political life in the new state.

5. What motivates Begin and his movement are not rational motives, but rather mystical forces which have nothing to do with actual political and social processes within the Jewish nation.

6. The Jewish people, its history, character, special qualities, aspirations, goals, and lofty spiritual values have nothing to do with Begin's ideas and actions.

In order to prove these absurdities, the professor read a multitude of books, articles and speeches, whose relevance to the subject is purely accidental. He brings proof from texts which have long earned their place in waste baskets, while the ones that do have some value have no connection whatsoever to the subject.

Here are some examples:

"The members of Betar in Poland wanted to form an organization whose main function was to prepare the members to become soldiers in the service of the motherland. They were convinced that military struggle was the only way to political independence."

So far he is right. But he goes on to say:

"In this respect, they were identifying with the views of Jozef Pilsudski, who, as the leader of Poland, was convinced that thanks to the military power of the Polish liberation movement, Poland attained her independence, and only a strong military power could ensure that independence."

A great insight, indeed!

The professor goes on with his prattle:

"[The Betarists] were influenced by the chauvinism that was spreading in Eastern Europe, particularly in Poland. Nationalism was the supreme value in Poland during that period. Its influence was so great that it became, according to historian Norman Davies, the source of prestige, the touchstone of human acclaim in all walks of life in Polish society. . . the extreme right version ruled. . .

"While most Jewish organizations, Zionists and non-Zionists alike, were repelled by these Polish national groups, which were imbued with bigotry and anti-Semitism. . . Betar imitated precisely the spirit of such chauvinistic and anti-Semitic groups."

About the leadership of Jabotinsky and Begin he says the following:

"The choice of a leader, as stated in the regulations, was ostensibly a democratic principle in the military organization, but it was only a symbolic act."

Here again the implication is that the rule of Pilsudski, who actually established the Polish republic in 1918 and later returned to power through a coup, was the model for Begin and his mentor.

Two types of ignorance are at play in all of the above quotes. First, ignorance of Jewish life in Poland. Second, ignorance of the nature, ideas, and dynamics of Begin and his movement.

Let us deal with the first type of ignorance first.

There were few Jews in pre-World War Two Poland who participated in Polish parties. Those few were mainly assimilationists and socialists. In the Polish Socialist Party there were a few Jewish leaders, but the number of Jewish members was miniscule. The masses of Jewish socialists in Poland formed their own Jewish socialist party, namely, the Bund, in order to attain their international, rather than Polish, aspirations ("Proletariat of all lands unite!"). This was due to the fact that the Jews in Poland did not feel they were part of the Polish people, and they weren't. They had their own political parties and communal and social institutions which operated under the purview of the community councils. They lived as a separate nation inside Poland.

If this was true about Jewish life in Poland in general, it was particularly true about ardent Jewish nationalists such as Begin and their movements. Their relations with the Polish environment was marked by friction, mistrust, and conflicts. The Poles, for their part, seemed to run the gamut from extreme overt anti-Semitism to refined subliminal versions thereof, which also applied to the Polish socialists.

The Polish right, which according to the aforementioned professor was a model and a source of inspiration for Menachem Begin, was in effect a sworn enemy of the Jews, and one of the causes for Begin to dedicate his life to establishing a haven for his people to be safe from the likes of the Polish anti-Semites.

The professor writes:

"The meeting of the minds on this question [that military struggle is imperative for attaining independence] between Betar and the ruling clique in Poland, resulted in encouragement for Betar by the Polish government, who even helped Betar with providing its members with military training."

This is an absolute lie! The Polish government at best tolerated Betar as it did other Jewish organizations, but no support was forthcoming for any one of them.

I myself was involved in Polish political and cultural life, no less than Begin. I also studied at the Jozef Pilsudski University in Warsaw, served as the secretary of the Jewish members to the Polish parliament, and wrote articles and even books in Polish. But in spite of all of this, the Polish environment did not leave any traces on my spiritual life or my ideology. On the contrary, for the most part I felt toward it revulsion and defiance. All my thoughts and deeds were different from those of the Poles, and quite often at odds with them. This was the general attitude of the Jews of our generation.

While Shapiro puts together an entire non-book based on his strange thesis about the role of the Polish political establishment in inspiring and moulding the ideology and activities of Revisionism, of Menachem Begin and the IZL, another leftist propagandist has recently come out with an even more fallacious theory (if such thing is possible. . .) Dr. Shlomo Avineri, political science professor at the

Hebrew University, has made the discovery that the "Jewish national renaissance in the nineteenth and twentieth centuries" is rooted in Central and Eastern European political movements and national culture." He writes:

> Israel as it emerged as a nation-state was to a large extent another example of the national renaissance which swept Central and Eastern Europe. . . Even the complex links between nationalism and religion—so vexing to many Israelis—have their origin in the complex interweaving between ethnicity and religion in Eastern Europe (*Jerusalem Post*, January 6, 1990).

According to Avineri, not just Revisionism and Begin, but *all* Israeli political parties and their ideologies are imitations of the Eastern European counterparts. Avineri, who in addition to his reputation as a leading Israeli historian, also occupied the high post of Director General of the Israeli Foreign Ministry under Shimon Peres, draws practical conclusions from his discovery. He recommends to the Israeli parties to follow in the footsteps of Eastern Europe, and predicts—and warns—as follows: "A revival of Eretz Yisrael. . . can also be expected: a country linked to the European [non-Jewish] heritage." He is quite euphoric about this Jewish revival resulting (again!) from the renaissance of the Polish and other Eastern European cultures, liberated from Communist domination.

There is still hope for Israel, he assures us. "With the disappearance of the Communist yoke in Eastern Europe, Israel too can come back into its own."

Avineri concludes prophetically: "Thus, the only hope of a cultural revival in Israel rests on the spiritual and ethical influence of Eastern European countries." In other words, it rests with the same people who together with the Germans murdered all the Jews in their own lands, whose culture and political movements, according to Avineri, they, the murderers, helped develop and shape. . .

What a remarkable proposition! What great promise for the uncultured Jews of Poland, Lithuania, the Ukraine, etc.! What absurd theories can be concocted by a spiritually rootless professor!

Another professor, Allan Shapira, instead of putting the hope for the revival of Israel's culture in imitating Eastern Europe, is afraid that the people of Eastern Europe may instead follow Israel's political and ideological example, which may be detrimental to their inborn and genuine democracies just freed from communist oppression. Shapira laments: "Socialist patterns of thought are largely discredited in today's Israel. Socialist institutions are in disarray, decline or dissolution. Instead a new tribalism is abroad in the land, nurtured by ethnocentric chauvinism and religious obscurantism." Shapira warns: "Are there no signs—ethnic conflicts, anti-Semitism—that this could be a pattern of development in Eastern Europe as well?" (*Jerusalem Post*, January 6, 1990).

In other words, instead of seeing Judaism as a "light unto the nations," the Israeli professor is concerned that darkness may descend on the just-liberated Eastern Europeans because of—of all people!—the Israelis!

This is not the only absurdity created by the queer and strange thinking of leftist professors. How weird this flimsy "scholarly" non-sequitur can be is seen in the following senseless postulate:

> If there was a strong influence by any people and its culture on their Jewish countrymen, this was, as we all well know, the German influence (and vice versa. . .) The Polish, Ukrainian, Russian, Lithuanian Jews (except for a very thin layer of assimilated intelligentsia), did not read literature by the masters of these countries. The Jews looked down on the population of the majority composed mostly of ignorant peasants and vulgar proletariat. And for a good reason. While there was almost no illiteracy among Jews, the overwhelming majority of the Polish, Ukrainian, Russian, Lithuanian population was illiterate, and certainly on a much lower level spiritually than the Jews. Not in vain the vulgar, uneducated, ignorant element was contemptuously despised as "goyish."

How strange it is that Avineri, Shapira and other Israeli professors came to the senseless conclusion that only the Eastern European people influenced the Jews and were the main ideological inspiration and political exemplars for creating the Jewish state!

The same learned pseudo-scholars completely ignore the real cultural symbiosis of Christian and Jewish Germans, which ended in the most cruel massacres in history!

I remember years ago I heard Aliza Tur-Malka, the wife of the greatest Hebrew poet Uri Tzvi Greenberg, a notable poetess in her own right, make some very harsh comments about the influence of Hebrew University teachers on Israeli youth. She accused them of denigrating Jewish heroes and values, and of debasing our glorious past and its great spiritual lights.

I thought then that this great poetess might have exaggerated. Now, after being subjected to these shameful diatribes by the above-quoted professors and their likes, I see how unfortunately right she was then, and even more so today.

It seems that their attacks on the lofty and authentic patrimony of our people has only gotten worse over the years. And again, one of the main targets of their hate-filled and poisonous arrows is the man who personifies the best in Jewish values, Menachem Begin.

Begin took his ideas from Jewish sources. His character, thought, actions, were shaped by historical and traditional Jewish thinking and values, and by Jewish national aspirations and goals.

With the exception of small groups of assimilated Jews, Polish Jewry lived on the other side of a chasm that completely separated it from the Polish people.

Clearly, Begin, like any of us who studied at a Polish university, read Polish literature and newspapers, and was acquainted with the politics of his native land. But he was not part of that environment, and had no share in Polish ideas, ideals and movements.

Even the commonly-held belief that Begin's gentlemanly European manners, such as kissing ladies' hands, are Polish in nature, is simply not true. This custom did not exist in Lithuania or in Congress Poland, where Begin hailed from and grew up. It did exist to some extent in Galicia (Southeast Poland), where his wife is from, and he might have adopted it from her native province.

Begin's late wife, Aliza Begin, his life-long companion, was also a staunch member of Betar. She grew up in a home where Polish was spoken, as in most Jewish homes of the professional intelligentsia in Galicia (her father, Dr. Arnold, was an attorney). But she gave up her native tongue and spoke only Hebrew. Begin studied law at Warsaw University, but in my conversations with him about Jewish life in Poland he never mentioned anything remotely related to Pilsudski, or to Polish political life. Those things simply were not part of his or our patrimony or ideological baggage.

No, Begin was anything but an imitator of Polish politics. More important, he was not an imitator of anything else, for that matter. He was the most authentic of Jewish leaders. While the Zionist left emulated European socialism, and borrowed its ideas from Marx and his successors, and, in the process, turned its back on the original culture of Judaism, Begin was an original and natural Jewish leader. In the thirties and forties, the top Zionist leader in America was Rabbi Stephen Wise; the top Zionist leader in Europe and the world was Dr. Chaim Weitzmann; and the top Zionist leader in Palestine was David Ben-Gurion. All three of them had to bend over backwards to try to please Great Britain and the United States, and all failed to provide true leadership to the Jewish people in its most tragic hour in all of history. The only Jewish leader at that time who realized that "quiet diplomacy" was not the right strategy for the time was Menachem Begin. He was a devoted and ardent disciple of Jabotinsky, but certainly not a blind follower, contrary to the assertions of such people as the above-quoted professor (see the account of Begin's clash with Jabotinsky). He was an independent thinker, who rather examined every question on its own merit and derived his own conclusions, usually the correct ones.

Begin's independent thinking was not divorced from the Jewish people's ideas and needs. He expressed their deepest longings, wishes and strivings. And he certainly did not put himself above the people, as some Jewish leaders did. On the contrary. He was rooted in his people, blood of their blood, flesh of their flesh, one of them, one of the masses of this variegated people.

Chapter Eighteen

Attacks on Begin Contributed to Anti-Semitism

The attacks by the Zionist antagonists of the IZL and the LEHI caused a domino effect that the antagonists either hadn't thought of or, in their fanatical partisanship, didn't care about. These attacks strengthened anti-Semitism. In certain instances, they turned friends of Jews into enemies.

A case in point is the transformation of Dorothy Thompson. Thompson was a great writer, perhaps the greatest in her field, in the 1940's and 1950's. She was a leading advocate of Zionism, the strongest Christian voice for the Jewish homeland. She was at the same time an ardent admirer of Professor Chaim Weitzmann, the recognized leader of world Zionism.

Weitzmann came out violently in the 1940's against the IZL and the LEHI; he condemned them in the strongest language possible.

Dorothy Thompson took her cue from the adored Zionist leader, whom she trusted implicitly. With her sharp, poisonous pen she produced a series of columns, syndicated in hundreds of papers across the country, assaulting the Jewish fighters savagely as "terrorists." Her outrageous calumnies, aimed initially at the "terrorists," eventually struck at the Zionists in general, and subsequently at the Jews as a whole. Her insinuations became anti-Semitic.

Her campaign reached such depths that the Zionist leadership became alarmed and tried to mollify her and moderate her attacks, but their efforts were in vain.

The anti-Zionist American Council for Judaism became her closest ally and supporter, and she became more and more vicious and uninhibited in her hate campaign against the Jews and, especially, against Zionism.

In thousands of letters, telegrams and calls, people protested

Thompson's defamatory columns. The editor of the *New York Post*, Ted Thackery (husband of Dorothy Schiff, the publisher) was a friend and supporter of the IZL and in 1944 he dropped Thompson's column.

Let us recall that to make things even worse, Thompson became a Germanophile, full of praise for the murderous nation, and sharply attacked Henry Morgenthau Jr.—then Roosevelt's Secretary of the Treasury—for his plan (the Morgenthau Plan) to turn Germany into an agricultural country after the war, and thus deprive it of the ability to start another war.

The transformation of Dorothy Thompson from an ardent Zionist supporter into a savage anti-Semite was a direct result of the attacks by the Zionist World Organization, with Professor Weitzmann at the helm, against the Jewish fighters. When these Zionist leaders realized the damage they had caused, it was too late to tame the unleashed flood of hate which poured forth from many segments of society hitherto free of anti-Semitism.

Chapter Nineteen

Renewed Assaults

In the guise of scholarship, leftist pseudo-historians and fake political scientists (who are more politicians than scientists) are trying to rewrite history à la Kremlin.

There appears to be no end in sight to the stream of distortions of the person of Menachem Begin and his role in our contemporary history. But while until now this unsavory work has been carried out by hired propagandists and unprincipled publicists echoing each other's hackneyed falsifications, lately a new breed of Begin "experts" has emerged: distortionists under the masks of "scholars," pseudo-historians and so-called political scientists who parade the usual credentials of university lecturers, researchers and other marginal appendages of the academic underworld.

One Sasson Sofer, for example, published a voluminous work in this vein under the deceptively objective title *Menachem Begin: An Anatomy of Leadership* (Basil Blackwell, Oxford, 1988). The author accumulated and assembled, with a diligence more suited to worthier causes, an abundance of falsifications and vilifications, culled from the tabloid newspapers and calumnitory and libelous leaflets and pamphlets of the party hacks and apparatchiks of the Jewish Agency—Zionist Organization and other professional slanderers and shameless muckrakers serving the leftist establishment.

Mr. Sofer clothes these mean insinuations and outrageous utterances in a "academic" babble designed to deceive the unsuspecting reader into believing that he is revealing the results of serious scholarship rather that merely reshuffling the usual phrases and juggling the same senseless and baseless contentions.

All these obfuscations and distortions have one essential aim: to deny and defuse the lasting beneficial impact of Menachem Begin's personality and leadership.

This historical truth has simply been considered unacceptable;

thus, mountains of printed trash continue to be produced in an effort to bury and erase undeniable facts.

Sofer's naming of his pastiche "Anatomy of Leadership," is, like the work itself, subversively misleading. The proper title should be "Anatomy of an Academic Fraud." The book opens with an outright libel. In the preface Sofer accuse Begin of ordering the bombing of the Iraqi nuclear reactor (designed to produce atom bombs to be used against Israel) for the sole purpose of winning votes in the upcoming parliamentary elections! Sofer writes:

> In the spring of 1981 (Prime Minister Begin) sent Israel's air force to bomb Iraq's nuclear reactor. Within a few months he had won an election in which he had appeared to face a certain defeat. (p. VII)

Even in the rough-and tumble Israeli elections no one of consequence had dared to impute to Begin such a monstrous deed—to endanger the Israeli air force with such a perilous mission, fraught with far-reaching martial risks—as a campaign trick!!

This irresponsible accusation will certainly not be overlooked by the anti-Israel forces (including the State Department Arabists who already harshly condemned the bombing at the time). Now these people can boast of having "proof" of the righteousness of their positions furnished by a lecturer at the Hebrew University, no less! Moreover, the nastiness of Sofer's attacks is covered and cleverly hidden under the dignified stamp of "Oxford."

This magnum opus is a product of a great number of professors and commentators who contributed to the research work, which was lavishly subsidized by the Leonard Davies Institute for International Relations and the Research Fund of the Faculty of Social Sciences at the Hebrew University!

There is no doubt in my mind that a few of the individuals and institutions involved in this work deliberately and consciously intended to support and abet Mr. Sofer's endeavors to blacken the activities and accomplishments of Menachem Begin in the emergence of the Jewish State and to pervert the public perception of his decisive and lasting historical role. But certainly there must be others who are embarrassed and even ashamed of their part in a work about whose purpose they may have been misled.

We wouldn't grace this deceitful publication with our attention if it weren't for the sad fact that it is far from a singular phenomenon.

Sofer is only one marcher among the dismal parade of biased leftist writers posing as historians and political scientists. Their "scholarly" camouflage cannot hide their essential similarity to the woefully familiar publicists and propagandists of the old and new left. They misuse their titles and chairs to validate their rewriting of history in the Soviet manner. More specifically, they persist in attempting to rewrite the history of the Irgun Tzvai Leumi, the LEHI and their leaders.

As they realize that the influence of Menachem Begin's ideas and achievements did not vanish with his voluntarily leaving the political scene, these decades-long hateful adversaries are continuing to labor to erase the indelible stamp that this leader left on our people, changing the course of history.

We must not allow this to happen.

Chapter Twenty

Begin's Persona

For one reason or another, there are many who have taken it upon themselves to attack Menachem Begin. But these individuals have not just criticized his ideas and dreams—they have criticized Begin himself. And in the process they have distorted his character, and made him out to be someone he is not.

In fact, I have read a number of books and articles about the Begin I have known through many years of personal contact, and I always come away with the feeling that I am not reading about Begin. Not only is there little in common between the Begin written about and the Begin I know, but the two radically contradict each other.

This phenomenon might be explained by the insight of Rebbe Nachman of Bratzlav who once said that when someone tries to criticize a righteous person he always criticizes him for things of which he is absolutely innocent (as Korach did when he accused Moses, "the most modest of men," of being conceited), or by the Sage's statement that his enemies were not attacking Nachman himself, but a Nachman they had created in their own minds who is *worthy* of attack.

Begin and his movement have been slandered and defamed by the powerful propaganda machine of the Zionist establishment. His reputation was sullied in the minds of innocent and uncritical readers, to say nothing of the minds of his adversaries. He was initially purported to be guilty of sins of which he was innocent, and he subsequently became an easy target.

He has been, for example, accused of having fierce personal political ambitions and of being self-aggrandizing and power-hungry. The truth is that he was a selfless and altruistic individual who was wholly dedicated to the Jewish nation and its needs. His assumption of the leadership of the Irgun Tzvai Leumi, of the Herut Party and finally of the State itself came about as a result of his personal charisma and self-sacrifice for his people which instilled confidence and trust in him. The confidence proved to be well-founded, and the trust never was betrayed.

Despite the personal harm Begin suffered from the maligning tongue of his arch-enemy, David Ben-Gurion, he nonetheless went to Ben-Gurion on May 29, 1967 (on the eve of the Six Day War) to beg and persuade him to take the helm of the Israeli government because Begin thought it was for the good of the country that Ben-Gurion do so.

The first thing Begin did when he became prime minister on May 17, 1977 was to offer full partnership to the opposing party, Mapai, in a gesture of national unity. (But because Mapai believed that it was only temporarily out of power and that it would only be a matter of time before it would regain it, it declined the offer). To the dismay of many in Likud who never forgave him, Begin then offered the nation's second highest office to the Mapai leader, Moshe Dayan.

He was said to be autocratic. But that was clearly untrue. In fact, he is an ardent (and some might even say over-zealous) and dedicated proponent of Democracy. He strengthened democracy in Israel and saved it from impending one-partyism.

Begin was accused of polarizing the parties, and polarizing the Ashkenazic and Sephardic communities, but the very opposite proved to be true.

Chapter Twenty-One

Authenticity and Integrity

Friends, opponents, and neutral persons alike, all have admitted that the man was endowed with a special kind of charisma, which affected those who came in contact with him. What was the secret of this charisma, which worked even on personalities with whom he totally disagreed, and who were poles apart in character, background, education, outlook, and especially political opinions? How did Begin manage to build bridges over so many personal differences, and at times even strike a friendship with adversaries?

The answer lies in his truthfulness. It might be characterized as authenticity. It illuminates some other traits of Begin's character. It was first cultivated in his youth, in the spiritual climate in which he grew up, in the atmosphere of Brisk, a spiritual center of religious Jewry, and later through his contact with his mentor, Jabotinsky, whose personality left an indelible imprint on his character.

Begin was always true to himself. Politicians, professional opportunists, men of short vision, call this quality rigidity. Begin, however, was never a man of devious maneuvers and stratagems, but always true to his ideas and principles. He would always derive his strength from his belief in his cause, and trusted his ability to persuade others, including avowed skeptics. To seasoned politicians he might have appeared naive in his conviction that "if they only knew the truth. . ." After all, there are always those who know the truth but choose to ignore it. It was this ignoring of the truth that he refused to accept. After all, his entire life was a struggle against lies.

Of course he understood the reality of politicians preferring the interests they represent to the truth. But he was convinced that the cause he served could not possibly be in conflict with justice. An example of his faith in his cause can be seen early in his career, when, in 1940, he was turned over to the Soviet secret police in Vilna, and did not hesitate to try to convince his communist, anti-

Zionist investigators of the merits and legitimacy of the Zionist idea.

Half a century later, it appears that his truthfulness was not only the result of personal traits, but also of a pragmatic approach. In the end it proved to be practical. It paid off.

As we review his statements, speeches and articles during his years in the underground, and later during his parliamentary career, we cannot fail to marvel at his faithfulness to the truth under all circumstances. This proved in the end to be the correct policy. It helped the commander of the Irgun gain the confidence of the public, even as his adversaries' lack of honesty in their attacks on him made them lose ground in public opinion. In his struggle in the underground he derived a special advantage from the credibility he acquired. The British Mandatory government could allow itself to lie and deceive with impunity, since it controlled enormous resources of coercion, as well as a military and political force, and powerful media, and did not depend on the public's trust. Great Britain did not need a moral basis for its policies and actions. Beginning in 1939, when it first issued the White Paper, the Mandate government based its rule on lies and deception, on cruelty and coercion, as can be seen clearly in documents now being declassified for the first time (Documents of the Foreign Office, 1946-1948, Government Printing Office, London 1976).

It was different with the Irgun and its commander, Menachem Begin. Since his resources were poor beyond comparison to those of the British, and since he depended strictly on volunteers, he had to depend on the trust Jews had in him and in his movement.

It is common practice during wartime for the fighting parties to hide their defeats so as not to endanger morale. Begin never pursued this policy. As a result, his men learned not only from successes by also from failures and setbacks, and made greater efforts each time to ensure the success of the next operation. The idealism of the Irgun members, their dedication to their aims, their faith in their ultimate victory, were so strong that an isolated setback could not dampen their spirit.

This attitude also characterized Begin's activities in the Knesset. It was also evident during election campaigns, in which he insisted on fairness and respect for opponents. It helped him survive 29 years in the opposition, and led him to victory in 1977. Even among those who did not vote for him, few doubted his honesty and integrity.

And, when he was elevated to power, these qualities helped him deal effectively with some of the most important decisions Israel had to face since the founding of the state.

Chapter Twenty-Two

Faith and Optimism

Our many and varied meetings took place during more difficult or less difficult times, never during easy times. But he was always in high spirits. He was always happy, always radiating faith and even overflowing with optimism, which always affected everyone around him.

Our meetings in Israel and in New York took place mainly during his years outside the government (except for my visit to his office when he served as minister without portfolio in July 1967, when he drew my attention, not without visible satisfaction, to the picture of Jabotinsky on the wall). Besides the fact that he was a member of the Foreign Affairs and Security Committee of the Knesset, he was obviously not in on what was going on, and certainly not "in the picture" of the decision making-process. In other words, he was looking in from the outside, rather than taking part in making decisions. When, in times of a national emergency, he was let in on secret information, he was not let in on the final decision. He was only told that, as head of the opposition, he should be kept informed, and that was all.

He had his doubts about some of those political decisions, and did not withhold his negative opinion on some of the government's actions. Despite some difficult situations, which he believed could have been prevented, his assessment was always optimistic. The same was true during eight Knesset elections. Although the polls predicted defeat for his party most of the time, he never lost hope.

He always believed in his ultimate victory, and when it finally came on May 17, 1977, and he had to face the difficulties and challenges that came with high office, he was ready and able to assume the heavy burden.

When he came to the United States on his first state visit as prime minister in July 1977, he radiated optimism. I recall a Friday afternoon in July 1977, when he left the UN building after his talk with

Secretary General Kurt Waldheim. When he noticed me he actually forced his way toward me through the ring of secret service agents. He came over to me and said: "With God's help, we were successful. We succeeded beyond our expectations. . ."

He explained to me that he was referring to his meeting with President Carter, from which he had returned the day before, not his meeting with Waldheim, which he did not seem to be too interested in. He asked me to convey the message to the Council of *Gdolei Ha'Torah*, the rabbinical authorities.

He did the same thing on December 2, 1977 in New York, after his meeting with President Carter. After he greeted me with great warmth, which was both an expression of sincere friendship and of his high spirits, he repeated: "We have succeeded, with God's help. . ." And he was glowing with joy.

I was certain he had won some great victory, although I did not know what it was. All I knew was that the Jewish public opinion was rather skeptical about Carter.

A few days later, when Begin came back to Israel from Egypt, he announced at the airport that "The United States is unconditionally opposed to a Palestinian state." On December 27, 1977, President Carter made the same statement in no uncertain terms. He added the remark that such a state would be "radical," which conformed with Begin's thesis that a Palestinian state would be a base for Soviet infiltration in the Middle East.

This was the result of Begin's impact in his talks with the President and his aides, who did listen for once (although the PLO itself made its own contribution to this decision. . .). Carter's security advisor, Zbigniew Brzezinski, who was considered the architect of the plan for a Palestinian state, went then even further than the President and declared that "The PLO removed itself from negotiations on the Palestinian problem."

There was, indeed, a basis for Begin's optimism.

This optimism started even before he went to Washington in July, and before he went to Egypt. When he came back from his meeting with President Sadat, which had its difficult moments, as he later revealed in the Knesset (when Sadat insisted on Israeli withdrawal from all the territories and agreeing to a Palestinian state), he said: "I came back a happy man."

Today, after we have found out about all the difficult moments and all the obstacles he had to face during those discussions, we may wonder why he felt so happy, and some may think that it was a calculated move on his part. But anyone who knew Begin and knew even a little bit about the way the discussions went in Ismailia, would understand why he was happy.

First, it should be made clear that he never pretended to feel something he did not feel. His son, Dr. Zeev Benjamin Begin, once said to me: "Dad behaves outside as he behaves at home, and behaves at home as he behaves outside." I myself in all my meetings with him, both private and public, never noticed any difference in his appearance. His public and private behavior were always the same. Therefore, if he said he was happy, he certainly meant it.

Secondly, he would always think in long-range terms. His vision was always far-reaching. and if at a given moment things appeared sad and somber, he would look further into the future and make plans which he felt had a good chance to succeed. His optimism was always quite practical. He did not rely on time to be on his side. He always strove to make it be on his side, bringing out every effort to achieve this goal.

Thirdly, and this is the most important point, he was always a believer. He believed in Divine Guidance. He was hopeful that the Lord would not abandon His people. Faith helped him confront the British and prevail. It helped him become prime minister after many years in the opposition, and it enabled him to make peace with Israel's most powerful enemy.

Chapter Twenty-Three

Master of the Word

In order to establish the significance of Begin as an orator—perhaps the last of the Jewish pleiade of masters of the spoken word in our time—we must contemplate the man who influenced him most in this area, namely, Ze'ev (Vladimir) Jabotinsky. Although Jabotinsky's influence was mainly in the realm of ideas, which attracted the young Betarist, his mastery of the spoken word had a great impact on Begin as well.

For Begin, Jabotinsky was a model. Not to imitate—Begin was never given to imitation—but to emulate. His innermost soul absorbed the qualities of the master by osmosis. He assimilated the substance of his teacher's ideology and learned from his oratorical style. It was part of what Jabotinsky called *Hadar*, a Hebrew word meaning splendor, both aesthetic and ethical.

There were basic differences in their respective backgrounds, way of life, and education. There were also divergences in opinion that led to a significant controversy on the question of the underground revolt, as was discussed in the previous chapter. Let us turn here to one aspect of the influence of the master on his disciple, namely, the art of public speaking.

Oratory, devalued in our time as "mere rhetoric," seems to be on the wane, having fallen into disrepute. There are a number of reasons for this.

Like every talent, oratory can be used for good or for evil. It can be a blessing or a curse.

Another reason for the decline of oratory is the fact that in the past speech was a highly individual expression of the speaker. It was often an intimate sharing of thoughts with the audience. Sometimes it was an extemporaneous inspiration, a spontaneous reaction to something just heard.

At present, a speech by an important public figure is often a product of scrupulous preparation, and the labor of one or more speechwriters. It is usually carefully planned, well researched and rehearsed, but the laborious preparation and reworking by a staff of hired phrase-makers deprives the word of the ring of sincerity. It strips it of any spark of authenticity and spontaneity, and often even of sincerity and truthfulness.

In Jabotinsky's time there were no ghost writers, at least not any that were known to the public, certainly not for speakers of Jabotinsky's caliber. It was an era when the impact of great orators was felt by masses of people around the world.

There were leaders of the free world who fought the German hordes, not only with arms and men but also with the power of the word which awoke and unified the people of the world, raising them to their finest hour. The British Prime Minister Winston Churchill and the American President, Franklin D. Roosevelt, were shining examples of this mastery.

The power of the word was even more important for the Jews, because it was their only power. Other people, living in a country they could call their own, had many means of communication at their disposal. Acts of the government are more telling. Deeds speak louder than words. But for the Jews and their leaders, the word was their only instrument, and therefore had special importance (at times the Jews ascribed excessive importance to the word, and fell victims to this overestimation).

Begin inherited many of his teacher's gifts and skillfully emulated his style. He used his talent which was augmented by his diligence and his natural enthusiasm and dedication.

Nevertheless, Begin's oratorical mastery is his own. It is a product of the harmonious blend of various ingredients. His is an art that combined penetrating perception with clear thinking, lucid reasoning with far-reaching foresight, depth and brilliance, logic and feeling, realism and vision. The clairvoyance of his insights matches the lucidity with which he conveys his ideas.

Begin's eloquence was not a mere flair for words. If a person mumbles, it is not simply because of a speech defect, such as stuttering. It reveals a lack of clear thought. It reflects incoherent thinking. It mirrors inner confusion and even insincerity.

Even in the days when great orators were held in high esteem,

Begin would have ranked among the greatest of them. How much greater he is in our time when most gatherings, under whatever name or guise, be they named "congresses" or "conventions," serve merely as a sounding board for the shallow, pedestrian, redundant orations of professional "delegates," "panelists," or "symposiasts" who frequently participate in these superfluous junkets at the public's expense. Their speeches are not designed to explain, convince or exhort, but are an end in themselves—the self-serving generating of cheap publicity for self-aggrandizement, and an excuse for superfluous trips. It is, therefore, much easier to book a throng of speakers than to attract a crowd of listeners. No wonder that the empty verbiage at these inane gatherings bores the public and empties the assembly halls.

In the light of all this, Begin, a superior speaker, is an unusual and unique phenomenon. First, his words do not lack substance. They are not meant to replace deeds, but are rather a call, an exhortation to action. In this sense, they are action.

Let us remember that during the crucial years of his fight for the Jewish state, he was in command not only of language but also of people. Those were silent years insofar as the spoken word is concerned, but he continued to alert and exhort the public with his written invocations in posters and widely-distributed leaflets.* When you read them today, you can actually "hear" Begin speak. You can almost listen to the sound of his voice, the palpitation of his heart, the ring of his anguish and anxiety, and of his indomitable faith.

No wonder that this resonance struck so deeply into the hearts of idealistic young men and women, and kindled an enthusiasm and a readiness for heroic deeds and sacrifice. Even today, almost half a century later, one can feel the power of those words.

When Begin emerged from the underground and was heard in public, we received the impression that his speeches were a continuation of all that preceded them, albeit in a different form, required by the new circumstances. The heroic years were not yet over for him and for those who had followed him and were part of his struggle.

When he came to power in 1977, his words bore much greater

---

* These messages have been published in *Bamachteret* by Menachem Begin, two volumes in Hebrew, Hadar, Tel Aviv 1975, and in *The Struggle of the Irgun Tzvai Leumi* by David Niv, Klausner Institute, Tel Aviv 1976.

weight, of course, but contained no less warmth. The official pronouncements of the Prime Minister were delivered with eloquence and with the typical individual imprint of his person. His speeches conveyed the authority not only of the high office of the prime minister, but also of the authenticity and integrity of the person. When the subject or the occasion warranted it, he could reach deep into his heart and cause the hearts of his listeners to tremble. He has been accused by his opponents of pretending to be rational while being ruled by his emotions. The truth is that he was always able to think rationally, without suppressing his feelings.

For those who listened to him closely, he always radiated more light than heat. While he could have used his great gift to inflame his listeners, he never fell into that trap. True, his voice moved his audience with its rhythmic, stirring cadences, reverberating with emotion, but it elucidated your mind and elevated your spirit.

He did not tell his audience what to think, as many politicians tend to do. Rather, he would present the argument, provide the background information, and let his listeners draw their own conclusions which, invariably, were inescapable. He would present his case like a lawyer in front of a jury, letting the members of the jury do their own thinking in order to reach the right verdict.

Quite often, the first reaction of his listener was emotional, but after some reflection the reason behind the emotion would emerge, and the listener would realize that he could not dismiss the argument. The best proof of this is the fact that when you read his speeches in cold print, without the magic of his charismatic personality and brilliant delivery, you are still impressed and convinced by his ideas and attitudes.

Whenever I heard either Jabotinsky or Begin speak—and I never missed such an opportunity—I would have a double reaction. My first reaction was one of admiration. I admired the magic of their oratory, the beauty of their diction, their brilliant delivery, their great sense of timing, their close rapport with their audience. I would say to myself: It is amazing how high the human mind can reach!

My second reaction would be: This is so obvious, so simple. Why didn't I think of it myself? . . .

Chapter Twenty-Four

Attitude Toward the Germans

I was present at the protest gathering at Zion Square in Jerusalem in January 1951, when thousands of Israelis expressed their opposition to the accepting of monetary compensation from West Germany for the murder of the Jews.

The gathering was addressed by Menachem Begin, and by Professor Joseph Klausner, the great historian.

From there a march was started to the Knesset. It was still the old Knesset seat, the Frumkin Building. Prime Minister Ben-Gurion, who advocated the acceptance of reparations from Germany, was overly concerned about the demonstration. He maintained that he had to "save" the government from the "fascists." When the angered crowd reached the Knesset, a few unruly demonstrators threw some stones at the building and broke two windows. Ben-Gurion seized upon the incident and accused Begin of attempting to overthrow the government. The false demagogic accusation was reminiscent of similar labels by the left, dating back to the murder of Chaim Arlozoroff and, more recently, to the sinking of the Altalena.

Mapai, Ben-Gurion's party, then summoned hundreds of kibbutz members to come to the capital the next day to defend the democratically elected government, and rescue it from Begin's "putsch"...

I happened to be that day in Tel Aviv. And whom do I see on Rothschild Boulevard leading a bunch of unruly preschoolers, trying hard to keep them in line, if not the old "conspirator" and instigator who urged people to topple the government, the leader of the alleged "putsch," Menachem Begin...

I found out that Begin, as a parent of kindergarten-age children, had to take his turn in the pool of bringing the neighborhood children to school. It so happened that the day when Begin was supposed to storm the government was his day to perform his parental duty.

Most of the press, incited by Ben-Gurion's hate-filled speeches, launched vicious attacks on the "fascist" Begin, and his alleged nefarious schemes to seize power. Even the thoughtful Dr. Azriel Carlebach wrote an editorial in his *Maariv* daily titled "Begin Lost His Political Mind."

I wrote an article for the New York Yiddish paper, *Der Tog*, reporting the facts of the event, and explaining the attitude of Menachem Begin, his actions and intentions, and his feelings.

How did I know his feelings? Simply because they were identical to mine.

In the choir of unbridled attacks, vituperations, and defamations, mine was a lonely voice. But, from the reactions of many, I must say it was quite a convincing voice and it expressed the opinion of many, perhaps of the majority. One of the most important, and, to me, the most gratifying reactions which I have cherished to this day, was the handwritten letter I received from Menachem Begin on that occasion:

Menachem Begin
Tel Aviv

To: Dr. Hillel Seidman
Jerusalem

Dear Friend:

I read and reread your article in original as well as published in *Der Tog*. My friends in America wrote me that the article—I am quoting—"caused a great stir in the city." Since friends wrote it to me I may assume with certainty that the "stir" was a positive one.

I am, of course, not worthy even of a part of all the great praise you bestowed on me. However, your words which could be thought of as "panegyric" if I would be in the government, are an expression of true sincerity, since I came out as a "rebel." They are a contribution to the revealing of the truth which was disturbed by the terrible negotiations with the murderers which look to me as a nightmare without basis in reality. For this contribution, which is the main thing here, not my mouth and not my pen but my heart says to you: Thanks!

Please convey my hearty wishes to your wife.

I shake your right hand in friendship and admiration.

Yours,
M. Begin

Tel Aviv   2 Shevat, 5712 (1952)

Begin's opposition to "normalization" of relations with Germany was based on the following:

a. He did not forget what the German people as a whole—eighty million strong—and not just the "Nazis"—conspired to kill every last Jew in the world, and succeeded in carrying out a major portion of their master plan.

b. Begin was aware of the shame of absolute helplessness of the Jewish people, being led like sheep to the slaughter, and was not about to forget this horrendous reality.

c. Begin was convinced, as I believe most Jews are, that the essential German nature did not change since the war, only the circumstances are different. The Germans, he argued, were not sincerely and genuinely sorry for what they had done to the Jews. He didn't believe in "new Germany."

d. Not only did the Germans fail to show any remorse, Begin argued, but they also showed distasteful hypocrisy by supporting the Arab mortal enemies of Israel on the pretext that by doing so they were serving the cause of justice.

e. Begin was deeply convinced as many of us were that there was no possibility of forgiveness for what the Germans had done to the Jews.

f. He further believed that if Israel would forgive and forget, it would not have learned the lessons of the catastrophe, or lessons vital to Israel's survival. He was afraid that forgiveness to the German murderers would encourage present and future enemies of the Jews. They could reason that if the German mass killings are forgiven, who was going to punish other murderers of Jews?

One of the assumptions and hopes of the Zionist ideologists was that the creation of the Jewish state would put an end to anti-Semitism. As a result, many Israelis made a conscious attempt to bury the past, as it were, and start a new leaf, *K'chol Ha'Goim*, to be like all other nations.

This way of thinking prompted many Israelis, particularly native-born, to draw a sharp distinction between themselves and the Jews of the Diaspora, or the *Golah*, exile, as Jews have traditionally referred to life among the nations. The Israeli was the new Jew, free, proud, an equal among equals. The *Golus* Jew was a second-class citizen, afraid of his own shadow, always one step away from persecution, from pogroms.

Begin did not fall prey to these stereotypes. He was not swayed by the delusion about the disappearance of anti-Semitism. He knew the simple fact that human nature did not change in 1945, after World War Two. He further knew that a strong Jewish state would make others respect the Jew and think twice before attacking him, but would not make the entire world love the Jews.

Israelis who drew a distinction between themselves and Jews of the Diaspora, initially thought that with the creation of the state anti-Semitism would disappear. How wrong they were! Anti-Semitism not only failed to vanish but was becoming even more widespread and more vicious.

Through the efforts of the Arab states and their supporters in the United Nations, the new code word for anti-Semitism is anti-Zionism. Their unceasing hate-filled attacks culminated in the passing of the UN resolution in 1974 which equated Zionism with racism. What a Jew was among non-Jews, the Jewish nation was among nations.

As for Germany, its criticism of Israel during the Lebanon War were among the most vicious of any other country with the exception of the Arabs.

In retrospect, what Begin did in 1951, putting up a strong and dignified opposition against the German reparations, was a lesson which needs to be repeated over and over again. *Zachor*! Remember! We must never forget and never forgive!

Following is a document proving beyond any doubt that the German army, as well as the German people as a whole, were the murderers of the Jews in Europe. The research was conducted by German scholars.

THE GERMAN ARMY KILLED THE JEWS

The former Secretary General of the U.N., Kurt Waldheim, the president of the U.N. Assembly for 1981, von Wechmar, the present chancellor of West Germany, Helmut Schmidt, and many other leaders of East and West Germany were officers of the German army, fraudulently called "Wehrmacht," during World War II. They are claiming now that they were innocent, and even unaware, of the killing of all the Jews under their rule.

Two noted German historians, Professor Dr. Helmut Krausnick and Hans

Heinrich Wilhelm published a detailed and thoroughly documented report on the role of the German army, of all its branches, infantry, air force and navy, in killing the Jews, men, women and children, especially in Soviet Russia, where Waldheim, von Wechmar and Schmidt, all major figures at the United Nations, served as commanding officers. Here, some excerpts:

In 1941-1942, no massive resistance was felt in the matter of the extermination of Jews in the German government offices of the conquered territories in the east. . . .

A commander of the 339th infantry division, General-Lieutenant Huelka, who criticized the mass slaughter in the city of Boryssov, reported a week later on November 5, 1941, on the food supply of local back-up units and proposed the elimination of "superfluous mouths of captured prisoners, gypsies and Jews."

Respected field commanders, such as Reichenau, Manstein, and Hueth, endorsed the proposal and issued an order requesting "understanding of this severe measure, but that justice was meted out to the worthless Jews . . ."

On January 25, 1942, the official appointed over the district of Slonim reported that he succeeded in "eliminating several thousand superfluous mouths" and added that "in a short time, the Wehrmacht has managed to clean up the district, but to my regret only in areas containing less than 1,000 people. Since the army is no longer willing to take action in the villages, I will concentrate the Jews of the area into two or three cities . . ."

In Byelorussia, according to S.S. documents, even before the region was occupied by Einsatzgruppe A, the army killed approximately 10,000 Jews. About the same number were killed in July in the district of Glubkoye.

In the Prypet Marshes, S.S. General Paglein, acting under the direct order of the army, massacred at least 13,788 Jews. In Laguisk, September 1941, an S.S. division under army supervision aided in the killing of 920 Jews.

In Brest-Litovsk, [Brisk] the 162nd infantry division participated in "actions" [euphemism for killing the Jews] in July 1941. In Libau, Latvia, the navy participated in a number of mass slaughters. On the Lithuanian border, hundreds of Jews were killed with the aid of the army.

In the district of Baranowicz, until February 1942 most of the "actions" were initiated by the army and the S.S. Waffen. The civilian supervisor of the district subsequently reported that "in the future, there will be no difficulty refuting the army command's claims regarding the excessive cruelty of the civil command."

[. . .] In Dinaburg and Riga, the Wehrmacht supplied the vehicles to carry out the "actions." In Libau, the navy participated in blocking off the area. In Boryssov, certain members of the air force who had come from a neighboring air-force base were eager and insistent upon helping in the slaughter.

[. . .] The Einsatzgruppe completed its task successfully; cooperation between the army and the police and security forces is essential for the army in order to secure the hinterland."

An example of the growing tendency of officers and soldiers to kill civilians, especially "Jewish Bolsheviks," was the occurrences in the city of Human in September 1941. The local Einsatzcommando scheduled a major action against the 8,000 remaining Jews for the 22nd and 23rd of the month. However, to the dismay of the Commando, who quickly complained, eager soldiers took action before that date. Already on September 21, the Ukrainian militia engaged in pogroms against the Jews, with the participation of many German soldiers. The destruction of the homes and the distribution of valuable spoils were accomplished practically by the Wehrmacht alone. . . . As a result of the unplanned nature of the pogrom, the action was not systematic enough and, among others, Jews and many Communist communal workers were warned in time and escaped.

Over this period, the active support of the army was consolidated into the ranks of the extermination units. On July 3, 1941, the infantry participated in the murder of 1,160 Jews in Lutzk; that same month 180 were shot in Zhitomir, and in the same city another 402 Jews were killed on August 7, in both cases with the participation of soldiers. Subsequently, the commander of the city, in cooperation with the S.D., decided to exterminate the remaining 3,145 Jews, and the army supplied twelve trucks for this purpose.

Prior to the mass murder in Babi Yar that totaled 38,000 victims, an agreement was reached between the military commander of the city and the Einsatzgruppe. The commander ordered all the Jews of Kiev to assemble by 8:00 P.M. on September 29; the proclamation was printed in the printing apparatus of the 6th army. The special "commandos" that carried out the slaughter succeeded in recruiting a unit of the [army's] engineering corps which, having completed the terrible act, dynamited the site of Babi Yar, such that the landslide buried all the bodies beneath and erased the traces of the deed. Thus, we have an example of perfect coordination [between the army and S.S.] in accordance with the explicit instructions to aid the murder units as much as possible."

[. . .] A certain commander in the 6th army unit was instructed to concentrate the Jews in the city of Bialocerkiev and requested that Einsatzcommandos be sent in order to destroy them. On August 20, 1941, the 295th infantry division passed by, and a dispute arose between the army and local commanders over the continuation of the slaughter, which included the surviving children. When the local commander claimed that he was not authorized to deviate from his instructions and was adamant in his refusal, the senior officer responsible for the extermination interceded and concluded that "it was necessary to conduct the campaign on an ideological basis, which necessitates the liquidation of Jewish women and children, because this race must be exterminated."

The cooperation between the army and the Einsatzgruppen grew steadily. The first major action in Minsk had already been conducted with the help of professional killers from the army police; this was the case in the village of Gorky, northeast of Mohilev, where 2,200 Jews were killed. In the villages of Dimar and Oster in the Kiev area, 'with the cooperation of the Wehrmacht', as stated in the report, 150 Jews and Partisans were killed. In Boryssov, at the request of the officer of the city, 146 imprisoned Jews were killed. It is incumbent upon anyone who claims that the Einsatzgruppen exaggerated the willingness of the army to join in the slaughter to read what the chief communications officer of the 6th army wrote on November 6, where he stated that although he opposes the evacuation of the civilian population from the occupied town of Charkov, he urged that "we must immediately capture all the Jews, the political commissars, all suspects, and the refugees. The ongoing treatment of these elements will be the responsibility of the S.D., but it is too weak to carry out the order and is in need of army support."

On October 29, the commander of the city of Mariopol reported: "8,000 Jews have been killed by the S.D. The homes owned by the Jews were expropriated by the local army headquarters. The clothes and underwear of the Jews have been collected by the soldiers and, after laundering, will be given to the army hospital."

Despite their reversal of fortune in the war, the army remained loyal to Hitler . . . A blatant and astonishing intertwining of the army in Hitler's plans and destruction and his politics of destruction. (TRANSLATED FROM GERMAN. Emphasis ours)

> Professor Dr. Helmut Krausnick and Hans Heinrich Wilhelm:
> DIE ARMEE UND DER IDEOLOGISCHER KRIEG.
> (Institut fuer Zeitgeschicte, Stuttgart, 1981)
> DIE TRUPPE DER WELTANSCHAUUNG KRIEGES.
> (Institut fuer Zeitgeschichte, Stuttgart, 1981)

THE WEHRMACHT AND THE MASS KILLING OF JEWS

(from T.H. Tetens, *The New Germany and the Old Nazis*, London: Secker and Warburg, 1962, pp. 109-112 *(excerpts)*

After the war a number of German Field Marshals and hundreds of high ranking Wehrmacht officers were found implicated in countless war crimes. Their signed orders proved that they were responsible for the mass shooting of civilians and prisoners of war, the burning of villages and towns, wholesale looting, and the deportation of millions to slave labor camps.

Among the prominent military figures whose cases won the most attention in Germany were Field Marshals Erich von Manstein and Albert Kesselring. Both had fair trials before British courts. Kesselring was sentenced to death (his sentence was later commuted) for having ordered the shooting of 335 hostages in the Ardeatina Grotta, near Rome, on March 24, 1944. Von Manstein was sentenced to eighteen years in prison for having ordered war crimes committed in Poland and Russia. Manstein's army command worked closely with SS Colonel Otto Ohlendorf, who was hung for the mass shooting of 90,000 Jews and Russians. One of von Manstein's corps commanders, General von Salmuth, dispatched 300 Wehrmacht soldiers with special instructions to assist Ohlendorf in the mass killing of thousands. . . . Field Marshal von Manstein issued the following order to his troops November 24, 1941:

> The Jewish-Bolshevist system must be destroyed once and for all. It must never again infiltrate our European Lebensraum. Therefore, the German soldier is not only charged with destroying the military might of this system. He also acts as an agent of the idea of racial supremacy . . . The soldier must show understanding for the necessity of severe revenge on Judaism, the spiritual carrier of the Bolshevist terror. This understanding is also essential in order to nip in the bud all uprisings, which are mainly instigated by Jews.

Similar orders were given by the other army commanders, such as Field Marshals Gerd von Rundstedt and Walter von Reichenau. The latter told his troops on October 10, 1941:

> The soldier in the Eastern Territories is not merely a fighter according to the rules of the art of war but also the bearer of a ruthless national ideology . . . therefore the soldier must have understanding of the necessity of a severe but just revenge on subhuman Jewry.

THE MILITARY AND OTHER MURDERERS IN THE "NEW GERMANY"

from T.H. Tetens, *The New Germany and the Old Nazis,* London: Secker and Warburg, 1962, pp. 48, 53, 109, and 111 (excerpts)

. . . It is indicative of the spirit prevailing in present-day Germany that the overwhelming majority of the people believe that officers like von Manstein, Reichenau, and Kesselring kept the German honor intact. *Times* correspondent Arthur J. Olsen reported from Germany that von Manstein is held in the highest esteem in the new Bundeswehr, where he is regarded as "the most prestigious German soldier who survived the war [and who] emerged in the soldier's view with honor intact."

In the Bundestag debate of October 23, 1952, Dr. Adenauer admitted that 66 percent of the diplomats in higher positions were former Nazis, but, he added, he could "not build up a Foreign Office without relying on such skilled men." (*Protokowlen des Bundestages,* Bonn, West Germany, 23 October 1959)

. . . Of thirty-eight newly appointed Generals in the Bundeswehr, thirty-one were members of the General Staff of the old Wehrmacht." These are the same Generals who served under the banner of the swastika and whose "responsibility for Hitler's rule is so heavy and so unmistakable." (Die Welt, *Hamburg, 8 September 1956*)

The militarists were assisted in their schemes by the diplomats and legal experts . . . They proclaimed . . . the dissolution of the Soviet Union as a state and nation, "whereby all positive norms of international law have become void and inapplicable." The author of the article was Ribbentrop's legal expert, Dr. Wilhelm Grewe, a member of the Nazi party and later Bonn's ambassador to Washington. (*Monatshefte fuer Auswaertige Politik,* September 1941).

Chapter Twenty-Five

Begin and Chaim Weitzmann

There were fundamental differences between the characters, beliefs, ideologies and policies of Chaim Weitzmann and Menachem Begin. It is amazing to what degree the former—born in the village Motele near Pinsk, in the heart of the Jewish community in Russia, brought up with a knowledge of Judaism, and attached to its main tenets—became almost an assimilated Englishman.

Weitzmann, a leader of the World Zionist Organization, became a British patriot, not unlike the German-Jewish assimilationists. He might have thought that there was no contradiction between Zionism and assimilationism. He even dreamed that the Jewish State be created in the image of the English, adapting their political culture, government system, laws and traditions.

But there weren't only differences between both peoples, but contradictions—and (according to the Foreign Office expert, Harold Bayley), even before Bevin's tenure, there was a genuine conflict of interests. The global interests of Great Britain, especially its oil supplies and its relations with the Arab world, were preponderant factors in the British international policy—in particular, its hostility to the strivings of the Jews in Palestine. Every other consideration, moral and ethical, every other obligation and promise, had to make way before these supreme demands of British global policy.

Even such an ardent admirer of Weitzmann as Sir Isaiah Berlin, who describes him as one of the greatest men of our time, is bound by his honest analysis of the relevant facts to come to the following conclusion:

> Bevin's Palestine policy had finally caused Weitzmann to wonder whether his own lifelong admiration of, and loyalty to, England and British governments had *perhaps cost his people too dear...* He wondered whether his own earlier trust in England had not *gratuitously lengthened the birth-pangs of the new Jewish state*

(emphasis ours)". (*Chaim Weitzmann*, by Sir Isaiah Berlin; Weiden-feld and Nicolson, London 1958)

Weitzmann went especially far in his submission to the British, even as his hopes and illusions were shattered by the brutish onslaught of Bevin. But other leaders of the Zionist establishment, even those critical of Weitzmann were basically not too far from his erroneous, and finally disastrous, policies. These policies led them to the shameful "Season" when the Socialist-Zionist collaboration with the British went so far as to lead them to capture IZL fighters and hand them over to the British.

The attitude of Dr. Weitzmann toward Eastern European Jews bor-dered almost on contempt. He despaired of them. On one occasion he used the word "dust" to describe them. Despite the fact that he him-self was one of them and certainly was aware of the enormous spiritual values and cultural forces which they possessed, he lacked respect for their uniqueness and greatness. (Compare this attitude with that found *The Earth is the Lord's* by Abraham Joshua Heschel, the great religious thinker.)

In Weitzmann's autobiographical *Trial and Error*, the mass killings of the European Jews by the Germans occupy only a marginal place, and are not treated as the most horrible catastrophe that befell any people in history.

Also, the relations between Weitzmann and Jabotinsky weren't like those between two antagonists. Weitzmann was overtaken by an ob-sessive hate and fear of his adversary. I was told by Rabbi Isaac Meir Lewin, the Agudath Israel leader and Social Welfare Minister in the years 1949 to 1952, that at a visit to Weitzmann, then Israel's first President, they discussed Heruth, the opposition party in the Knesset. Weitzmann admitted to Lewin that his hatred of Jabotinsky had be-come a paranoic obsession. It was sufficient for him to read in the morning an article on a a statement by Jabotinsky for his whole day to be spoiled. He couldn't get Jabotinsky out of his mind, and became unable to concentrate to the degree that he almost grew sick. Finally, this obsession had a disastrous effect on his nervous system and he consulted a psychologist. He was advised to totally put the man out of his mind. He should make himself believe that such a man by the name Ze'ev Jabotinsky doesn't exist. Then the staff of the Zionist Ex-ecutive, and every friend, co-worker and associate, should be warned and forbidden to ever mention his name. Every printed word by or about Jabotinsky should be kept away from Weitzmann. This man should completely disappear from his conscience. He shouldn't exist!

Weitzmann scrupulously followed this advice, and he became another man, as he glowingly recounted the experience to Rabbi Lewin.

However, long after Jabotinsky's death, something of this animosity lingered in Weitzmann. He couldn't suppress his distaste for the men of the underground fight. When the King David Hotel was bombarded or when Lord Moyne was executed, his terrible outburst showed traces of his obsession.

Chapter Twenty-Six

Why the Hate?

We are asking ourselves: Why? Why, after these events are far away from the present problems and are superseded by more timely, acute and relevant events, and after the principal figure went into seclusion? Why this flood of venomous vilifications? Why this fury of hate?

In part is it a further result of Ben-Gurion's enmity against Begin which even some of his followers couldn't help but define as an obsession.

But there is another reason which is less irrational. For years before the creation of the State, and afterwards, old adversaries and enemies of the IZL repeated the Big Lie that the IZL's struggle was detrimental to the efforts for a Jewish State.

Now, from the perspective of over 40 years, and as a result of many facts and documents lately revealed, and of conscientious research and objective lucid evaluation, it is becoming more and more obvious that (let us put it straight and bluntly) Begin's war was the decisive factor in forcing out the British out of Palestine, and as a result of the creation of the State of Israel.

This requires elaboration. We are far from belittling the historical merits of the Halutzim, of the Hagana, the Palmach, or the merits of the historical role of Ben-Gurion. They laid the foundations, they built the basis, they created the framework for the Jewish State. As they say in Israel: Kol Hakavod! All the honors!

It would be inexcusable not to bow our heads in awe before the heroism and sacrifices of the fighters of Hagana. Begin himself always went out of his way to give these heroes full credit for their courage and accomplishments.

Having said this, we shouldn't allow the following fundamental historical facts to be obscured:

The Hagana prepared and partially waged war against the Arabs; the IZL—against the British.

The latter was more brutal and the second enemy more dangerous. Besides, the British encouraged the Arabs in many devious ways to fight the Jews. They built up the Mufti, King Hussein of Jordan. They provided them with arms, they helped them in every possible way and disguise.

However, the Zionist establishment acquiesced to the devious tactics of the Foreign Office which maintained a fictitious semblance of non-partisan arbiter in the Jewish-Arab conflict. The Jewish Agency leaders continued to maintain the fiction of negotiations, the possibility of compromises, arrangements. Even the protests, the critical statement played in the hands of the British in their nefarious play of deceiving and deluding the Jews and misleading them into the false belief that there still is a possibility of mutual understanding and peaceful accommodations.

Menachem Begin put an end to these dangerous illusions. He unmasked mercilessly and effectively the true character of Perfidius Albion, of the "pro-Zionist" Labor and even of the "Zionist" —Winston Churchill.

Let us not forget, as many do, that the most outrageous and cruel closing of Palestine was perpetrated by the Churchill coalition government, with the conservative Foreign Secretary Anthony Eden. In this matter there was not the slightest difference between the aristocratic Eton-Oxford educated Anthony Eden and the brutal, uneducated longshoreman, Ernest Bevin.

One footnote to Churchill's "Zionism." When Lord Moyne, the British satrap of the Middle East, who closed the gates of Palestine before the Jewish escapees from the German murderers was justly executed. (there is no more just execution in history). Prime Minister Winston Churchill noticed this outrage against the Jews, against the Zionists (who condemned the execution) with his cruel threats. But on hearing of the murder of millions of Jewish men, women and children, he issued, through one of his henchmen, a hypocritical routine "condemnation."

Here we have a most telling example of the double standard, how he felt at the loss of one of his own cast, and how he felt about the must cruel slaughter of millions of Jewish men, women and children not of his people and class!

In the IRANGATE and NICARAGUAN Contra affairs some officials conducted their own policy outside the legal framework of the
Constitution of the United States and the proper authorized government authorities. We may look back in disbelief at the dealing of
State Department officials in 1946-1948 and later, in the Palestine,
then in Israel question.

The Constitution of the United States says clearly that the foreign
policy of the U.S. should be conducted by the President through the
State Department.

This provides that the State Department is an instrument of the
President in his dealings in foreign policy.

Yet in the Palestine question, State Department officials not only
didn't implement the President policy in the matter but worked at
cross purposes to it; they audaciously and utterly sabotaged it and
reversed his direct orders.

They maintained that while the President worries about Jewish
votes, so someone has to take care of the interests of America; thus
they fulfilled the function of guarding the interests of America against
the President of the United States.

However, behind these patriotic excuses lurched plain anti-Semitism. Sometimes covered up, camouflaged, sometimes more open.
Truman himself wrote in his Memoirs that there is anti-Semitism in
the State Department.

If you'll look back at the darkest years of the German mass murders of the Jews, when the head of the Immigration Division of the
State Department, Breckingridge Long, with the then Secretary of
State, Cordell Hull, closed hermetically every entrance for Jewish escapees from the German killings, you'll not be too surprised of the attitude of the people of the same kind and way of thinking toward
Jewish survival—in spite of them. . .

Let us note that this attitude prevailed when President Franklin
D. Roosevelt was considered a staunch friend of Jews, and got the
overwhelming majority of the Jewish vote in the election of
Governor of New York State, and later of President of U.S.A. The
hypocrisy of this "friend of Jews" with Henry Morgenthau, Jr., his
Treasury Secretary, with Samuel Rosenman as his principal speech
writer, with Herbert Lehman, the Governor of New York and other
prominent and staunch supporters of his who acted as Jewish

leaders and delivered to him the Jewish vote, is a sad chapter in itself.

(Let us note in parenthesis that F.D.R.'s relatives, with Mr. Kermit Roosevelt, were active against Israel before its creation and after. In contrast the First Lady, Eleanor Roosevelt, was a sincere friend of Israel, but without influence in the White House.)

Chapter Twenty-Seven

Revolutionary Event

The emergence of Menachem Begin, and the impact of his leadership was a revolutionary event. It changed the course of Jewish history. It transformed the fate of the Jewish people, of its thinking and acting.*

Yet in spite of an abundance of articles and books on the subject few did justice to this event and even fewer grasped the full significances of the phenomenon called Menachem Begin and its real meaning and larger repercussions.

The reason: historians, political scientists, commentators, most of them prisoners of their routine methods and of their sterile narrow-mindedness, are treating Begin's Revolt like another unusual occurrence. They are looking at it as another clash of conflicting forces. They do not see its uniqueness. They are like this tourist in Israel who, unimpressed by the Western Wall, reacted: "What is here to be excited about? A Western Wall like every Western Wall. . ."

These historians and researchers are wrong.

Begin's resolve under the impact of the Holocaust was not only "Never Again." It was also "Never Before." Never before since Israel lost its independence 2000 years ago, did Jews wage war against their enemies. They were unable to. They were utterly powerless. They were not a subject but an object of history, which was shaped by others for their own aims and purposes.

By necessity Jews submitted to this passive role. They had to. They did not have any alternative. They tried hard accommodate to this reality. They used different ways to ease the pressure from the blows aimed at them.

---

* Curiously, Toufiq Toby, the Communist member of the Knesset, when he resigned from his office in June 1990, said: "In order to be a leader you have to be able to change. Menachem Begin had the courage to change the course of history." (*Yediot Achronoth*, June 6, 1990)

The "Jewish Condition" relative to the peoples and rulers of their countries of residence was one of passivity. At best they were reacting to other people's acts. But this was quite limited.

Some Jews certainly deplored this situation, but they were forced by conditions to acquiesce.

Generally they made of this necessity a virtue. Many peoples worship power. Jews worshiped powerlessness. They turned calamity into superior value. They converted sufferings, torture, murder into Kidush Hashem, the sanctifying of G-d's name. This concept was a result of Jewish total devotion to faith, to keeping the faith in the face of enormous powers bent on forcing them to abandon it.

When Jews faced the alternative between abandoning their faith and losing their life, they choose the latter.

Of this freedom of choice they were robbed by the German onslaught. This was another unique aspect of the German mass murder. Even converted Christians, even infants were killed in the gas chambers.

Another unparalleled uniqueness was the enormity of the discrepancy between the power of the Germans, the mightiest in the world at this time, and the absolute and complete powerlessness of the Jews.

Then when the heavy curtain was lifted from the abyss of the demonical atrocities committed by the Germans, by all the Germans, against all the Jews in Europe, we witnessed, as victims of an unbelievable strange occurrence. Britain, which indirectly, albeit consciously, made it easier for the Germans to commit the mass murders of the Jews, by closing the gates of their homeland in Palestine before the Jewish escapes—went on with its war against the Jewish remnants.

Never mind the tricks of the vocabulary by deception, deceit, duplicity covering the brutal, violent assault on the ships with the remnants on their way to Palestine with a smokescreen of diplomatic semantics. We read and heard of "illegal immigration," White Paper, economic absorption capacity, negotiations, etc. . .

All this was camouflage of a cruel war against broken, helpless, homeless people, which escaped only by miracles the German killings. This assault was perpetrated by the British socialist government uninhibited by compassion, by any humanitarian and moral principles, and by elementary decency.

This war was constructed on a global scale. We will quote only some of the more telling examples: In July, 1946, Ernest Bevin's Foreign Office asked the State Department in Washington to order the Justice Department to issue the following three rulings:

(1) To forbid newspaper advertisements appealing for funds for illegal immigration organized by the Hebrew Liberation Committee with Ben Hecht, Peter Berson, Hillel Cook and Shmuel Merlin.

(2) To annul U.S. tax deductions for charitable contributions related to Palestine Jewish causes.

(3) To prevent acquiring, outfitting, or manning transport shipping for Jewish immigration to Palestine.

The State Department, infested with anti-Semites (according to President Harry S. Truman in his memoirs) under the disguise of Arabists, willingly obliged. However, the then Attorney General, Tom Clark refused these demands. He replied that creating technical cases against newspaper advertisement for charitable fund-raising related to Palestine, and cancelling tax deductions for their contributions, will only invite charges of anti-Semitic discrimination and thus perversely benefit the Jewish national cause.

Now comes the most revealing aspect. Treating the British persecution of the ships with Jewish survivals for Palestine we characterized it as "war." Perhaps too strong a word, some may have thought. But this definition came from the British Foreign Office. Its request from the State Department to prevent the shipping of Jewish immigrants to Palestine was justified in these words: "Because these ships go to war against Britain."

As everyone knows, these ships were unarmed. The war was waged against them by the armed English forces. War it was, but a one-sided one, mainly by the British against Jewish immigrants.

The U.S. Attorney General rejected London's request, implying that war was waged by the other side. He wrote:

"To characterize the ships carrying these hundreds of displaced refugees as vessels of was is to torture the fact" (*Ibid.*).

Thus war was relentlessly conducted by the British government against the Jewish survivors. While the Zionist establishment protested and negotiated, Menachem Begin saw in this onslaught against the martyred people what it really was, war.

And he responded accordingly: "A la guerre comme à la guerre."

Chapter Twenty-Eight

The First Steps on the March to Freedom

Begin first appeared in a major public Jewish forum at the Betar conference in Warsaw in October 1938. He was at the time the head of Betar—the Revisionists' youth organization—in Poland. He was 25 years old.

This conference had special significance for four reasons:

a. The head of world Betar, Ze'ev Jabotinsky, attended the conference.

b. There was a sense of crisis and a desire for change on the part of most of the participants.

c. A confrontation took place between the head of world organization and the head of Polish branch.

d. The magical and stirring word, Irgun Tzvai Leumi, was mentioned for the first time in public.

Any meeting or conference attended by Jabotinsky was greatly influenced by his personality and oratory. But this time it was an unusual occasion. The young members of the movement were in a state of frustration and apprehension. The grave danger posed by the nation of murderers—the Germans—had already been translated into atrocities inside Germany. Yet the Jewish organizations and institutions were in a state of mental paralysis and passivity. Betar, whose entire raison d'être was to fight this kind of paralysis was yet to act and effect a radical change.

Jabotinsky ran head on into demands of Betar's youth, who looked to him for daring solutions. Their spokesman was the young leader of the Polish branch, Menachem Begin, who was the catalyst and the main advocate of those demands, both by virtue of his office and because he had started to emerge as a great orator.

His task was far from easy. First, he deeply admired Jabotinsky, whose very presence acted upon him as a restraining force. Second, Jabotinsky was a master of the art of polemics, one of the best in Europe, at an age when the Zionist movement had more than a few great orators and polemicists. Third, Jabotinsky was a highly charismatic leader, recognized as such by all the members of the movement, including those who opposed some of his thoughts and tactics.

At the root of those differences of opinion were the educational and psychological differences between the world leader, imbued with the spirit of European liberalism—his image as a "fascist" notwithstanding—and known for his dedication to democratic values, on the one hand, and the representative of the national Jewish youth in Poland, exposed to growing anti-Semitism, on the other.

Jabotinsky was being accused at that time by his adversaries of trying to bring about a Jewish homeland by force, and was now trying to tone down this accusation. It was now the rank and file of Betar that demanded an armed struggle. Begin gave expression to this demand, which became the stated wish of many delegates and an urgent matter which could no longer be delayed.

Begin's underground colleague who served during the revolt as the idealogue of the LEHI splinter-group, Dr. Israel Eldad, wrote in his memoirs (*Maaser Rishon*, in Hebrew, Jerusalem, pp. 21-22) about the conference and about Begin's role in it:

> Begin goes up to speak.
>
> *Enfant terrible* of Polish Betar. A rare combination of a romantic lawyer, he is to Jabotinsky what a Roman disciple is to a Greek teacher. He tries to emulate the teacher, but because of his own nature he cannot reach his level of refinement. . . He is more given to overdramatizing. . . Jabotinsky was a man with a distilled sense of tragedy. His follower is more simple in his thinking and his words. Jabotinsky would often close his eyes in order to see, and keep quiet for a long time in order to think. Not so his pupil. The master was much better looking than the student, but reality is much uglier than both, and there is a need to act.
>
> Menachem has become the spokesman of the opposition within Betar. If he does not pull Betar out of the paralysis which Propes and Isaac Remba had put it into, the Irgun Tzvai Leumi will gobble it quickly, whether or not there is an agreement between the two bodies. The youth is tired of sitting in their clubs, writing petitions,

shouting slogans against the methods of the Jewish Agency. Shlomo Ben-Yosef* is the first expression of the revolt in the land of Israel. He did not receive an order from Betar or from the Irgun. In Poland, the power center of Betar, many Ben-Yosefs are growing up. The head of Betar made a wonderful gesture during the eulogy. he said: "I am *now* giving you, Ben-Yosef, the order to do what you did." His words are drowned by ecstatic singing, but it is not made clear whether they represent a political commitment for what's to follow or rather do not prove anything, and it doesn't mean that from now on the head of Betar would give the order to put an end to inaction. Betar clubs are in deep crisis. The leaders are being ignored, and boredom causes members to quit the organization. The Irgun's clandestinity, on the other hand, its courses, and its incipient action over there in the land of Israel attract the youth to the cells of the Irgun which are being established everywhere. The alternatives are the disintegration of Betar, especially the older groups, or the pursuit of an activist line.

Menachem is the spokesman of the activist opposition.

And as often happens with such polemics, they focus on an expression or a formula, sometimes central, sometimes accidental.

Menachem uses as his formula the Betar vow, composed by Jabotinsky himself. The vow says: "I shall not lift my arm except in defense." Menachem opposes this restriction and demands that it be changed to read: "I shall lift my arm to defend my people and conquer my homeland."

Obviously, behind the old formula there is a very practical problem. The formula means a commitment, and Begin argues it is time to live up to the commitment. One can expect nothing from the world—it is a pack of wolves. And here Begin shows his last and strongest card—a few months earlier Czechoslovakia was abandoned following the Munich agreement. The good, liberal Western democracies committed the unconscionable and heartless act of abandoning Czechoslovakia who had trusted them and relied on them. The world is cruel. It only understands the language of power and facts. It is time to declare the revolt.

This was the essence of Menachem Begin's words.

After several side discussions, the word was finally uttered at the conference. Loud applause. Very loud. Especially in the corner

---

* Ben-Yosef was the first Jew executed by the British authorities in the land of Israel for committing a "terrorist act," viz., retaliating against Arab marauders.

where—as I am told—the delegates from the land of Israel were
sitting together. I am talking about the hall. I cannot yet see who is
sitting in the balcony.

The head of Betar asks for the floor immediately after Begin is
finished. But he cannot wax poetic after hearing what Begin had to
say. This is a time for prose, not poetry. His prose is biting, his
knife is always sparkles, but now it also cuts. (Eldad)

Responding to Begin's call to arms, Jabotinsky cautioned: There is
an arithmetic. There is a balance of power. Our power is not yet sufficient and therefore we must not engage in idle talk about a revolt.

There was another difference of opinion. Jabotinsky had not yet
given up his faith in the conscience of the world. Begin had lost that
faith—even back then—and had put his entire trust in his people and
in the Divine Providence.

Jabotinsky called out at his young disciple: "If you, Mr. Begin, do
not believe that there is any conscience left in the world, you have no
choice but to go and drown yourself in the Vistula River. . ."

But Begin chose another alternative. Rather than go to the river, he
went to the Jewish people and prodded them to start the revolt for the
liberation of the homeland.

As I had mentioned before, I was present at Jabotinsky's rebuttal,
but I had missed Begin's speech. Most of the Betar's members sided
with Begin. The above-quoted Israel Eldad certainly gave him his
whole-hearted support, went even a few steps further. Eldad, the future ideologue of the LEHI, the Fighters for Israel's Freedom, the
group headed by Abraham Stern and then by Yitzchak Shamir, Dr. Israel Eldad and Nathan Yellin-Mor would try to outdo Begin in its
fight against the British, recognized Begin's courage and gave the
revolt his blessing.

Begin's clash with his revered leader at the Betar conference in
Warsaw in October 1938 can now be seen as a turning point in
Begin's life and in the chain of events that led to the birth of Israel.
After that conference events began to take a new course, and through
Begin's efforts the Irgun Tzvai Leumi was given a clear line of ac-
tion, which, among other things, led to Begin's appointment as the
commander of the Irgun shortly after his arrival in Palestine in 1943,
and to the final victory.

The first news we received in Warsaw about the activities of the

Irgun in the land of Israel was armed response to Arab assaults on Jews. I clearly remember the feeling of relief following the first reports about reprisals against Arab marauders. The Arabs paid with many casualties and learned to fear the Irgun. It was the beginning of the end of the traditional Jewish policy of paralyzing inaction, called *Havlaga.*

At that time I was a contributor to the Warsaw Jewish daily *Der Moment*, which published a weekly article by Ze'ev Jabotinsky. As we began to receive some of the news about the activities of the Irgun shortly after the debate between Begin and Jabotinsky, we were curious to find out what would be the reaction of the head of Betar to the Irgun's reprisals. When Jabotinsky's weekly contribution arrived, titled "Amen!" The title told the whole story.

Dr. Eldad writes in his aforementioned book (page 37) that the poet Uri Tzvi Greenberg, who at the time was a regular contributor to *Der Moment*, had edited Jabontisky's article and took out all the "soft" paragraphs. I am not sure that it was possible for him to do such a thing, since the paper was committed unequivocally never to change a single word of Jabotinsky's. Then again, given Greenberg's indomitable character, it is possible that he might have overlooked the agreement that once. . .

The young Begin, at age 25, was laying the groundwork for the revolt. It will take five more years—one of them in a Soviet prison— before he finally arrives in the promised land and assumes the command of the Irgun. But events, in which for the next half a century Begin will continue to play a central role, were now set in motion.

Chapter Twenty-Nine

Destruction of British Seat of Power

As was suggested before, historical events rarely result from a single act. They are usually the outcome of the confluence of many factors which combine in complicated ways to yield the ultimate results. One can therefore understand the frequent disputes and differences of opinion as to which of the multiple causes or components of a certain event was the decisive one. The Sages settled this dispute as follows: In Talmudic law, the responsibility for committing certain transgressions on the Sabbath rests with the one "who struck the final blow of the hammer." (*Makeh b'patish*).

From the perspective of four decades of research and insight, and from the evidence which has recently come to light concerning events which ensued, we must come to the following inevitable and undisputable conclusion: The *decisive* factor in the creation of the State of Israel was the armed struggle of the Irgun Tzvai Leumi against the British Mandate government in Palestine, a struggle which reached its peak on July 22, 1946, with the bombing of the English Administrative Headquarters at the King David Hotel. If I were asked to pinpoint the exact moment at which the State of Israel became possible, if not inevitable, I would say, July 22, 1946, at 12:37 p.m., when the explosion crushed the southwest wing of the King David Hotel, burying the seat of the British Mandate government in rubble.

Rabbi Aryeh Levin, the Tzaddik of Jerusalem, repeatedly comforted imprisoned Irgun members with these words: "The Almighty's help comes in the blink of an eye." Some historical reversals, even very major ones, undergo a long gestation period, yet occur very quickly (witness the breaching of the Berlin wall). The Viennese Jewish writer, Stephen Zweig, titled one of his books *The Stellar Hours of Humanity (Die Sternenstunden der Menschheit)*. In the struggle for the Jewish state, 12:37 p.m., July 22, 1946 was the "stellar hour," or more precisely, the "stellar moment" of Jewish destiny.

On July 22, 1986, at 6:37 a.m. New York time, or 12:37 p.m. Israel time, I telephoned the man who had been the commander of the Irgun on July 22, 1946, to congratulate him on the 40the anniversary of that historical moment. Menachem Begin was glad that someone overseas had recalled the event. Yet this day should have been engraved in the memories of all Jewish people as the date of one of the most crucial events in Jewish history.

To sum up briefly what took place: Amichai (Gidi) Paglin, the main planner, organizer and implementer of the operation, had seven milk cans stuffed with TNT delivered by truck to the basement kitchen of the hotel. At 12:37, the milk containers were detonated. The huge explosion shook the city. The entire southwest wing crumbled. One floor crashed into the next in a roar of collapsing masonry and woodwork.

Over the deafening noise of the crumbling walls, ceilings and floors, could be heard the screams of the trapped and injured. With a final tremendous crash the whole Secretariat General was turned into a pile of rubble. Ninety-one people were killed, among them British, Jews and Arabs. British rule in Palestine, supervised by the brutal, anti-Semitic Foreign Secretary Ernest Bevin, and the vicious regime of the mediocre Labor Party hack, Prime Minister Clement Attlee, was virtually crushed with the collapse of the building.

With the publication of documents and research on this period, certain facts have come to light. We now know for a certainty that anti-Semitism governed British policy in Palestine. We also know the decisive impact of the hotel bombing on the decision of London to quit Palestine. On July 28, six days after the bombing, Winston Churchill, then the opposition leader, asked the House of Commons: "What more has to happen that we should get out of the mess the Attlee policy caused?"

Another important issue which has since been completely clarified is the efforts made by the Irgun to avoid casualties. Today there is no doubt that the Irgun issued a triple warning half an hour before the assault, allowing enough time to evacuate the building. One warning was telephoned to the hotel, a second to the Jerusalem daily Palestine Post, and a third to the nearby French Consulate. But Sir John Shaw, the Secretary General of the Government to whom the warnings were immediately conveyed, refused to evacuate the building with these words: "I am here to give orders to the Jews, and not to take orders from them." Menachem Begin, who was, of course, glued to the radio listening to the reports of the bombing, was deeply shocked and grieved to hear of the casualties. He thought, with horror, that they were the result of some oversight or negligence on the part of his people in issuing the warning. Haim Landau, the deputy of Begin who was with him at the time, disconnected the radio and told him that the radio had stopped functioning, since he was worried about Begin's extreme emotional reaction to the news about the victims.

Even later, when Irgun members had convinced Begin that the casualties were not their fault, and that they had sent the warnings on time, Begin was overwhelmed by the gloom at the loss of human lives in the bombing. We, who can share his distress over these deaths, should nevertheless not permit grief to obscure the enormous significance of the event. We have to recognize it as the determining force generating the later developments which eventually led to the emergence of the Jewish state.

When I called Begin exactly forty years to the minute after the bombing, I couldn't help but express my regret that the import of this climactic event in the struggle for the liberation of the land of Israel was not sufficiently understood and appreciated.

Begin agreed. He spoke again of the pain caused him by the loss of lives, which the Irgun tried very hard to avoid, a pain which obscured his own appreciation of the act.

Looking back in time it becomes clear that despite the regrettable casualties, those who carried out the attack on the British seat of power drove the last nail into the coffin of Great Britain's failed policy in Palestine and opened the door to the UN vote that led to the establishment of the state.

Chapter Thirty

Emerging from the Underground

After the creation of the Jewish State in 1948, the Irgun Zvai Leumi was voluntarily dissolved and its fighters were incorporated in the newly formed Israeli army. It now appeared that Menachem Begin had completed his mission, at least as a commander of a fighting paramilitary force. His activities as head of the newly founded Herut party would henceforth be relegated to the parliamentary arena, as the first parliament was about to be elected.

Begin played a key role in the early weeks and months of the state, a role more decisive than had hitherto been known or acknowledged. Particularly in strengthening the resistance of Israel to the enormous pressure by Britain and her supporters within the U.S. Department of State. There were two main areas of pressure. One was the concentrated campaign to deprive Israel of her capital, Jerusalem. The second was the attempt to nullify one of the principal objectives of the struggle for independence—free Jewish immigration to Israel.

The provisional government of Israel was naturally opposed to both of these attempts. But there was always the possibility that the government might yield to pressure. And here Begin exerted great influence. He warned against surrender, and he still retained sufficient power so that his warning could not be ignored. Furthermore, at the same time, the government, in resisting foreign pressure, cited as one of its reasons for not surrendering Jerusalem or limiting Jewish immigration the opposition of Begin still wielding substantial power, particularly in Jerusalem, where the Irgun still maintained an independent military unit.

Consequently, the British Government and the State Department saw in Begin, and to a lesser degree (because of its smaller numbers) in the LEHI, the main, if not the only obstacle to the implementation of their plans. Let us recall that concerning Jerusalem these plans foresaw either the internationalization or, according to the UN mediator Count Folke Bernadotte's program, the immediate occupation of the old and parts of the new city by King Abdallah of Jordan. Naturally, the government of Ben-Gurion rejected both of these plans as well as the British demand, acquiesced to by the State Department (behind the back of President Harry Truman), for the surrender of the Negev to Jordan. The British and their American supporters, however, saw the main obstacle to the realization of these plans in Menachem Begin, since they assumed that they might still come to terms with the more flexible Israeli Foreign Minister, Moshe Sharett, were it not for this "terrorist" Begin who still aroused their hate, fear and—respect.

Declassified 1948 documents made public by the State Department reveal a Begin who is an obstinate pursuer of a strong viable Jewish state, a still unyielding fighter opposed to any surrender and—a pro-communist! Or, as the reports by American diplomats and by British Foreign Miniser Ernest Bevin label him, a "Soviet-oriented leader" of whom "the USSR will take advantage."

One of the U.S. officials in the area who was particularly hostile to the Jewish state was the U.S. Vice-Consul in Jerusalem, Mr. William C. Burdett. In his frequent reports to the State Department, he tried most assiduously to persuade his superiors to maintain and further reinforce their already negative attitude towards the new Jewish state. His biased reports, full of unfounded allegations, willful distortions and false assumptions fell on fertile ground. Mr. Burdett endeavored to alert his superiors to the "communist" danger embodied in Menachem Begin and his Irgun. True, Begin had dissolved his military organization immediately after the founding of the Jewish state, and had integrated its members in the new Jewish army, but Mr. Burdett warned Washington that the Irgun was still very much alive in Jerusalem. He also alerted the U.S. Secretary of State, General George C. Marshall to the danger of Mr. Begin's "pro-Soviet policy."

In his secret telegram to the Secretary, the U.S. Vice-Consul reported on June 24, 1948: "Menachem Begin, Commander of IZL, has ordered his followers to orient themselves towards Russian recognition and Russian support of the Jewish state."

To protect himself against a possible rebuttal, Burdett cautiously added that: "No concrete evidence is available to substantiate [the report]."

Let us add here that attempts were made by the Ben-Gurion government (and met with considerable success) to obtain vitally necessary arms from Czechoslovakia. These efforts were made in the face of a U.S. embargo on arms to Israel, an embargo which Washington strenuously tried to impose on many countries including Prague as well. At the same time, Britain continued to deliver weapons to the Arab states under the pretext of previous contractual obligations to Iraq and Jordan. To put the "blame" for Israel's efforts to obtain arms from the USSR (actually through Czechoslovakia) on Begin, shows the lengths to which some American officials actually went in order to denigrate the already defamed IZL leader. Those very same sources which alerted Washington to the "pro-communist orientation of Mr. Begin" did not hesitate on other occasions to describe him as "an extreme rightist, a 'fascist.' "

But a further point made by the same Mr. Burdett in the same telegram officially confirmed the role played by Mr. Begin in the early days of the state. That is, Begin was responsible for the government stiffening its resistance to pressures from without. He reported that:

> A reliable Jewish source indicates that two groups are augmenting their forces here in Jerusalem to serve as a threat and reminder to the Israel Government that IZL and Stern will not tolerate any concession on immigration or on the status of Jerusalem. Regarding latter, it is possible that IZL and Stern will reject international status for city believing that Jerusalem should be capital of Jewish State which they regard as ultimately including all of Palestine.

Since the "reliable Jewish source" mentioned in the above telegram could not be other than pro-government or government circles, it is obvious that the impact of Begin's "presence" in Jerusalem was felt within the Israeli government. Moreover, the same used the threat of Begin as a further argument in its strong stand against hostile demands, particularly on the subject of immigration and the status of Jerusalem.

In the same telegram, Mr. Burdett quoted Dr. Bernard Joseph, chairman of the Jewish Jerusalem Emergency Committee, and David She'altiel, Jerusalem commander of the Haganah, who stated to the United Nations Truce Commission that: "Haganah is unable to cope with the situation [concerning the Irgun]."

The support of the Irgun and the LEHI for the Ben-Gurion government was "conditional," according to the same telegram, "upon the
assurance that that policy does not weaken or change."

It is obvious from these reports that while Ben-Gurion fought the
Irgun and made every effort to liquidate it completely, he simultaneously
used the presence and influence of Begin, and the fact that Begin's organization and the Sternists still held considerable power in Jerusalem,
to ward off British and American pressure. Begin therefore served well
as a reason for the provisional government of Israel to be adamant in its
rejection of British and U.S. demands for the internationalization of
Jerusalem, the limitation of Jewish immigration to Israel, and the surrender of the Negev to Jordan (which was under British control).

On June 28, 1948, a secret memorandum was sent by acting
Secretary of State Robert A. Lovett (the Wall Street banker associated
with the obsessive paranoiac anti-Semite, Defense Secretary James
Forrestal, who later committed suicide while suffering from a mental
illness) to Clark Clifford, President Truman's special counsel and a
staunch supporter of Israel. Its subject was "Activities of IZL and
Stern Gang in Palestine." Mr Lovett wrote:

> As you know, we are working on a plan for the internationalization
> of Jerusalem. . . Telegram [by U.S. Vice-Consul Burdett in
> Jerusalem of June 24, 1948] no. 963 presents a rather alarming pic-
> ture of the activities of the Irgun and Stern Gang. . . Dr. B. Joseph
> has informed the Truce Commission that he is unable to be respon-
> sible for the acts of the Irgun and Stern Gang in Jerusalem.

Lovett asks Clifford to show President Truman the telegrams from
U.S. Vice-Consul Burdett alerting them to the danger called Begin.
Presumably, this was in order to deflect the President from his objec-
tion to the Bernadotte plan, which according to the Irgun and others,
was initiated and authored by the implacable enemy of Israel, Harold
Bailey, Bevin's advisor on Palestine. (In Truman's biography *Plain
Speaking* [by Merle Miller], this great American president reminisces
on the experience: "I told him [Rabbi Stephen Wise, president of the
Zionist Organization of America] I knew all about experts [the State
Department officials]. I said that an expert was a fella who was afraid
to learn anything new because then he wouldn't be an expert
anymore." (page 233). On another occasion Truman remarked that
there were some anti-Semites in the State Department.

Later, British Foreign Minister Ernest Bevin himself alerted Washington to the threat of the "Soviet-oriented" Begin.

In a top secret cable dated August 6, 1948, from the U.S. Ambassador to Great Britain, Lewis W. Douglas to Secretary of State George C. Marshall, the former conveyed the content of a conversation in which Bevin warned the United States about Begin:

> Evidence [of keen interest of the USSR in Begin] is supply of arms to Israel through Czechoslovakia. . . and Menachem Begin's speech August 3 in Zion Square, Jerusalem, during which Begin said that fighting underground resist any international regime that attempts to wrest Jerusalem from Jewish control. . . It would be naive to suppose that USSR would refuse to take advantage of a personality such as Begin. . .

At the same time, while Bevin conveyed to the U.S. Government the threat of Soviet penetration of the Middle East through—of all people!—Menachem Begin, the British press, being unaware of this top secret document, referred to Begin as "the fanatic rightist and 'fascist'. . ."

The American Ambassador to London, who must have been aware of the absurdity of this accusation of Bevin's—anti-Semitism had become an obsession with Bevin at that point—did not cast the slightest doubt on the Briton's strange contention. On the contrary, he accepted British Palestinian policy and made every effort to win the approval of Washington for it, in order to avoid a "divergence between British and U.S. policy."

It is amazing how Begin, a commander without an army, an embattled opposition leader without government power, constituted such a major resistance force against the enormous pressure of a great power, Britain, and to a somewhat lesser degree, the United States, through its State Department.

In the early and crucial months of the newborn fledgling state, Begin played both a direct and an oblique powerful role in shaping Israel's resistance to the conspiracy to destroy her viability through the Bernadotte plan. This plan, viciously conceived by the British and supported by influential pro-Arab State Department diplomats, provided, as mentioned, for the surrender of Jerusalem, the Negev, and part of the Upper Galilee to Jordan, with all the implications and consequences of such actions.

It was nineteen years later, on June 7, 1967, the day of the Six Day War, that Menachem Begin, then a member of the government, was once again destined to give a hard push—this time to the somewhat timid Prime Minister Levi Eshkol, and to the hesitating Defense Minister Moshe Dayan, towards the final thrust for the liberation of the Old City and the reunification of Jerusalem, the capital of Israel and of world Jewry.

Chapter Thirty-One

What Forced the British Out of Eretz Yisrael?

What forced the British out of Eretz Yisrael? Historians are pondering this question. There were, of course, many factors and causes of this historical event. One of the decisive ones, perhaps the most decisive, was, of course, the weakening of the rule of Palestine by the British Mandatory government. Thus, the crucial question focuses itself. *What and who forced the British to abandon Eretz Yisrael?*

The British were then at the peak of their might and prestige. They came out victorious in World War II. The assurance by Churchill that he is "not going to preside over the dissolution of the British empire" was also valid for the Labor government at the helm. The empire was still intact.

The various interests of Britain in the Middle East were seen as vital, and Palestine was the key to the region, according to their estimate.

The Attlee-Bevin government was stubbornly obstinate in its determination not to relinquish or weaken its iron grip on the country.

What, then, forced them out of Palestine?

It took forty years of "rewriting history" (in the Kremlin method. . .) by some Israeli historians, political scientists, publicists, journalists, to distort and pervert the historical facts. Many of these writers were propagandists hired and dominated by the leftist establishment, whose power encompassed all the sectors of the political, social, cultural and economic life of the country, not excluding the academy.

Many of the official historians and political scientists, enslaved by their stiff doctrines and narrow prejudices, and often motivated by personal interests, degenerated into partisan fanatics, Etzel being the subject of their hate.

In these circumstances it would be naïve and futile to expect historical truth to emerge from these writers.

Thus, after many historians, political scientists, publicists, answered this question, mostly tendentiously and incorrectly, after many distortions and falsifications—it is time for a sober look at the historical truth.

This is necessary not merely for a correct perspective and outlook, but for learning the right lessons from the past for the present and future. Especially at this time of turmoil in Israel when the struggle for its very existence, which we thought—erroneously, as we see—was definitely won, is still going on.

The above question is answered thoroughly and clearly by the book in Hebrew "What Caused the British to Leave Eretz Yisrael?" by Dr. Yosef Nedava (Tel-Aviv, 1990).

I didn't read it—I swallowed it. And I am still engrossed in it and delighted by it.

After encountering so many base misinterpretations and utter falsehoods on the subject, it was like a breeze of refreshing air, a breath of the truth, the undiluted historical truth.

Dr. Nedava presents us with a clear definitive, and irrefutable final answer to the baffling question why the then still mighty empire abandoned its crucial position in a crucial for it region, the Middle East.

The straight and lucid explanation is amply and solidly documented and proved beyond any doubt by the vast wealth of research encompassing all relevant factors, causes and aspects.

And this is the answer: the British were forced out of Eretz Yisrael by Etzel (Irgun Tzvai Leumi) and LEHI (Lochmei Heruth Yisrael).

These heroic fighters, initially seen merely as an insignificant nuisance, eventually overcame the overwhelming power of the English led by the unscrupulous, brutal anti-Semite Ernest Bevin, their infamous Foreign Secretary, and by Clement Attlee, the most mediocre, narrow-minded and evil-spirited of the otherwise illustrious chain of the British Prime Ministers!

The greatest and best educated Jewish journalist of the time, Dr. Azriel Carlebach, was right when he published May 16, 1948, in Maariv, the Hebrew daily edited by him, an editorial under the heading, "Menachem Begin, you liberated [Eretz Yisrael]!"

If someone moved by ignorance, lack of sound judgement of by any nefarious motives will doubt this truth, let him read Dr. Nedava's book.

The great historian, perhaps the greatest of contemporary Israel, and certainly the most honest and unbiased, avoided in his book any trace of polemics or partisan coloring. He really did not answer himself the question he puts as the topic and the content of his book. He did not assume the role of a judge in the court of history.

Instead, he put on the gown of the lawyer he was (with a JD from London University, but not practicing)—and what . . . caliber of witnesses he is calling to testify:

Winston Churchill, Franklin D. Roosevelt, Cordell Hull. And then Ernest Bevin, Clement Attlee, Lord Moyne, Baker, Cunningham, the last British High Commissioners of Palestine, and a horde of other Bevinazis bound to make Hitler's Final Solution final! . . .

Nedava lets also testify such sworn enemies of Etzel like Chaim Weitzmann, David Ben-Gurion, Moshe Sharett, etc. . . in their speeches, statements, notes, correspondence, secret communications.

Their testimony is supported and affirmed by other vast documentary evidence, amplified by recent disclosure from British and other archives. There are also in my possession many documents and sources, partly published, a result of long time research and study. Some of them were used in my articles over many years, in Hebrew, English and Yiddish publications (see appendix).

Chapter Thirty-Two

"Received from Irgun Zvai Leumi"

"Received from IRGUN ZVAI LEUMI: one JAFFA (signed) Haganah commander." This somewhat unusual "receipt" was presented by the Haganah commander to the IZL commander, Shraga Ellis, upon the transfer by the latter to the former of one of the sandbagged positions along Alen Street in Jaffa, liberated by the IZL in April 1948.

If objective historians will have their way, they will, after thorough research and evaluation from a safe distance in time, have to present a similar receipt to Menachem Begin, the Commander-in-Chief of the IZL, which will say in essence: "received from the IZL: one State of Israel."

However, as a state is not presented on a "silver platter" and its emergence is the result of a combination of several factors and situations, the above form of acknowledgment will have to be trimmed with certain qualifications. The recipient himself, never claiming exclusively something not wholly belonging to him, would be the last to accept such acknowledgment without further ado, because a state is not born of a single factor. It is a product of several divergent forces, an outcome of many developments, events and situations. Far be it from any honest student to deny, or even belittle the efforts, sacrifices and the heroism of the other fighters and builders, foremost among them, the Haganah and its striking units the Palmach, or for that matter the LEHI. Nor could the fighters for Israel's freedom, known as the Stern Group be overlooked; or the work and achievements of the Chalutzim, the founders and builders of the settlements, the Kibbutzim and Moshavim. Neither could the political negotiations and activities of the Jewish Agency, the Va'ad Le'umi, nor the merits of the Zionist organizations be ignored. Is it also possible to disregard the blunders resulting from the blatant anti-Jewish obsessions of the

Labor Prime Minister, Clement Atlee and his Foreign Minister, the brutal Ernest Bevin, who contributed so largely to the bankruptcy of British rule in Palestine?

Likewise, the support, at the crucial moment, by the Soviet Union, of the partition resolution of the United Nations in 1947 and sub-sequently—albeit for their own reasons and purposes—could not be overlooked. In addition, the arms and planes delivered through Czechoslovakia to the fledgling Jewish State facing a one-sided arms embargo (the British supplied arms to the Arabs) also applied by the U.S. Government, cannot be omitted.

All this should be duly recorded and acknowledged and to each his due be given.

However, in the final analysis, the verdict of history will ascribe the decisive role in "persuading" the British—against their intention and determination—to leave Palestine, thereby enabling the Jews to achieve sovereignty over their land—to Menachem Begin. In the long chain of events which led to May 15th, 1948, *his* was the final thrust which made the Declaration of Independence unavoidable, compell-ing, imperative!

At that time and later too, the decisiveness of the IZL struggle was overlooked by many and its adversaries even denied its role as a contributing factor. The Establishment (it later became the Government), which had fought the "dissidents" for many years on the ground that they were a disruptive and destructive force, detrimental to the Yishuv and its aims, could and would not later admit any positive share of the same in achieving statehood. Such an admission would be tantamount to an admission of guilt in cer-tain actions against the IZL. Thus the powerful propaganda ap-paratus of the Government, the Jewish Agency and the World Zionist Organization, dominated by the leftist, Socialist parties, maintained the "official" pre-State line, distorting the role of the dissident fighters. Most of the press cooperated consciously or un-wittingly in this distortion.

"Official" historians with leftist leanings had their share in this manipulation of history too. As a result, the heroism of the fighters and martyrs of the IZL, along with the role and image of its com-mader-in-chief, remained uncomprehended, unappreciated and misrepresented. The calumnies and falsifications persisted.

The few books authored by participants in the dissident underground struggle, like: *The Revolt* and *In the Underground* (4 vols.) by Menachem Begin, *The Woman of Violence* by Ge'ulah Cohen, *Long is the Way to Freedom* by Ya'akov Meridor and *The History of the IZL* by David Niv (some of these were translated from Hebrew into other languages including English), did something to bring out the truth of the matter. But their impact was limited. They did not reach the larger public. They were considered rather personal accounts—memoirs by their nature subjective. They were not successful in erasing the partisan propaganda which continued for decades, and could help little in eradicating deep-rooted prejudices and correcting the distortions and outright falsifications.

Fortunately, the public is in a better position today to judge the events of the time of the struggle for a Jewish State and to grasp their real significance.

As a result of the publication of the official secret documents of the British Foreign Office and the U.S. State Department of the years 1944–1948, it became clear that the British Government of Prime Minister Clement Atlee and Foreign Minister Ernest Bevin, was not only determined to prevent Jewish sovereignty over Palestine and to stop Jews from entering the country, but that there were also blatantly anti-Semitic pronouncements of the British commanders in Palestine, such as those of General Baker ("hit the Jews on their pockets. . ."), were only a echo of the voice of their masters. . .

in spite of all this, the heads of the Jewish Agency, Professor Chaim Weitzmann, David Ben-Gurion, Moshe Shertok (later Sharett), still believed in the possibility of an understanding and eventual accommodation of and cooperation with the British. But Begin saw the enemy in them and indeed, we now know without doubt, that the enemy they *were*. It was proven beyond any doubt by their own since-published documents and by subsequent events.

Once the British Government announced its decision to relinquish its mandate over Palestine and handed the problem over to the United Nations, it used every subterfuge and trick to prevent a solution which might be favorable or acceptable to the Jews—in fact, any solution. When, on November 29th, 1947, the Special Assembly of the United Nations adopted a resolution for the partition of Palestine into a Jewish and an Arab state, London, which had previously maneuvered against the resolution, did everything possible to sabotage its implementation. After the declaration of the State on May 15th, 1948, the British collaborated with the invading Arab countries against Israel, by supplying some of them weapons, supporting the Jordanian Arab Legion with arms and commanders and at the same time, by persuading the United States (not too formidable a task, considering the State Department's sympathetic leanings towards them), to enforce the embargo on arms deliveries to Middle-East countries which was specifically directed against Israel.

Simultaneously, British diplomacy, again with some help from Americans such as the Ambassador to London, Douglas and the Under-Secretary of State, Robert Lowell, worked hard to deprive Israel of large and vital tracts of territory assigned to the Jewish State, like the Negev and the Upper Galilee. Count Folke Bernadotte, who was supposedly the neutral United Nations mediator, was a willing instrument in the hands of the British. The infamous and fortunately abortive Bernadotte Plan was actually conceived and authored by Harold Bailey, the chief strategist of Bevin's war against the Jews.

But, we might now hear an objection, namely the Declaration of Independence was not made up by Begin. He was not even present in the Tel-Aviv museum at this fateful event on May 15th, 1948; his signature does not even appear on (we are tempted to say: does not grace) this historic document.

This is true. However, there was a declaration *before* the declaration—a declaration which made the historic act inevitable. On May 6th, 1948, seven days before the British promised (threatened?) to relinquish the mandate and evacuate Palestine, the Irgun issued the demand which bears the unmistakable imprint of its commander, Menachem Begin (by now, we *know* that he *was* the author), that the sovereign Jewish State should be proclaimed and come to full life. In case the Jewish establishment will not abide by this demand, the State will be proclaimed by the Irgun.

Here we have a demand coupled with a warning, veiled into a threat, which in fact was no less than an ultimatum. The Irgun threatened that in the event that the establishment would desist or postpone the proclamation of the State, it would take place neverthe-less and a Jewish Government would be formed. Such an ultimatum could not be ignored.

In fact, the top leaders of the Yishuv, David Ben-Gurion and even Professor Chaim Weitzmann, who were usually inclined toward reconciliation with the British, were this time inclined not to delay the fateful act. But powerful forces in Washington were exerting enor-mous pressure on the Jews, forcing them to desist from proclaiming Independence. Secretary of State, George Marshall, summoned Mr. Moshe Shertok to Washington and tried hard to compel the Jews not to do so. Marshall, together with the Under-Secretary of State, Robert Lowell and Loys Henderson, head of the department's Division for South Asian and Near Eastern Affairs (whose wife was a White Rus-sian, not too friendly to Jews. . .), made use of the stick and carrot method on Shertok. They argued that if the Jewish State were to come into being, the Arab neighbors would invade it and the United States would have to come to its rescue. This would lure Soviet Russia to the side of the Arabs and then there would be a Third World War.

This, said Marshall, we cannot afford. In addition to all else, the U.S. armed forces who were then in the process of demobilization, were not prepared for a confrontation, according to the Joint Chiefs of Staff.

(The writer had the above relayed to him by Rabbi Yitzchok Meyer Levin, the first Israeli Minister of Welfare, then in New York, to whom Shertok reported daily on these happenings and whose advice he sought and received.)

Marshall hinted that the United States may not only withhold its own support for the State, but also the support of the American Jews, through the United Jewish Appeal and other similar institutions. On the other hand, the Secretary said, if the proclamation were to be postponed for a more propitious time, the U.S. would then lend its support.

These arguments could not fail to make their impact on the heads of the National Council under the chairmanship of Ben-Gurion.

But then there was this other warning—the warning of Menachem Begin. It certainly bore its weight on the scales of the difficult decision. It helped greatly to counterbalance the pressure difficult decision. It helped greatly to counterbalance the pressure and the threats, and to free the decision-makers from whatever hesitancy may have lingered in their minds.

Thus Begin's act was a decisive one. His was the final thrust for the historic Declaration of May 15, 1948.

Chapter Thirty-Three

Begin's Revolt—A War of Liberation

The British did not leave the land they called Palestine in 1948 of their own free volition. What led to their departure from that corner of the world was a series of events which—by their own admission— made their continued presence there intolerable not only to the *Yishuv* but also to themselves.

On the night of May 15, 1948, as the British Mandate over Palestine came to and end, the Colonial Office and the Foreign Office of His Majesty's Government published a statement which included the following paragraph:

> His Majesty's Government had now striven for twenty-seven years without success to reconcile Jews and Arabs and to prepare the people of Palestine for self-government. The policy adopted by the United Nations had aroused the determined resistance of the Arabs, while the States supporting this policy were themselves not prepared to enforce it. 84,000 troops, who received no cooperation from the Jewish community, had proved insufficient to maintain law and order *in the face of a campaign of terrorism waged by highly organized Jewish forces equipped with all the weapons of the modern infantryman* [my emphasis]. Since the war [World War Two] 338 British subjects had been killed in Palestine, while the military forces there had cost the British taxpayer 100 million pounds. . . the declared intentions of Jewish extremists showed that the loss of further British lives was inevitable. . .
>
> In these circumstances His Majesty's Government decided to bring to an end their Mandate and to prepare for the earliest possible withdrawal from Palestine of all British forces.

The "terrorists" and "Jewish extremists" referred to in the above statement were of course the IZL and its offshoot, the LEHI. The most notorious "terrorist," for whose captain the British were willing to pay a reward of thousands of pounds, was Menachem Begin.

In 1948, Begin's revolt was in its fifth year. Far from having "all the weapons of the modern infantryman," the IZL, also known as the Irgun, was a small organization of a few hundred fighters equipped with the a pitiful arsenal, including mostly pistols, some rifles, a few submachine guns, and some explosives. This "fearsome army" confronted some 100,000 British troops, including paratroopers, armor, aircraft, and the celebrated British intelligence. Yet, under the command of the invisible, anonymous "Reb Yisroel Sassover," alias Menachem Begin, those young men and women managed to inflict devastating blows on the foreign occupier, blowing up police and army headquarters, military airfields and aircraft, railroads, and other military installations, and staging some of the most incredible jail breaks in all of history.

Was Begin a terrorist or a freedom fighter? To the British at that time he was, of course, a "terrorist." No doubt, if he had a few divisions and some armor and aircraft of his own, he would have challenged them on the open battlefield. But since—unlike the Jewish fighters of the Warsaw Ghetto—Begin was not engaged in a suicide mission, but in a war of liberation, he had to use guerrilla warfare tactics.

In judging the events of the twentieth century, future generations will pass the ultimate judgment of who were the freedom fighters and who were the terrorists of this century.* A few things, however, are clear even now:

a. The British, in the 1917 Balfour Declaration, made a pledge to the Jewish people to establish a Jewish national home in the land of Israel. In 1939, with the publishing of the White Paper, they reneged on that pledge, closing the gates of Palestine to the doomed Jews of Europe. By doing so, they had forfeited their right to the Mandate and became a foreign occupier and oppressor.

b. The Irgun declared war of liberation against the British occupier.

c. During that war, known as the Revolt, the Irgunists focused only on military targets, not on civilians, even if it meant risking their own lives or giving up the opportunity to eliminate some of their top enemies.

---

* It is my contention that the real terrorists were the British themselves, who during the years 1939 to 1947 closed the gates of the Mandate to the Jewish refugees of Europe, thus indirectly cooperating in the German murder of the Jews of Europe.

d. The stated goal of the revolt was Jewish sovereignty over the land of Israel. This was necessary in order to enable the survivors of the German "Final Solution" and those who were potential victims of similar murderous threats by some East European peoples, like the Poles (such as the pogrom on the few remaining Jewish survivors in Kielce July 4, 1946!) find a safe haven. The Jewish people had the moral right to take up arms and fight for their right to their own homeland.

e. The revolt of the Jews against the British occupation of their ancestral homeland signalled the beginning of other wars of liberation against British, French and Portuguese colonial rule throughout the world, resulting in some 50 new independent states. Several of those states have acknowledged their debt of gratitude to the Irgun and its leader for showing the way and providing an example of self-sacrifice and heroism.

f. The revolt was Israel's War of Liberation, while the 1948 war was Israel's War of Independence. Begin fought to liberate his country from foreign rule, while the newly formed Israel Defense Force (IDF) fought in 1947-48 to defend the newly formed state against the invading Arab armies and the murderous Arab gangs inside the infant state. In Hebrew the war of independence is commonly known as *Milhemet Ha'shihrur*, or the war of liberation. This is incorrect. The war that followed the proclamation of the state on May 14, 1948 took place after the country had already been liberated from British rule, and its main objective was to defend the infant state and secure its independence against the onslaught of the Arab states.

When Begin arrived in Palestine in 1943, he assumed the command of the Irgun and took personal charge of two key areas: First, military commander and planner of military operations; second, writer of the propaganda wall posters, *Herut* (freedom), which were illegally pasted on walls in the cities and towns of the Mandate. He was the paper's only writer, regularly filled it up with messages, calls to action, and discussions of completed military operations. He was a one-man propaganda department, an ideologue, a military spokesman, a political commentator, a polemicist, and a public orator (in print), who at the same time commanded and oversaw the Irgun's daring operations and conducted negotiations with representatives of the Jewish establishment, and later with the UN Special Commission on Palestine (UNSCOP).

When I read today some of those *Herut* wall posters, which were pasted on walls by teenagers risking their lives, I can understand why those young people were willing to put their lives on the line so that the word of their commander could be brought to the attention of the public. As I read them I can almost hear the sound of explosions. Every word of Menachem Begin is as charged with dynamite as the bombs that were planted and thrown by his soldiers. Both the words and the bombs had their double impact on the British enemy, destroying its strongholds and its prestige.

When we consider under what conditions Begin wrote those words, and in what state of mind—under constant danger to his life, mourning the death of his people in Europe, and feeling rage toward the oppressor, we cannot help but admire the precision of the language, the beauty of the style, the masterly use of the spoken Hebrew language by someone who had just arrived from Europe. One can feel his restless spirit, his boiling anger, and yet one can also perceive his iron logic, the lucidity of his ideas, and the clear and exact analysis of political events, their causes and repercussions.

Today, looking back on what had taken place, and judging from official British documents which only recently have been made public, one must marvel at Begin's accurate analysis of the situation. His predictions were fulfilled, and his political line has proved itself to be justified by subsequent events and led to the eventual victory and vindication of his struggle.

Compared to all this, the endless meetings and resolutions of the "official leaders" of the *Yishuv* appear pale, insipid and ill-conceived. For, at the bottom of those activities there seemed to be faith, albeit shaken ("in spite of everything. . ." "after all. . ." "they will eventually realize. . .") in the British rule. Begin never trusted the British, whose political double-dealing, deception and fraud convinced him that he was faced with a cunning and cruel enemy. He drew his own conclusions. Instead of negotiations—war; instead of false hope—facing reality; instead of speeches—an iron fist. He certainly had enough steel in his character to follow up on what he advocated.

The secret protocols of the 1945-1948 Attlee regime were recently made public. They show how sophisticated leaders like Ben-Gurion and Sharett, who were in constant touch with the British authorities had fallen prey to illusions and deceptions in regard to the British policy, and how correct was the man in the underground, who had little contact with the outside world.

Begin's sense of reality is seen today not only in the light of the newly released documents of the Attlee-Begin government, whose actions cannot be defined by any other word except criminal, but also in the political developments in various countries who have no direct relationship with the Jewish cause.

Of the approximately fifty new states that have come into being since the days of Begin's revolt, having shaken off English, French and Portuguese colonial rule, not one achieved its independence through negotiations, statements, speeches, resolutions, or through the good will of the colonial rulers. When you meet the representatives of those Third World states, as I have several times at the United Nations, you can hear each one of them tell his own story of an uprising and an armed struggle, and of a long and difficult fight. The diplomatic activities and the negotiations and agreements usually accompanied or followed the armed struggle as a sideshow, rather than a factor determining the course of events and assuring final victory.

In the maze of political moves there is never one single factor at work. Many and varied factors collide and interact, and what happens in the end is the result of all the various factors, courses, actions and events. But in a final analysis, from the vantage point of distance of time, one can single out one factor out of many as being the decisive one. No doubt, the various forces active in the *Yishuv* during the time of the revolt contributed to the ultimate liberation of Israel. But what gave the *decisive* push was the revolt headed by Begin.

In his book *Palestine Triangle* (London 1979), the British statesman and historian Lord Nicholas Bethell asks the question, What would have happened if the British had not evacuated Palestine in 1948? In his conversations with Haganah veterans and Jewish Agency leaders, there were a few who were willing to admit that "The Irgun made an important contribution to putting pressure on Britain, and that its members helped hasten the decision to evacuate." If this is the case, the author adds, "If indeed the Irgun and LEHI hastened Britain's withdrawal by one year, they may have well affected the course of history." The author goes on to explain that in 1948 the geopolitical picture changed radically, Soviet expansionism became a real threat to the west, and the West might have decided that it was in its best interest to have Britain continue to keep the Mandate.

Britain decided to terminate the Mandate (or rather to turn the matter over to the United Nations, hoping till the last minute that it would become evident that the only hope for that corner of the world was for Britain to remain in control). Thus, the revolt proved to be justified, well-timed and effective.

One can only regret the fact that the Irgun did not enjoy broader support in the Jewish world during and immediately after World War Two, particularly in the United States, where a pro-Irgun organization was created by Peter Bergson (alias Hillel Cook) and Shmuel Merlin, with the participation of some influential people and public figures, notably the author Ben Hecht. This group encountered no less opposition by the Zionist establishment in America than did the Irgun in the land of Israel. But what matters, in the final analysis, is the end result. In this instance, the end result was the fulfillment of a two-thousand-year-old dream, the Jewish State.

Chapter Thirty-Four

Altalena—Crime and Tragedy

The most controversial thing Begin did during the early months of the new state was to bring a ship loaded with vast quantities of the most modern weapons and carrying several hundred men who had undergone military training to beef up the woefully ill-equipped army of the new state engaged in battle on all fronts.

The ship, named Altalena (after Jabontinsky's pen-name), was a project that had taken a long time to bring into fruition. It was the result of efforts made by Irgun supporters in Europe and the United States, partly in collaboration with French government circles.

For the past forty-two years the Altalena debate has raged in Israel and throughout the Jewish world, and it is far from over. Hundreds of articles and a few books have been written about it, arguing both sides of the issue. The event has been studied down to the minute or even the second of each of the several fateful days during which this grim saga unfolded on the shore of Tel Aviv. It has been looked at from every angle. Every motive and factor was analyzed and reanalyzed. What is missing, however, are some critical pieces of the drama, such as: Did Israel Galili, who served as Ben-Gurion's liaison with Begin in negotiating the fate of the Altalena, actually relay to the prime minister Begin's offers and counteroffers, or was Ben-Gurion, in the final analysis, misled by his seconds-in-command?

Ben-Gurion is alleged to have told General Yigal Allon that the ship posed a threat to the very existence of the new state, since Begin intended to run his own separate war, which would signal the end of Jewish unity and the fall of the state before it had a chance to take its first breath. Ben-Gurion ordered Allon to open fire on the ship and sink it. This was done. But as the ship went down to the bottom of the sea, it took down with it the only chance of saving the Old City of Jerusalem and other territories, such as the Etzion Bloc, which were subsequently lost to Jordan.

To understand the critical need for the enormous amount of arms on the Altalena at that fateful moment in the battle for Jerusalem, one must realize that the most severe problem facing the newly born state was not a lack of determined fighters, but a lack of sufficient weapons to repel the attacks of the invading Syrians, Iraqis, Jordanians, Egyptians, Sudanese, as well as numerous Arab gangs in Jerusalem, Jaffa, Haifa, Acre, Tiberias, and many other towns throughout the country.

These forces were not only numerically vastly superior to the Haganah, but also incomparably better armed. In many battles of the 1948 war, Jewish defenders faced tanks, armor, airplanes and artillery with rifles, Molotov cocktails, pistols, and light machine guns (witness the battles of Degania, Yad Mordecai, and countless more). The Arabs also had the advantage of large reserves of materiel accumulated over many years by sovereign states unhindered by foreign control. In addition, while the bloody battles went on, these armies were supplied with great quantities of weapons by various countries, mostly Britain. Thus, the embargo which was ostensibly imposed on all the parties was in reality only implemented against on Israel.

Ironically, this embargo was imposed on Israel even by its so-called "friends." The U.S. Department of State was not satisfied with merely prohibiting any supply of arms to Israel from the United States. It played, in addition, the role of "Policeman of the World," and did everything in its power to prevent other countries from sending arms to the embattled Jewish state. Various American government agents, including intelligence and diplomatic officials, made sure American influence was felt by countries such as Czechoslovakia and France, the main sources of arms for Israel. The Jews, desperately in search of weapons for defense, encountered these inimical efforts everywhere in Europe. Thus the State Department continued its anti-Jewish policy of the war years.

The unusual zeal these American officials displayed in order to deprive the beleaguered Jews of the vital means of defense must lead inevitably to one conclusion: the State Department, which consistently opposed the creation a Jewish state (because of Arab interests, particularly oil) in the first place, and which, together with certain American and British military efforts predicted that such a state would not be able to repel the Arab armies, acted in this matter to enhance the fulfillment of its own dark prophecy. Strong elements of anti-Semitism, in the tradition of Defense Secretary James Forrestal, were also a factor in this withholding of vital arms from the beleaguered state.

The heroism of the Jewish defenders was legendary. But in many places—particularly in the Jerusalem area—inadequate arms led to defeats. This was the situation in June 1948 when the Altalena arrived at the shores of Israel. "The Altalena carried more weapons than the Haganah and the establishment leadership had accumulated in Palestine in all previous years," wrote Yitzhak Ben-Ami, the executive director of the American League for a Free Palestine, the organizations that supported the Irgun in the United States. The Israeli government was well aware of the tremendous amount of weapons on the Altalena, since the Irgun dutifully and trustfully reported to it its contents and cargo. These arms could have played a decisive role in the War of Independence. With these weapons, all of Jerusalem and all of Judea and Samaria could have been conquered, as military experts assert.

The decision to destroy this precious cargo was prompted—as was mentioned previously—by fanatical partisanship, and, possibly, by a series of misunderstandings. What remains clear is that the hatred some Labor leaders felt for Begin had prevented them from thinking rationally. For years they had hammered home the calumny that the Revisionists, and even more so the Irgun, were fascist totalitarian organizations bent upon destroying democracy and imposing a dictatorship.

If fascism and dictatorship were always hateful to Jews, this hate was intensified as these totalitarian systems embodied the most horrendous murderers in the history of mankind, the Germans. The connotation of fascists appended to the Irgun became even more abominable during the German massacres of the Jews. To accuse the man who taught Jews to fight for their lives at a time when they were being exterminated by fascists of being a fascist himself, was truly a useless, mindless and absurd accusation.

The accusers fell victim to their own vicious propaganda. They started to believe their invented lies. They whipped up a frenzy of hate and convinced themselves that they were fighting fascists bound to take over the government by force.

This nonsensical belief was consistent with the character and ideology of the Irgun and its leaders—as they perceived them and as they described them. The reason given by Ben-Gurion's people for destroying the Altalena was in essence that Menachem Begin planned to use the weapons on the boat to arm his men for a "putsch" intended to cause the fall of the government and to seize power.

These allegations were proven to be utterly baseless. They ran contrary to the long held policy and acts of Menachem Begin, and were diametrically at odds with his deep belief in democracy and his character of a true liberal.

During the dark days of the revolt, particularly during the "Saison," when the Haganah, carrying out the orders of the British, rounded up Irgun members and turned them over to the foreign ruler, there were many instances when Irgun members demanded retaliatory action against their tormentors and persecutors. Begin never acceded to such demands. Furthermore, during the entire revolt Begin always made it clear that his goal—for which he kept risking his life—was an independent Jewish government, democratically elected by the entire population. Now that this goal had just become a reality after centuries of striving, praying, suffering, Begin, with his keen sense of Jewish history, was the last person to harm it.

There was another essential element of his character that had made such a conspiratory act improbable. Begin studied law at the Josef Pilsudski University of Warsaw. From conversations with him, from his speeches and articles, it is obvious to me that these studies were not merely a preparation for a career. They became a way of life, as Begin became imbued with the lofty ideas and ideals of jurisprudence, with the humanistic principles underlying the legal system, the foundations of justice.

Ironically, this man, dedicated to legal rules, became an underground leader who was misunderstood by many of his own fellow-Jews. According to his deep convictions, however, the British Mandatory government was in itself a system that had violated the legal foundations and spirit of the mandate was based on, as he had kept emphasizing in his underground messages and calls.

Begin possessed a vast knowledge of the legal systems of democratic regimes, and of the historical legal principles of Judaism, a religion and culture which contains the seeds of Western democracy (see Max Dimont, *Jews, God and History*). Disobedience to tyranny, defiance of injustice, were according to him not only a moral but also legal imperative. His was a legitimate fight against despotism which is by definition illegitimate. The unlawfulness was in the oppression and persecution perpetrated by the occupants of his country was unlawful, and the fight against it was, therefore, just and lawful. Ironically again, in later years Begin will be accused (at the Camp David accords talks) of being too legalistic. . .

Another example taken from Begin's life prior to the revolt is illuminating. When he first arrived in Palestine in 1943 he was a soldier in the Polish army of General Wladyslaw Anders. The Polish republic did not exist any longer, Poland was then totally occupied by the Germans. The Polish army was not free from the stain of anti-Semitism, so it would have been a natural thing for Private Begin, about to become the top commander of the Irgun, to leave this army-in-exile without even saying goodbye. Others, Jews and non-Jews, did so without any qualms. But not Begin. "I am not going to be a deserter," he said to his associates in the Irgun. It took many arduous efforts and complicated formalities on the part of his close associate from Warsaw, the lawyer Mark Kahan, until he obtained a legal release.

Another example from the days of the revolt: Two British sergeants were hanged in retaliation for the hanging of Irgun members, and as a warning against a repetition of this crime against Jewish prisoners of war. But before the execution of the British sergeants, Begin insisted on having a duly appointed court and putting those men on trial. This procedure increased the risk to the Irgun. But only after they were handed down their death sentence were they allowed to be executed.

What Ben-Gurion and other leaders on the left of the Zionist spectrum probably failed to understand about Begin was a very essential point: Begin fought the British because he was saw in them an illegal foreign ruler. He was far from fighting or subverting the newly born Jewish government, which was the fulfillment of his own dream, a government which represented his own people.

Even before that government was created, Begin proclaimed his unswerving loyalty to it, knowing that it would be formed by Ben-Gurion and other implacable adversaries of his. And as we look back today, forty-two years later, we know that Begin never broke his word.

It is safe to say that Begin, in his 36 years in the Knesset, both in the opposition and at the head of the government, holds the finest record of adhering to democratic principles and parliamentary procedures. Add to this his personal integrity and his zealous guarding of the authority of Israel's parliamentary system.

After the Altalena was sunk, Ben-Gurion talked about the cannon (a small caliber howitzer, one of the few Israel owned at the time) that sunk the "illegal" ship as a "holy cannon" which saved the state, and which should be kept in a museum of Israeli history for future generations. . . Absurd! It was an unholy cannon! It was a cannon that caused Israel to lose hundreds of its best sons and daughters on the battlefield unnecessarily; it was the product of *Sin'at Hinam*, groundless hatred among brothers which, we are told in Jewish history, led to the destruction of Jerusalem by the Romans in the first century. This time it led to the loss of old Jerusalem and other parts of the historical land of Israel. While it is true that Ben-Gurion was a forceful leader, that he did play a decisive part in winning the War of Independence and getting the new state started, it is equally true that he was harsh and vindictive, his vision was often a narrow partisan tunnel-vision, the loss he caused to the new state by sinking the Altalena.

Begin, on the other hand, who stood on the deck of the Altalena as it was going up in flames, as some of his best men lay dying on the deck; Begin, who had to be taken by force off the ship by some of his aides, did not become bitter, did not lose his faith. Begin went on to become the head of the loyal opposition for the next thirty years, and was given the unique privilege of becoming Israel's prime minister and the signer of the peace treaty with Egypt.

Chapter Thirty-Five

Constructive Opposition

After the War of Independence in 1948, the newly created State of Israel faced the challenge of shaping a democratic political system. The economy of the new state was controlled by the labor movement, headed by David Ben-Gurion. Free enterprise, typical of most Western democracies, was severely limited if it existed at all. The Israelis were split into several parties. The only party that had enough seats in the Knesset to form a coalition government was Ben-Gurion's Mapai (Israel's Workers' Party). In fact, one could call the fifties—the first full decade of the new state—the Ben-Gurion era.

During those years Ben-Gurion left an indelible mark on the character of the new state. As Begin observed years later, history would always remember Ben-Gurion as the man who had the courage to proclaim the state. One might add that the Labor leader also deserves credit for bringing and settling hundreds of thousands of Jews from the DP camps in Europe and from Arab lands, and for laying the foundations of the Israeli army, only to mention two of his greatest achievements.

But Ben-Gurion was also an autocratic leader who did not easily tolerate opposition either inside or outside his own party. Looking back to the early years of the state, it becomes clear that the man who made the major contribution to the establishment of a truly democratic system in the Jewish state was the leader of the opposition, Menachem Begin. Ben-Gurion, in fact, once speculated that the new state did not need a political opposition altogether. He felt that a free press could actually take the place of an opposition. (See *Menachem Begin* by Eitan Haber, page 242).

It is possible that were it not for Begin's active participation in the political life of Israel in the fifties, Israel would not have become the kind of a democracy it is today. It would instead be closer to a one-party regime. No other leader in the opposition had the stature of

Begin; no one took Ben-Gurion to task on the Knesset floor the way Begin did; no one created a real alternative for the three-decade rule of Labor, as Begin did.

During the fifties Begin was asked by different people why did Ben-Gurion seem to hate him so much. Indeed, Begin even asked himself the same question. For years after the birth of the state, the prime minister refused to address the opposition leader by name, and referred to him as "the man sitting next to Dr. Bader" (a long-time Revisionist leader and Herut Member of Knesset). Clearly, Ben-Gurion had a personal dislike for Begin (and, for that matter, for many of his own Labor colleagues). But it seems to me—from the vantage point of hindsight—that it was more than a typical Ben-Gurionite personal animosity. Somehow Ben-Gurion must have felt in his guts that this young leader, nearly half his age, was the only real alternative to his leadership. During the entire fifties, with only a short interlude of the Sinai Campaign in 1956, Ben-Gurion referred to Begin in the most demeaning terms, using such epithets as "fascist" and "hooligan."

The fifties were a very difficult time for Begin. He saw the fortunes of his party, the Herut (Freedom), decline; he became engaged in a bitter public debate and parliamentary fight over the question of accepting reparations from West Germany; he faced opposition within his own party, which became disillusioned with its lack of an active participation in leadership in the new state. A lesser man would have quit. There were occasions in the fifties, at least once or twice, when Begin seemed to be at the end of the road. He considered quitting, but was always able to bounce back. He realized that the role he played, albeit in the opposition, was vital for the infant state. Even though it was not the lead role, it was nonetheless vital. Once again, Begin had learned well the lesson taught by Jabotinsky, who had insisted that a just cause, no matter how few people support it, is bound to win out in the end. Begin did not doubt for a moment the rightness of his cause.

Ben-Gurion at that time refused to issue a state order—as requested by Jabotinsky in his will—to bring the remains of the great Zionist leader for internment in the State of Israel. It was clearly part of his personal campaign to deny the Revisionists and Herut legitimacy in the new state.

And yet, ironically enough, what Ben-Gurion was busy doing in the fifties was to a great extent a fulfillment of Jabotinsky's vision rather than that of such labor philosophers as Katzenelson, Borochov, or A. D. Gordon. While the socialist thinkers envisioned a Middle East where social justice prevailed, and where Zionism would convince the Arab population that solidarity of the proletariat was a historical imperative, Jabotinsky realized that without a strong army the Jewish state could not survive in a hostile and dangerous environment. Ben-Gurion—fortunately for Israel—was enough of a realist to grasp this assessment of the future. He proceeded to lay the foundations for the strongest army in the Middle East, which enabled the small state of Israel to win several major wars and move the United States to accept Israel as an important ally.

But while the fifties were clearly the Ben-Gurion era, in time they might also come to be regarded as the time of Begin's considerable achievement, namely, creating Israel's viable political opposition and bolstering the democratic foundations and regime of the state.

Here again the model the Israeli legislature is bound to follow is that of Begin. Ben-Gurion, great leader that he was, was also intemperate, obstinate, opinionated, downright abusive of his opponents, and at times even paranoic. He certainly did not set a good example of democratic parliamentary behavior. The one who always commanded the respect of friend and foe alike (except for Ben-Gurion's) was Begin. His tongue was sharp; his barbs were well aimed. But he invariably addressed issues, not personalities. His deep respect for the democratic process was always in evidence. His placing of the interests of the country above partisan ones is a matter of historical record.

The most bitter confrontation between Begin and Ben-Gurion took place in 1951, during the debate on accepting "reparations" from Germany. To Begin, accepting money from the murderers of the Jewish people meant infringing on Jewish dignity. To Ben-Gurion, it was *realpolitik*, an imperative of a financially pressed young state, justified by the biblical quote, "Have you both murdered and inherited?". . . The issue of the "reparations," like the Altalena, belongs to the past. But Begin taught his nation a lesson. No money in the world can atone for the most cruel murders in the annals of mankind. The German mass massacres, committed by an entire nation, could never be forgotten or forgiven!

Chapter Thirty-Six

In the Government, 1967–1970

Observers of the Israeli political scene remember Begin as the outspoken, eloquent leader of the main opposition party, frequently locked in battle with the ruling Labor Party. It is often presumed that Begin waited twenty-nine years, the entire period since the establishment of the State of Israel, in the opposition camp, outside the government, until he became prime minister. He did, however, join the Government of National Unity in June of 1967, shortly before the Six Day War, and remained in the government until 1970, when he resigned in protest over the Eshkol cabinet's deviation from the foreign policy which had originally been outlined at the formation of that government. (The Rogers Plan.)

The public is acquainted with Begin's role as a leader of the opposition, but little is known about his function as a member of the cabinet. This is due to the fact that cabinet deliberations are generally classified, and Begin took great precautions to make sure the discussions did not reach the ears of members of the press, while other cabinet members have been known to leak information.

Ministers in the Israeli government have a twofold task: they head their respective departments and they form the cabinet, which makes policy. At his own request, Begin served in the government as minister-without-portfolio. Since he did not have the responsibility of heading a department, he could devote all his time, thoughts, energy and experience to his cabinet duties. He was not absorbed by day-to-day problems and administrative functions and details. His attention was focused on the broad picture of Israel's foreign policy. In this area, he felt that he had the ability and therefore the duty to contribute decisively to the security of the state.

There were two ways in which Begin accomplished his mission. First, he utilized his political acumen and clarity of thought to expound and explain the policy agreed upon by the consensus of the parties which formed the government coalition. He was careful to observe another master of formulations, Israel Galili, a leading member of the Labor Party and also a minister-without-portfolio, with whom he had had dealings in the underground. Begin made every effort to maintain and strengthen national unity and to interpret and implement the national consensus in foreign policy.

The second role that Begin took upon himself was to guard zealously and conscientiously the position of the government against any erosion of its determined attitude and against any surrender to external pressures that aimed at extracting from Israel concessions detrimental—in his opinion—to Israel's national security. He was particularly alert to any decision or pronouncement that might signify some weakening of the unyielding refusal to relinquish any territory in that part of Israel which he considered liberated Judea and Samaria, and which the outside world calls the occupied West Bank. It was in 1970, when Begin felt that the government was yielding to outside pressures to relinquish those territories, that he caused the withdrawal of GAHAL, the Herut-Liberals bloc, from the government. The decision to leave the government was not supported whole-heartedly by the Liberal wing of the bloc, which was very reluctant to return to the "wilderness of the opposition." Begin, however, demonstrated consistency of policy and close adherence to his principles, and strongly insisted on the departure of his colleagues and partners from the government, a decision which eventually was reached by the majority of the GAHAL.

The discussions held regularly at each Sunday meeting by the cabinet, and occasionally during the week as well, would usually be lengthy and frequently heated. This was in part due to the large number of ministers, twenty-two in all. The controversies would mostly be over foreign relations, and the main initiator and participant would often be Begin.

He was most scrupulous and painstakingly meticulous in his every utterance on behalf of the government's foreign policy. He would spare no effort to put more strength and bite into the government's pronouncements. He showed particular interest and alertness in regard to the statements of the Israeli representative to the United Nations, which meant both the foreign minister, Abba Eban, and the permanent delegate to the UN, Yosef Tekoah (a former member of

Betar). His insistence on precision extended to each and every sentence and word of the speeches delivered by Israel's representatives at the UN. Begin was a great believer in the power of words. He had good reason to think that words lead to action, particularly words that are carefully thought out.

Begin was very clear and adamant in his arguments during cabinet debates. His discourses and rhetorical tone often tended to annoy some members of the majority party. But these were minor notes of discord which did not disturb the basic harmony within the government. It was Begin himself who contributed greatly to this good feeling and the more-than-correct relations among the members of the government. Whenever possible, he did his utmost to avoid friction and disagreement. He went to the limit in trying to find common ground with the Mapai and other left factions. The Labor Party in particular appreciated his effort. They may have been somewhat surprised that this man, noted for his unbending obstinacy and inflexibility, was searching for understanding, for a common denominator, for concurrence and agreement, whenever his convictions and principles permitted.

Twenty years earlier, these very persons confronted Begin as the commander of the Irgun. Later, they faced him as leader of the main opposition, across the benches of the Knesset. But now, as they sat with him at the cabinet table, they encountered a personage quite different from the one they and others always seemed to misread.

On the level of personal relations, he was courteous, gracious, affable and genuinely friendly. He gained not only respect, but also a certain friendship among otherwise stiff officials not given to camaraderie in their relations with outsiders—those not of their party, circle or clique.

They needed to guard themselves against showing outward signs of their congenial relations, lest these be damaging to the propaganda theses expounded in their election campaigns, when they were compelled to conjure up the old and fallacious image of their chief adversary.

Begin's natural friendliness, however, could not be tamed by political calculations, and his sense of fairness would not be repressed by electoral considerations. Once in the government, he started to gain respect, even among his longtime adversaries, and could no longer be dismissed as part of the "fanatic fringe" of Israeli politics. He was now a recognized partner in the Israeli policymaking process, and he was beginning to cultivate powerful political allies inside the socialist camp who would later enable him to accomplish such momentous tasks as the signing of the peace treaty with Egypt.

Chapter Thirty-Seven

Begin and the Reunification of Jerusalem

In the weeks leading to the formation of the national unity government, particularly during May and the first week of June 1967, Israel and the Jewish world were in a state of deep anxiety bordering on fear. Egypt's dictator, Gamal Abdul Nasser, had closed the Red Sea straits to Israeli navigation, and was preparing for a war of annihilation against Israel. Syria was Egypt's staunch ally. There was a distinct possibility of Jordanian participation in a coordinated attack on the Jewish state.

Begin was now a member of the unity government. Levi Eshkol, the Prime Minister, was afraid of war, and hoped till the last minute that the situation could be resolved through negotiations. Eshkol was particularly concerned about possible Soviet intervention on behalf of its Egyptian client, an intervention that could threaten the very existence of the Jewish state. The Cabinet and the High Command of the IDF were divided on what course of action to follow. At the same time, however, careful plans were being drawn by the military experts in preparation for the imminent Arab aggression, particularly Egypt and its allies. Every detail, every step, every possibility was meticulously planned, researched and analyzed. Israel braced itself for the threat of war, and was fully prepared to deal with the imminent aggression.

While the military planners focused on the Egyptian and Syrian fronts, Begin's thoughts also turned to Jerusalem, a city divided by walls and barbed wire fences, behind which armed Arab Legionnaires stood guard. He thought of East Jerusalem, where all the Jewish holy places—the Western Wall, David's Tower are located, made inaccessible to Jews; a city breathing the words and spirit of Israel's prophets and the Psalms of King David, yet where Jews could not move freely, let alone worship; a city mentioned in every Jewish birth, every Jewish wedding, every Jewish funeral throughout the world, yet where Jews were not allowed to live; a city which was lost to the Arabs in 1948 because a ship called Altalena was sunk as it was about to deliver substantial quantities of arms; a city which for nineteen years Begin hoped and dreamed to restore to the Jewish people.

Begin had believed that the IDF, led by Israel's outstanding team of generals—Defense Minister Moshe Dayan, Chief of Staff Yitzhak Rabin, Air Force Commander Ezer Weizman, and such field commanders as Ariel Sharon—could win a decisive victory, routing of the Arab forces. What he—or anyone else in the world, for that matter – did not know at the time was how total and devastating Israel's victory would be. But anticipating victory as he did, Begin's thoughts reached further than the immediate military objectives, to the old dream of a liberated and reunited Jerusalem.

In the total picture of the impending conflict, Jerusalem was not a top military priority. On the contrary. Prime Minister Eshkol had let King Hussein of Jordan know through the UN that if Jordan stayed out of the war, Israel would honor Jordan's non-belligerence. Dealing with Egypt and Syria, the strategic thinking went, was enough.

In the first three hours of the war the Israeli Air Force destroyed the combined air forces of Egypt and Syria on the ground. Being now in complete control of the skies, Israel's military leaders knew that the war was won. Jordan's King Hussein, however, received a false intelligence report from Cairo during that stage. According to his sources, Nasser's forces were dealing Israel devastating blows. The little king ordered his artillery to shell Jewish Jerusalem and every other Jewish community within its range. Around noon of June 6, the Jordanians achieved a success, their only one during the Six Day War: they conquered the headquarters of the UN command in Jerusalem (it had been previously the seat of the British rulers during the Mandate). This conquest created a dangerous situation for the Jewish part of the city, and caused concern on the Israeli side.

Begin reacted instantly. He knew that the danger presented the opportunity long waited for. He further knew that such an opportunity may not present itself for many years to come. He immediately got in touch with Education Minister Yigal Allon, former commander of the Palmach, who had carried out Ben Gurion's orders in sinking the Al-

talena. He knew that Allon had Eshkol's ear, and he persuaded Allon
to ask the Prime Minister to wage battle for the liberation of the Old
City. Allon, who was buoyed by the news of victory in the south,
went into Eshkol's office and told him,

"Begin and I want Jerusalem."

Eshkol answered in Yiddish:

"*S'is a gedank*" (it's an idea).

Eitan Haber writes in his book, *Menachem Begin, the Legend and
the Man* (Delacorte Press, New York 1978):

> "Later that afternoon, Begin, accompanied by his secretary Yehiel
> Kadishai, drove up to Jerusalem on a side road to avoid Jordanian
> shells aimed at the main highway. His destination was the Knesset,
> where the new members of the National Unity Government were to
> be sworn in. At the entrance to the building Begin asked Kadishai
> to wait for Eshkol, and to tell him the moment he arrived that he,
> Begin, was asking for a cabinet meeting before the full session of
> the Knesset began.
>
> The meeting convened in the Cabinet Room, but not for long; the
> sergeant-at-arms drove the ministers out with a warning that the
> room was too exposed to Jordanian shellfire. The leaders of Israel
> trooped down to the basement of the building, where they accepted
> Begin's proposal to liberate East Jerusalem and the Old City. Then,
> and only then, were Begin and Yosef Sapir sworn in as the two
> ministers representing Gahal—Begin's union with the Liberal
> Party." (pages 271–272).

At that moment the bulk of the IDF was engaged in a fierce battle
in the south of the country against the Egyptian forces. Only in the
evening could the paratroopers under the command of General Mordecai Gur leave the front in El-Arish after repulsing the Egyptian
units, and come to the aid of the Israeli defenders of the central region
against the assault of the Jordanian Legion. The Israeli paratroopers
did not go into the city but decided to surround it, with the idea that it
would fall into their hands without a battle on the narrow, sniper-in-
fested streets, which could claim many casualties.

In the early dawn hours of June 7, Begin heard on the BBC broad-
cast that the UN Security Council had adopted a resolution at an
emergency meeting calling for an immediate ceasefire in the Middle
East.

Begin was afraid that again an opportunity would be lost. He woke up the Prime Minister at 5 a.m., and urged him: "We have to start an attack on the Old City immediately!"

Eshkol replied: "Speak to [Defense Minister] Dayan. If he agrees, I will too."

Begin called Dayan. At the same time General Motta Gur ordered an attack on the site of the Western Wall, which was led by Generals Uzi Narkis and Arieh Ben-Ari, and in a few hours the whole country was electrified by the unforgettable message: *"Har Habayit b'yadeinu!"* (The Temple Mount is in our hands!)

It should be mentioned that at Camp David, where President Carter waited for the Israeli delegation to agree to some kind of "accommodation" that would put into question the sovereignty of Israel over Jerusalem, Begin vehemently rejected the suggestion and reaffirmed Israel's official position that united Jerusalem was to remain forever Israel's capital.

Chapter Thirty-Eight

Begin and the Diaspora

Another area of grave concern in Israel today is the relation between the Israelis and Diaspora Jewry. Many Zionist leaders have looked down on the Diaspora as the galut, or exile, which they considered an abnormal and debased condition which must be liquidated. The term used in the Zionist lexicon to describe this attitude is "*Shlilath Ha'galut*," or the "negation of the exile." According to Abba Eban, writing in the *Moment* magazine, the greatest failing of the Jewish people in this day and age is the fact that after the establishment of the state millions of Jews failed to immigrate to their homeland and remained in exile.

Begin stands out among Israeli leaders as one who has always shown understanding towards, and close ties with, Diaspora Jewry. Here again the key word is "Jew." Some Israelis leaders have advanced the thesis that they had become "Israelis." Begin has always insisted that he was a Jew first and always.

Begin, the nationalist, never weakened his ties with his native Jewish culture of Brisk, Poland. He continued all his life to be part of Polish Jewry, indeed of world Jewry and its rich spiritual legacy. Over the years, he strengthened his ties with Jewish communities around the world, and has been at home among Jews in Paris, New York, Buenos Aires, Bucharest, practically everywhere. He was always aware of the fact that the State ties together all the Jews of the world, and made it his mission to be the emissary of the State who helps promote this tie. It is ironic to consider the fact that the man who was accused of dividing the Jewish people, has brought greater closeness and unity between Israel and Diaspora Jewry than ever before. This is one of the fundamental values of his lasting legacy.

While Diaspora Jewry has been united with the State of Israel from the very beginning, and played an essential role in the establishment and upbuilding of the state, there seemed to be some sort of an invisible barrier between Israelis and Diaspora Jews. Begin removed it. Since the day he took the reins of government into his hands, the Diaspora became an even more active partner of the state.

He has called upon Jews to come and live in Israel, but he accepted the reality of flourishing Jewish communities around the world. He has been aware of the problems of those communities, and has been particularly concerned about assimilation and about Israelis leaving Israel. He insists on the need for Jews to cultivate and strengthen identity and spiritual values both in Israel and in the Diaspora. It is no wonder that on one of his visits to the United States some Jewish leaders and journalists referred to him as the "first Jewish prime minister of Israel."

One might add that he may be also the first prime minister of Israel whose political orientation was not partisan, but national, dedicated to *"Klal Yisrael,"* in other words, the totality of the Jewish people. He did not make distinctions between Oriental Jew and European Jew; between religious and secular; or even between a Jew living in Israel or in the Diaspora. His love for Jews has been all-pervasive. His understanding of being a Jewish leader was to be a leader for all kinds of Jews. One can only hope that his successors in the office of prime minister of the State of Israel, regardless of their particular political affiliation, follow in his footsteps as leaders of all Jews, rather than one segment of this highly variegated people.

Labor Zionism, no doubt, played an enormous and decisive role in the building and establishment of the State of Israel. But the legacy left by Labor, of failing to integrate the Sephardim in Israeli society, finding a common language between religious and secular Israelis, and establishing deeper understanding between Israeli and Diaspora Jewries, is gradually being changed by the legacy of Menachem Begin. His political and social outlook, his personality and example, and his national leadership have transcended all partisan and sectarian interests and left us an enduring model not only for future prime ministers of Israel, but for every Jew in Israel and abroad to emulate.

Chapter Thirty-Nine

What He Restored to Them

"He restored to me my respect for my grandfather." These are the words of a noted American writer of Jewish descent. They sum up the impact of the emergence of Menachem Begin upon alienated Jews, both in the American-Jewish community and in other countries outside Israel.

The spell of his personality and the resonance of his message sowed the seeds for a meaningful re-examination of the relationship of many Jews estranged from Jewishness, not merely to Israel, but to their own people, to their past, to their roots and ultimately to themselves.

The appearance upon the international scene of the phenomenon Menachem Begin, mirrored something sublime and by now deliberately buried but which had been alive in the ancestors of Jews now entirely submerged in a culture not their own. He raised from the depths of conscious escapism and unconscious estrangement that essential Jewishness within themselves which had hitherto been repressed and which was now little short of obliteration. The inexplicable shame of being what they are or were, was replaced by an unequivocal pride in their values—essentially Jewish ones. Against the centrifugal force which had dominated most of them, emerged a dam, which at least to some extent stemmed the massive flow. The dam was, of course, the State of Israel. But its presence in the Jewish world and in the life of Jews individually, was made more consciously apparent by Menachem Begin as Prime Minister. His presence itself reminded them of their ancestors and reflected both their martyrdom and the glory. While the reminiscences of the past were permeated by memories of suffering, Begin introduced an ancient and at the same time quite novel dimension, which had long been absent—namely, the glory of the heroic fight, of the supreme sacrifice, this time crowned with splendid victory.

Fully saturated with innumerable accounts of cruel persecution and suffering, right up the very mass murders of recent years in Europe, many Jews may naturally be somewhat apprehensive of these horror stories. They would rather prefer *not* to be reminded of them. But Begin, himself a survivor of the German mass murders, will not let us forget—if only for the sake of being alert to new threats and dangers, and in order to safeguard the remnant of the slaughtered people from both present and future dangers.

"Never again" is for him a distress call, particularly in view of the inimical forces against the Jews—both overt and covert. While this struggle was against British rule over Palestine, in the background there loomed constantly the unspeakable horrors of the German mass killings of Jews in Europe.

At variance with the predictable outcome of the Warsaw Ghetto uprising, which could but end in defeat considering the very hopeless situation for the Jews at that time, Begin's revolt resulted in victory and in the rebirth of the Jewish State.

Often weary of martyrdom and defeat, and longing for some tangible, durable achievement, Jews saw in the Irgun leader a perfect "success story" brought about by idealism, courage and self-sacrifice.

Thus, the oft-frustrated and defeated cling to the victor and his heroism so that they too may become a part of the victory which is the triumph of the common cause. And so, Begin's rise to power on the national as well as on the international scene, returned many estranged Jews to their people, restored to them their lost pride and imbued them with the glory of the revival and renewal of the Jewish State and its people.

Chapter Forty

Emancipation of the Sephardim

In another chapter we discussed Begin's contribution to the changing of the Jewish character—from a largely passive people depending on the good (more often not so good) will of others for their security and well-being and for their very existence, to a people who took their fate into their own hands, and prevailed. In this chapter let us take time out from discussing Begin's political activities, and look at the impact he has had on the Jewish people.

His influence was felt in areas which were critical not only during the first decades of the state, but also today, as Israel continues to evolve and define itself at the close of the twentieth century. Those areas include in particular the place of the Sephardic Jews in Israeli society; the relations between religious and secular Jews; and the relations between Israeli and diaspora Jewry.

In 1948 there was a deep gap between the European Jews already entrenched in the country, and the Oriental immigrants arriving from Arab countries after the founding of the state.

On the surface, both were inspired and moved by the same desire to return to the land of Israel. But in reality, there were two kinds of movements, essentially different and even contradictory in many ways.

The establishment of Israel was achieved by European Zionists with a pronounced strain of leftist elitism, as contradictory as this may sound. Its moving forces, especially in Russia (the land of origin of most of those Zionists) were at odds with the old religious order. They revolted against the domination of religion and the rabbis. They strove to put an end to the homelessness of the Jews and to gain a national home. At the same time, they aimed at a change of the socioeconomic structure of the masses, mostly engaged in small business as merchants or artisans, eking out a poor livelihood.

The socialist-Zionists—who borrowed their socialism from the East European models—strove to change these occupations to agriculture and industry in the land of Israel. This change, aimed at and partially achieved in the kibbutzim, moshavim, and various industries, was not only socioeconomic. Its further purpose was a fundamental transformation in the way of living and thinking and in the character of the immigrants, especially of the youth. This Zionism was, hence, linked to socialist ideologies and trends, and opposed to religious faith, practices and tradition.

The secular socialist establishment of Israel, which dominated every part of the country and every aspect of society, endeavored to eliminate the gap between Oriental and European Jews by doing away with the culture of the Sephardic immigrants, which, according to the ruling establishment, was not a culture worth preserving. Socialist-Zionists looked down on the Sephardim as "primitive" masses, denigrated their religious faith and practice, and despised their age-old traditions and customs. The establishment proceeded to pursue vigorously, and by force, its task of "civilizing" those "uncultured" people, and transforming them into Europeans similar to their European brothers and sisters, especially to the socialists.

They gave up on the elderly. Those were considered a "lost generation," as David Ben-Gurion defined them, "the generation of the desert," which did not spiritually and mentally reach the Promised Land.

The following paragraph written in Israel in the fifties is indicative of this attitude:

> There is a people whose primitiveness reaches the highest peak. Their educational level borders on absolute ignorance. Still more serious is their inability to absorb anything intellectual. . . There is no hope even with regard to their children to raise their general level out of the depths of their ethnic existence—this is a matter of generations!

This attitude prevailed for a long time. As late as the sixties, Ben-Gurion spoke of the Sephardim as primitives without cure: "These Moroccans had no education. The Moroccan Jews have been very influenced by Moroccan Arabs. I don't see what contribution they have to make. . ."

The one who did succeed in bridging the gap between the Sephardim and Ashkenazim was Menachem Begin. Many factors enabled him to accomplish this difficult feat.

At an encounter with Leibele Weisfish, the Neture Karta leader who was, strangely, a Nietzschean, Begin was asked by Weisfish, "Are you a Brisker or a Zionist?" (Brisk, Begin's hometown in Poland, had a special meaning to Weisfish as a strictly Orthodox and anti-Zionist community).

Begin answered: "Both" (see *Jerusalem on Earth*, by Benjamin Rabinowitz, McMillan, N.Y. 1988). This may have sounded like a blatant contradiction to Weisfish, an extreme adversary of the Jewish state, but herein lies the secret to Begin's understanding and acceptance of the Sephardic Jews. Unlike other East European born Zionist leaders, Begin, though not a strictly Orthodox Jew, was nonetheless deeply religious. He did not regard the religious customs of the Sephardic Jews—which often differ from those of European or Ashkenazic Jews—as primitive and obsolete. Oddly enough, it was the "egalitarian" socialist-Zionists who suffered from a sense of elitism, while the "right-wing nationalist" Begin regarded all Jews, Sephardic and Ashkenazic, religious and secular, living in Israel or living abroad, highly educated or semi-illiterate, rich and poor—as absolutely equal.

Begin's contribution to the emancipation of the Sephardic Jews in Israel was decisive and far-reaching. This accomplishment, like so many other of his activities, was so distorted by hostile journalists, writers, agitators and politicians, that it was turned into another trumped up charge against him. Instead of the praise he deserved for incorporating the Sephardim in the state and doing away with the barrier between this "Second Israel" and the rest of society, he was blamed for the antagonism between Israeli Sephardic and Ashkenazic Jews, created primarily by the Zionist left.

When Sephardic Jews throughout Israel thronged to Begin's election campaign rallies in 1977, 1981, and 1984, as a way of protesting their treatment by the Labor party, Begin was accused of "polarizing" the two groups, of inflaming "the mob," as the left contemptuously continued to refer to those Jews.

Some trivial incidents of unruly behavior by some individual Sephardic Jews, quite common during election campaigns, were blown out of proportion, and depicted hate mongering as "threats against democracy" by the "fascists."

All these attacks were clearly aimed at Begin and his Likud party. But they were also used to play down the legitimate grievances and justified protests against discrimination and the indignities suffered by these groups for many years at the hands of the political left.

In the Arab countries from where the Sephardic Jews hailed, there were no Jewish political parties and no Zionist organizations. Zionism was a quasi-religious belief, and *aliyah*—immigrating to Israel—meant the fulfillment of a messianic dream. Consequently, Sephardic Jews did not have the political connection with the Israeli left which meant better jobs, housing, and political influence.

Begin's relations with the Sephardic community began shortly after his arrival in Palestine in 1943. In fact, his mentor, Jabotinsky, was the only top-echelon Zionist leader to visit Jews in Arab countries like Morroco, Algeria, Tunisia, Syria, Iraq, and Lebanon. He was interested in the descendants of Spanish Jewry, and studied Ladino, the Jewish Spanish dialect, enough to be able to converse in it. With the formation of the Irgun, a significant number of Sephardic Jews joined its ranks and distinguished themselves in military operations. Enough to recall that Rabbi Ovadia Yossef, the great Talmudic scholar and the highest rabbinical authority among the Sephardim, as his brothers were fighters supporters of IZL.

In his book *The Revolt*, Begin points out that a "large number of the members of the [Irgun's] Shock units were Oriental Jews" (page 118 of the Hebrew edition). He goes on to explain that Ben-Gurion told Ernest Bevin that the entire Irgun consisted of "black" Yemenite Jews, "trying to prove to the British Foreign Minister that the 'terrorists' are quantitatively or qualitatively insignificant." Begin explains:

> In the Shock Units and other units of the Irgun Tzvai Leumi we had men from all ethnic groups and social classes. They came from Harbin and Tunis, from Poland and Persia, from France and Yemen, from Belgium and Iraq, from Czechoslovakia and Syria, from America and Bukhara, from England and Argentina and South Africa, but especially—for those were the majority—they were native born. . . We were a microcosm of the melting pot of the nation being forged on the soil of the homeland despite all the ethnic origins. We did not ask anyone about his or her origins. We were

only interested in loyalty and ability. Our Sephardic brothers and sisters felt at home in the Irgun. No one addressed them with ludicrous superior airs, and so they were completely freed from their unjustified inferiority complex. They were fellow fighters, period. They could, and they did, attain the highest command ranks. Daniel was "Sephardic," and until he was turned in he was chief of staff. His brother, Uzi, after returning from the detention camp in Eritrea, was the Tel Aviv district commander, and he commanded thousands of men until he fell heroically and exaltedly in the decisive battle of Jaffa. Shimshon came from Persia, and was, until his capture, the commander of the Haifa district. Besides Gidi [Paglin], we had another Gideon, a "Sephardic" Jerusalemite, who commanded the historical attack on the headquarters of the high command of the occupation army, where he showed incredible courage and self-control. Our warriors executed by the British, Alkashi and Kashani, were "Sephardic". . . The thing with which our enemies and adversaries tried to denigrate us, was for us a source of pride. Those men, who were humiliated and oppressed, became proud warriors in our proud fighting family, bearers of freedom and honor. Statistics? We never counted, but I believe I would be right in saying that between 25 to 35 percent of our warriors were "Sephardic." In the Shock Units, which had a special task, there seemed to be a higher percentage, about 40 to 50 percent Oriental Jews (*ibid.*, pp. 119-120).

The Haganah, on the other hand, and its own shock units, the Palmach, recruited from the kibbutzim and other agricultural settlements, as well as from high school students and graduates who were almost exclusively of European stock, mostly east European. Between 1948 and 1950, hundreds of thousands of Sephardic Jews were brought to Israel from practically every corner of the Arab world. Most of them were poor, or even destitute. For several years they lived in transition camps called *Ma'abarot*, and were gradually settled in towns and villages, and in new development towns. In the early years of the state they knew little about the European-styled Israeli political system. In the fifties, Ben-Gurion's ruling Labor party would bus thousands of new-immigrants from the *Ma'abarot* on election day, and "arrange" for them to vote for Mapai. In time, the Sephardim became better acquainted with the system, and in 1977 they played a decisive part in bringing Begin to power.

Even today, the Sephardim constitute the vast majority of the "weak classes" of Israeli society. Their problems are far from over. But they have been gradually integrated in the general Israeli society and in the highest echelons of the government. One of their leaders, David Levy, occupies the office of foreign minister. This is in no small part due to the leadership of Menachem Begin.

Chapter Forty-One

Begin and Religious Jewry

Many observers of the Israeli scene have expressed the opinion that one of the most serious long-term problems facing Israel is the relations between religious and secular Jews. Over the years there have been conflicts and clashes between the two segments of the population over questions of religious observance by the state, such as the observance of the Sabbath, prompting some Orthodox extremists to turn to stone-throwing, burning of bus stops, demonstrations, and various forms of violence. Clearly, the secular national ideology of the great majority of Israelis, and the religious national ideology of between 15 to 20 percent of the Jews in Israel, are at odds with each other. What Israel needs is a common ground to accommodate both, rather than allow the differences become greater and more divisive.

Here again Begin has served as a model of a modern nationalist Jew with a deep respect for religious Jewry, a model which is imperative if Israel is to function as a state in which Jews of differing ideologies are going to live in peace and harmony with one another.

Begin's respect and high regard for religious Jewry is not merely a personal preference. His movement, Betar, was taught by its founder, Jabotinsky, to respect the tenets of the Jewish religion, at a time when the Zionist left did not only fail to show respect for religion, but was outright hostile toward it. In Betar camps in Poland before the war, the Sabbath was observed. While Betar was a Zionist-nationalist movement, it did not predicate Zionism on secularism and anti-tradition. When Begin proclaimed the revolt against the British in 1943, the Chief Rabbinate in Palestine, which was part of the establishment, seconded the condemnation of the Irgun by the Jewish Agency-World Zionist Organization, using quotations from the Bible and Talmud to decry the IZL attacks. Thus, for example, after six British policemen were killed in a battle with the Irgun, the Chief Rabbinate reacted with the following words: "In the name of the Almighty God of Israel and His Torah, and in the name of all that is holy in the people of Israel, we call upon all those who are caught up in this craze to desist from these abominable and dangerous acts, which may cause, heaven forbid, a catastrophe for the entire Jewish people."

But behind the public statements there was another reality. The Chief Rabbi, Isaac Herzog (father of Israel's current President, Chaim Herzog), felt admiration for Begin. While serving as director of the Israeli Ministry of Social Welfare, I found out that Rabbi Herzog helped the Irgun in clandestine ways, mainly through his son, Yaakov Herzog, a gifted diplomat who served in high government positions under Ben-Gurion, Golda Meir, and Levi Eshkol, and died in 1972 at the age of 51.

During the revolt, the chief rabbi's son, who was a member of the Haganah, travelled to Africa to see Irgun members who had been exiled by the British and kept in detention camps. The families of the exiled had appealed to the Chief Rabbi to visit their sons. Yaakov Herzog was then the official secretary of the Chief Rabbinate, and he undertook the trip. The British authorities granted permission for the visit in Nairobi on the condition that he would not bring any messages to and from the prisoners. Before his trip and afterwards, Herzog met secretly with Menachem Begin. He recounted to the Irgun's commander the deep impression that the prisoners had made on him.

He then met, at his request, with Chaim Landau, who was the Irgun's second-in-command. Herzog revealed to him that he had brought a coded message from the prisoners from Nairobi, but he had promised not to reveal its content.

Landau told Herzog that "the exiled are resolved to escape under any conditions. But we are able to help the escape. . . We can eliminate dangers that not only can have serious consequences but even result in a tragedy." Landau goes on to say: "I tried to convince him that there was danger to their lives, and he was in possession of the key. Then Yaakov gave me the message." (Radio interview with Chaim Landau, March 1973, *Memorial Book for Yaakov Herzog*, pp. 16-17).

My close acquaintance with Yaakov Herzog helped me gain insight into the attitude of the religious community in Israel towards Begin and the Irgun. I found out that religious Jews were outraged by the

"Saison" campaign when some Haganah members informed on Irgun members to the British authorities, and even captured some Irgun fighters and turned them over to the British. The leaders of the Mizrachi (Orthodox Zionists), Rabbi Yehuda Leib Maimon, Moshe Chaim Shapira, and David Tzvi Pinkas, strongly opposed this collaboration with the British, and even resigned from their posts in the Jewish Agency in protest.

The attitude of the Mizrachi leaders was especially outspoken in the Altalena affair. Ben-Gurion and the ministers of his party, Mapai, as well as the leftist Mapam, were intent on physically liquidating the Irgun and its commander. Their main objective was Begin himself. The outrage of the Mizrachi leaders was very clear and sharp, as described in Shlomo Nakdimon's well-researched book, *Altalena* (in Hebrew, Idanim, Jerusalem 1978).

Ben-Gurion was at that time at the peak of his power and prestige. Despite this, the two Mizrachi ministers, Rabbi Y. L. Maimon and M. Ch. Shapira, vehemently opposed this action against IZL by Ben-Gurion and his leftists ministers, aimed at total destruction of the Irgun by use of a vastly superior military power.

• • •

Over the years I undertook a rather gratifying task of serving as a conduit between Begin and the leaders of religious Jewry in the United States.

As I have mentioned before, my active role in Jewish religious organizations dates back to pre-war Poland, where I served as the national political secretary of Agudath Israel, and as the secretary of the Jewish members of the Polish parliament (the Sejm and the Senate). At the same time, I wrote extensively in the Jewish press in Yiddish, Hebrew and Polish.

In the United States, I maintain close ties with the various Jewish religious organizations. These organizations as a whole have shown support and admiration for Menachem Begin. I took it upon myself to channel those sentiments into a cohesive force in support of the interests of the State of Israel.

I arranged get-acquainted meetings in my house between Begin and American Jewish religious leaders and educators. Those leaders gave Begin an enthusiastic reception, and his words were always received warmly, with understanding and appreciation. Begin formed lasting relations with the leaders of American religious Jewry, which strengthened the ties between them and the Jewish state.

One such meeting in my house included the religious writer, scion of the Sandzer Hasidic dynasty, Rabbi Eliezer Halberstam. I first met him in Paris in 1946 at the home of Ben-Zion Chomsky, at a secret gathering of IZL supporters, where I found out that he was a dedicated IZL activist. I introduced him to our honored guest, and told him about the rabbi's "past," which had remained a secret until that evening. I said that he was the only remaining member of IZL who was still in the "underground". . . Before he was hiding from the British, now he was hiding from the Satmar Hasidim, who were antagonistic opponents of the State of Israel. . .

In 1970 I used my connections with the Lubavitcher Rebbe to arrange a meeting between Begin and this great Hasidic leader. I accompanied Begin to the Rebbe's residence in Brooklyn, and after I introduced him to the Rebbe I waited outside. The meeting lasted almost three hours. Begin came away greatly impressed. Since then there has been a close and warm relation between the two, and when Begin became ill in 1977 after he became prime minister, and was hospitalized, the Rebbe took great interest in his health, and prayed for his recovery, conveying him through me warm concern and blessing.

Afterwards I arranged more meetings between Prime Minister Begin and the Lubavitcher Rebbe. I also arranged meetings with Rabbi Moshe Feinstein, Rabbi Yitzhak Hutner, and other great Torah luminaries. When Rabbi Feinstein passed away, Begin expressed his sorrow over the loss in a special letter to me.

Begin's support of religious education was not merely the result of coalition agreements with the religious parties. In 1970 he spoke at a dinner for Chinuch Atzmai, the school network of Agudath Israel in Israel, with the participation of Rabbi Joseph Dov Soloveichik, at the home of Oscar Gruss in New York. I accompanied him there, and later agreed with Rabbi Soloveichik that his speech was one of the greatest paeans for Torah education.

At the helm of the government he lent his full support to religious education, beyond the agreements with the Orthodox coalitions partners. In 1982 when the Beth Jacob Teachers Seminar was in dire straits, I went to Israel on a rescue mission. Begin lent his full support to this institutions and to other centers of religious education.

When we are witnessing the growth of religious education—the number of Yeshivot, Kollelim and other Talmudic learning institutions in Israel being the greatest in Jewish history—we should remember Begin's helping hand during the years, especially as head of the government.

Chapter Forty-Two

Begin and the Working Class

The socialist economy of the State of Israel during the first three decades of labor political domination produced some interesting anomalies. Ben-Gurion and some of his followers argued that Begin "hates the working class." They saw their mission as one of protecting the "proletariat" against the attacks of such right-wing "capitalists" as Begin and his party, who, they argued, sought to promote the interest of the employer at the expense of the worker. The socialists defended the "hegemony of the worker," which was allegedly threatened by Herut.

Begin represented, in their opinion, capitalist interests, while they represented socialism and the struggle of the oppressed working class.

What was the reality?

During the fifties and sixties Israel became one of the few democracies in the world where the working class owned most of the means of production, among them the industrial and agricultural complex of the country. The so-called bourgeois class owned a very small portion of the country's industry, that paled by comparison to the labor-owned giant concerns, such as the construction company Solel-Boneh, the shipping company ZIM, the industrial giant Koor, Tenuvah, to mention only a few.

Begin the "capitalist" lived on his modest salary as a Knesset member (the honoraria of his books were donated for IZL's former fighters), he rented a modest apartment on the ground floor, almost a basement. He was, in effect, much closer to the living standard of the working man than many a socialist party hack, official, bureaucrat and politician. Labor, which amassed enormous economical power during the first decades of the state, became in many ways callous and unfeeling in its attitude toward the worker. As of this writing, the labor-dominated economy has been going through a severe decline, resulting in the collapse of many Labor-owned companies.

The failing of labor unions is not a new thing. It has happened in many countries, including the United States. When Begin reached power in 1977 he had to deal with a host of economic problems created by the labor economy. Those problems will still take years to overcome.

Far from being an enemy of the working man, Begin has been what may be described as a populist. He was never seduced by socialist theory, but was interested in the welfare of each and every individual, no matter how humble, as a human being deserving respect and a chance to improve his way of living. Begin would accept invitations of Knesset workers—the ushers and the waiters and the cooks, to their family events. The Israeli leftist satirist Silvi Keshet, who is not known for paying compliments to anyone, much less to politicians, and least of all to rightists like Begin, wrote in her book *An Arrow from Silvi Keshet* (Keshet is the Hebrew word for bow) (in Hebrew, Schocken, Tel Aviv 1969):

> "Menachem Begin is the only one among Knesset Members who twice a year, on Passover eve and on Rosh Hashanah eve, goes to the cafeteria to wish the workers a happy holiday. He goes into the kitchen to kiss the hands of the female cooks, and sends them and the waiters, rather discretely, in a sealed envelope, a gift for the holiday."

In another chapter we discuss Begin's attitude toward the Sephardim, who have and continue to constitute the majority of Israel's underprivileged class. The highly idealistic socialist leaders, the defenders of the humble and the downtrodden, have had questionable credentials when it came to the proper treatment of the *Edot ha'mizrach*, the Oriental communities, as the Sephardic Jews are often referred to. Begin and his "elitist" party, on the other hand, have little to be ashamed of when it comes to attitudes towards the Sephardim or towards any of the underprivileged classes of the society.

Chapter Forty-Three

Begin and Children

Is Ephraim not My precious son, the child in whom I take pleasure? Whenever I speak of him, I remember him yet more. therefore, my heart has turned to him and I will show him compassion, says the L-rd. (Jeremiah 30:19)

I

You cannot know Menachem Begin without being aware of his special attitude toward children. Whether in their company or whether talking and thinking of them, he becomes another person— or, rather, some of his innermost traits shine through.

A few episodes will suffice to illustrate this.

In 1972, Begin has become enmeshed in a very difficult situation not of his making. Tel-Chai, the Herut's financial institution, went into debts that it couldn't satisfy. It was a strange situation for Begin to be involved in. When it comes to finances, the man is simple and detached. In his own life, the needs of his family were the exclusive domain of his wife, Eliza.

But now Begin, as head of Herut, became its great debtor. He couldn't bear the thought that people might suffer because the party had gotten into monetary difficulties.

For the first time in his life, Begin became engaged in fund-raising in order to pay back Tel-Chai's debts. I had never before seen him so unhappy as he was then, visiting America to collect funds. I remember that the late Samuel Wang from Queens, New York, a wealthy shipping tycoon and devoted adherent of IZL who contributed to this fund, shared with me the pain he felt on meeting with Begin in this situation. (Incidentally, despite his name, Wang was not Chinese, but a Jew from Sanok in Galicia, where he had been a friend of the famous Rabbi Meir Schapira.)

When Begin went back to Israel, I saw him off at the airport. His daughter, Hasia, her husband, Milo, and their baby daughter, Osnath, who had also been visiting the States, were accompanying him back to Israel.

At the airport, Begin was a changed man, full of obvious joy. He carried the baby, dancing and singing Nossim Habaitha ("Going home. . ."). All of his troubles and worries seemed to have disappeared. I saw the happiest man in the world.

II

During one of the most difficult stages in the Camp David talks, in September, 1978, it seemed as though all the participants' efforts would fail. Carter and Begin each indicated to his staff that the talks may end without achieving any results.

At this desperate moment, Carter devised an ingenious idea, one which may have been inspired by a recollection of Begin's affection for Amy, Carter's seven-year-old daughter.

Carter took a few photographs of himself and went over to Begin's quarters. He asked Begin the names of each of his eight grandchildren, autographed a picture for each of them with a friendly inscription, and presented these to Begin as gifts for his grandchildren.

Begin was very moved by this gesture, so out of place in the strenuous and sometimes bitter atmosphere of diplomatic arguments and bargaining. With tears in his eyes, Begin said to the President, "All my efforts, all my thoughts, and all my toil have only one purpose: to make the children of Israel safe from the cruel lot of their brothers and sisters, the million and a half Jewish children in Europe who were tortured and murdered by the Germans. This is what motivates all my actions in striving for a true and lasting peace."

This emotional outburst of the seemingly inflexible Israeli leader left its mark on President Carter. From then on, as participants later testified, the talks continued in a more relaxed mood.

Who knows? Perhaps this occurrence was the turning point that eventually led to the Camp David Agreement of September 17, 1978.

III

Begin paid a visit to former President Jimmy Carter in Atlanta, Georgia. Every move and every step was, of course, worked out by the protocol people of the United States and Israel. But something happened that dislodged all their plans. A teacher of the Hebrew School in Atlanta wanted to surprise the Israeli Prime Minister with an expression of his and the children's feelings toward Israel and its leader.

He gathered the children in the street not far from Mr. Carter's residence, and when Mr. Begin arrived, they burst out in song: *Heveinu Shalom Aleichem*—"We welcome you in peace."

On hearing the singing and seeing the children, Begin left his numerous entourage and the dignitaries, including the former president, and went over to the children, hugging and kissing many of them. People present noticed tears in Begin's eyes.

IV

Observing Menachem Begin's attitude toward children—or, rather, the effect that children have on him—I came to the following conclusion: because Begin never forgets the murder of the Jews of Europe, the sight of children reminds him of the Jewish children tortured and killed by the Germans in the ghettos and death camps—their pain and their cruel end.

What leads me to this conclusion? Two things: First, seeing him when he looks at children. And second, drawing on my own feelings and experience.

Whenever I come into the presence of Jewish children, there emerges from my innermost soul the memories and images of Jewish children in the ghettos and death camps tortured and killed by the Germans—put in gas chambers or thrown live into graves and pits.

I never talk in terms of numbers—one and a half million children killed, six million Jews. The human mind is unable to grasp the enormity of these horrendous numbers, of so many sufferings and deaths.

Thus, whenever I face Jewish children, playful and charming, I recall individuals. Images of children I knew in the ghettos and death camps appear vividly in my mind, in all their beauty and wisdom, and in their unending agony.

The Midrash, *Eichah Rabati*, on the destruction of the Second Temple, contains wonderful tales of the children of that disastrous epoch. those children were exceptional in their intelligence and understanding.

I assume that under hard conditions people's dormant abilities are brought out and put to use. And there were no times as hard as those under the Germans.

Thus, under the most extreme stress and danger, there came out in even very young children extraordinary abilities and qualities. Their darkest hours were, as regards their behavior and acts, their finest as well.

Many Jewish children aged five to ten provided food for entire starving families. Their emaciated bodies were an advantage in this mission: they managed to slip through small holes in the walls and narrow slots in the fences surrounding the ghettos, and to smuggle whatever meager food they managed to obtain, often by searching for left-overs in garbage cans. These child-providers showed such a measure of concern and responsibility for feeding their families that they served their parents and siblings before satisfying their own hunger.

The poet Chaim Nachman Bialik said: "There are no Jewish children—only small, young Jews" (*kleine Yidelech*). These times proved the truth of his words.

I described some of this in my *Diary of the Warsaw Ghetto* (in Hebrew, Tel-Aviv, 1946).

One instance left an indelible imprint on me. In January, 1943, when there were almost no Jewish children left in the ghetto, a girl named Rochelle, about five years old, appeared from nowhere at the place where we, a small group, were staying. We gave her a piece of bread, at that time a precious gift, but she didn't eat it. Knowing her hunger, which showed on her face, I asked her why. Her answer: "I am keeping it for Mommy."

She didn't know that her mother was gone already, taken away by the Germans to her death in Treblinka.

Instead of dwelling on the so-called Holocaust and other braggadocio of political science, I would propose that the German Chancellor, Helmut Kohl, the president, Richard von Weizsaecker, and other German leaders, historians and thinkers, keep before their eyes this little girl of the Warsaw Ghetto, as well as the countless others tortured and gassed (not by a band of Nazis as the Big Lie would have us believe, but by Germans of all parties and persuasions) and answer the unuttered question of Rochelle of Warsaw: Why? Tell me why!

The Last Dance

This happened on the last Simhat Torah, in 1942. Only a handful of Jews remained alive out of the five hundred thousand, formerly inn the Polish capital.

Twenty Jews were gathered in the home of Rabbi Menachem Zemba, the last remaining rabbi in Warsaw, to observe Simhat Torah. Among them was Judah Leib Orlean, former director of the Beth Jacob Teachers' Seminary, who had devoted his lift to religious education. At the proper time they brought forth the Scrolls of the Torah; and, sorrowfully recited the verses, which in former years had been joyously chanted, they wearily plodded the *hakafot* about the table.

Suddenly a boy of twelve appeared in the room. This was astonishing, for the Germans had already slain or deported all the Jewish children in the ghetto. Who could he be, and where had he come from? No one knew.

Orlean ran to the boy and, embracing him together with his Torah, cried out, "Young Jew with the holy Torah!" he swept him along in an exultant *hassidic* dance. The others joined the dance one by one, until all had formed a circle about the unknown boy, Orlean, and the Torah.

Bereaved fathers who had lost their entire families danced, with tears rolling down their faces, while the great educator reiterated, "Young Jew with the holy Torah! Young Jew with the holy Torah!"

This was the last dance of the Jews on their last Simhat Torah in Warsaw.

(Reprinted from *The Glory of the Jewish Holidays* by Hillel Seidman Shengold Publishers, Inc., New York, 1962.)

Chapter Forty-Four

Followers

There are political leaders who attract disciples, devotees, admirers. But none of them possesses what one calls *Hassidim*. The relationship between the Hassid and the Rebbe is unique. It elicits enthusiastic devotion and unlimited trust. Indeed the Hassid's faith in his Rebbe can be so profound that his personality may ultimately be cast in the Rebbe's mold.

Menachem Begin hails from a family and milieu of *Misnagdim*, that is, opponents of Hassidim. Historically, a *Misnaged's* disposition is rational, critical, dry and objective. However, Begin, by his nature and spirit, is an enthusiastic follower, a disciple, a *Hassid* of Ze'ev Jabotinsky. Moreover, Begin himself generates a kind of devotion, a relation typical of Hassidim with their Rebbe.

Hassidic leaders tend to fall into two separate streams. There is the Rebbe who stands aloof from his followers, who is unapproachable and distant. He evokes more awe that love. The other is close, even intimate, with his Hassidim, so much so that he is one of them. This is not to say that he does not tower above the crowd. He does. But his closeness to every individual to whom he happens to relate, and his accessibility may initially hide from view the unique spiritual heights he has attained.

Begin belongs in the second kind. He excels in *human* relations, which differ from public relations. For him, the concept of a people is not the sum total of many but a mosaic of individuals, each of whom has distinct traits, each of whom is more a friend than a party member, more a brother than a brother-in-arms.

As a result, there has evolved around Begin an association similar to that of Hassidim and their Rebbe. Political connections are elevated to spiritual bonds.

Of course, they are tied by a common world-view, identical ideas and goals. Begin represented an ideology and he knew how to articulate it. But in the process of implementing that ideology, through turbulent actions and events, the ideology was transposed to the level of a belief, an almost religious faith. For Begin and his followers labored hard to make the idea a reality. Personal dedication, supreme sacrifice were necessary.

All this created an especially close bond between him and the individuals who formed his movement. More that the shared goals and ideas, the core of the link between him and his followers lay in Begin himself. One can, at times, disagree with the opinions of the revered leader, but how can one distance oneself from a leader who radiates personal warmth and who emanates spiritual elevation?

The *Hassidic* Rebbe deals not only with the spiritual worlds and concerns of his constituents and supplicants but with every manner of problem they face, be it material, financial, marital. He is asked for advice on everything. His concern embraces the totality of human needs.

The ordinary political leader is so overwhelmed with issues of a general nature that there is neither the time nor the inclination to display interest in the individual. Not so Begin.

I was privileged to have witnessed the interest Begin takes in the lives of his friends and followers. I experienced it myself in our personal relations.

In the tough rumble of impersonal politics, he preserved human feeling. Paradoxically, the man who was a *zoon politicon* par excellence managed to somehow preserve the traits of a family man, not only toward his own family.

These traits reflected, incidentally, in his only son, Benny, whose jealously guarded privacy shields him from any "taint" of politics, even when he became lately an active political figure.

However, as the national Polish poet, Adam Mickiewicz, said: "There was no happiness in the family because there was no happiness in the fatherland." (Pan Tadeusz) Begin's love for his suffering people would not allow him to remain comfortably ensconced in his family. His inner revolt against the subjugation of his people, against the persecutions and murderous attacks—these were the moving forces behind his efforts and struggles. His ambitions were never strictly political.

If a political career had been his aim, he could easily have gained public recognition and prestige. Endowed with unusual talents, particularly in the art of rhetoric (an indispensable political tool for a stateless people) and writing, he decided to cast his lot not with the establishment, not with the big, influential parties, but with the opposition. This, despite the fact that the Revisionists were out of office and power and lacking financial means.

As a man of convictions and principles, Begin dared not challenge his revered leader and mentor, Jabotinsky. They did, however, diverge on the question of the underground movement, which Jabotinsky opposed on the ground of his faith in the liberal, enlightened tradition of Europe. ("If you lose this faith," Jabotinsky said once to Begin, "there is no choice for you but to drown in the Vistula. . .")

Tragically, Begin was forced by circumstance to cause suffering and to send young men into martial dangers when he became commander of IZL, the Jewish fighting forces. All this was inspired by a love of his people, by his determination to put an end to their inhuman suffering and—to passive submission to sufferings. For these, there was only one solution, he believed, a sovereign state in the homeland.

It is towards the realization of this supreme goal that Begin has devoted all his efforts—his whole life.

Chapter Forty-Five

The Land of Israel

Begin has been known to be an ardent advocate of the concept the "complete" land of Israel. For years, his movement has been ridiculed by the Zionist left for its fantasies about a Jewish state on both banks of the Jordan.

Throughout time, the borders of kingdoms and states have expanded and contracted. As of this writing there is considerable talk in Europe about the reunified Germany, and the Warsaw Pact countries have just issued a statement insisting that the borders of central and eastern Europe are not to be changed as a result of the new political trends in that part of the world. In the USSR, some national groups are asserting their right for national independence.

The Middle East has been no exception to this rule. On the contrary, because of its long history and its multitude of nationalities, religions, ethnic groups, clans and tribes, it has been notorious for border changes throughout antiquity and modernity, and particularly in the twentieth century. At this very moment, if the various groups living in the little country of Lebanon had their way, Lebanon could break into a Shiite, Sunni, Druze, Maronite, and Palestinian ministates.

In 1921, as the British were consolidating their domination of the Middle East, they felt the need to create a new political entity east of the Jordan, which they could better control. They invited a Bedouin leader from the Arabian Peninsula, named Emir Abdullah ibn Hussein, to become the puppet ruler of the new "kingdom." The concept of a "Jewish home" was now redefined as applying only to areas west of the Jordan.

For the next three decades, the British would keep revising their proposed map of the Jewish state, culminating, at one point, in a tiny enclave around Tel Aviv, which looked more like a ghetto than a state.

In 1922, when Great Britain redefined the concept of a Jewish na-

tional home, the leader of the Zionist movement, Dr. Chaim Weizmann, accepted the definition, realizing that the only hope for attaining a Jewish state was reaching an agreement with the British.
Another Zionist leader, Zeev Jabotinsky, realized during the twenties
that the British were not serious about establishing a Jewish national
home. He further foresaw that a minimalist Zionist policy was leading nowhere. The real objective of the Zionist enterprise, as he understood it, was not to create a Jewish ghetto in an Arab region, but
rather to establish a viable Jewish state.

This viable Jewish state, as Jabotinsky understood it, included
Jerusalem as its capital and the Jordan as its major river. Jabotinsky
reminded the Jewish people that the Jordan had two banks, and that
historically Jews lived along both of them. The historical land of Israel did not exist west of the Jordan, but rather on both sides of it.

Jabotinsky's credo, "The Jordan has two banks," was bequeathed
to his successor, Menachem Begin. By 1947, however, the Zionist establishment in the land of Israel had given up its claim to the land east
of the Jordan, and accepted a UN partition plan which left the Jews
with three loosely connects areas west of the Jordan. Those areas did
not include Jerusalem, which was to be internationalized, or either
bank of the Jordan River.

Begin, who was emerging at the time from the underground, opposed the partition plan and especially the internationalization of
Jerusalem. Neither Begin nor Ben-Gurion at that time considered the
mutilated boundaries of the partition plan final, but political reality
dictated accepting the plan and worrying about boundaries later.

The present population of Jordan is about 70 percent Palestinian,
and, indeed, in 1970 Jordan was on the brink of becoming a Palestinian state, but the Palestinian uprising was quelled by King Hussein
in September of that year, which came to be known among the Palestinian Arabs as "Black September." After Israel won its War of Independence, Jordan annexed those parts of Mandatory Palestine which
Israel was not able to conquer, namely, the West Bank and East
Jerusalem, while Israel's neighbor to the south, Egypt, occupied the
Gaza Strip.

In 1967, after beating an alliance of Egypt, Jordan, and Syria in
the Six Day War, Israel occupied the West Bank, the Golan
Heights, and East Jerusalem. Israel incorporated East Jerusalem as

part of its capital.

Ten years later, when Begin became prime minister, he did two things. The first thing was his agreeing to granting an autonomy to the Palestinian Arabs living on the West Bank and in the Gaza Strip, as part of the Camp David accords, which led to the signing of the peace treaty with Egypt. The second was the annexation of the Golan Heights, a small area formerly occupied by Syria, which, in effect, has no Arab population to speak of, only some Druze villages, and which turned out to be indispensable for the defense of the north of Israel against the implacable Syrian enemy which had inflicted death and destruction on the Jewish settlements at the feet of the heights.

The agreement to a Palestinian Arab autonomy was not accepted by many elements in the Israeli political right. But Begin, realizing that an accommodation must eventually be reached between Arabs and Jews in the Near East, went along with Egypt's President Sadat and U.S. President Carter in agreeing to an autonomy plan.

Begin agreed to the proposed autonomy arrangement, but absolutely opposed a separate Palestinian state sandwiched between Israel and Jordan. In effect, Begin and the Israeli right have long given up the idea of a Jewish state on both sides of the Jordan. They have come to realize, as has the Israeli left, that the historical land of Israel is destined to have two peoples living side by side on its soil, namely, a Jewish nation and an Arab one.

In his book *The Israelis, Founders and Sons* (New York, 1975) Amos Elon argues that the founding fathers of Zionism, including Herzl and Ben-Gurion, paid little attention to the existence of an Arab population in the land of Israel. This, Elon argues, is at the root of many of the problems Israel has been facing in its dealings with the Palestinians and the rest of the Arab world. Again it was Jabotinsky, the "ultranationalist," who spoke about the "Son of Arabia living in peace alongside with my son." And, quite recently, Begin in his retirement in Jerusalem, happened to see some Jews pursuing some Arab youngsters who—as part of the *Intifada*—had just thrown stones at them, and in a rare instance of breaking his silence, sent a message to the Israeli authorities asking to prevent Jews from committing violent acts against Arabs.

Chapter Forty-Six

The Lebanon War

The war that caused Begin to retire from public office was the Lebanon war in 1982. This war actually consisted of two different stages. The first was the advance of the IDF 40 km from the northern border of Israel into Lebanon. That was the "good" stage. It resulted in the destruction and expulsion of the PLO military buildup in southern Lebanon. This buildup which included long-range artillery, large underground arsenals of materiel, fortified positions, was a military threat that during the preceding months sent thousands of Israelis fleeing from their homes in northern Israel because of katyusha attacks and terrorist infiltrations, and could have escalated to an aggressive war in cooperation with such long-time enemies of Israel as Syria.

The second stage was both good and bad. Begin's defense minister, Ariel Sharon, ordered Raphael Eitan, the IDF chief of staff, to move north to the Beirut-Damascus highway and to surround West Beirut, where the high command of the PLO and its chairman, Yasser Arafat, were esconsed in the midst of a large civilian population. Sharon's objective was to destroy the viper in its own nest, and to enable the leader of the Lebanese Christian militias, Bashir Jemayel, become president of Lebanon and subsequently sign a peace treaty with Israel.

Sharon, one of Israel's most brilliant generals, proved to be a less than brilliant analyst of political conditions in Arab countries. Jemayel was not a dependable ally. Begin, an ailing man (he had just broken his hip and was in pain for weeks) about to turn seventy, whose most trusted life-long companion, namely, his wife, Aliza, was on her death-bed at the time, did not watch closely his defense minister's moves. Yet, he kept reminding his second-in-command he did not wish to engage in any military action that would result in more than the most minimal loss of life.

Sharon kept reassuring him he was not about to engage in any risky operations. But as the IDF kept advancing, the list of Israeli casualties grew, and several field officers realized that the campaign may be getting out of hand.

Finally came the most devastating blow of the war, which seriously injured Israel's image in the world. It has come to be known as the Sabra and Shatila massacre. Briefly, after the IDF entered Beirut and forced the PLO to leave Lebanon, the would-be ally and piece partner, Bashir Jemayel, was to assume power in Lebanon. He was assassinated, and Israeli troops were posted at the refugee camps in west Beirut. For reasons which were later on investigated by an Israeli commission of inquiry, known as the Kahan Commission, Christian phallangists were allowed to enter the camps of Sabra and Shatila, presumably to look for PLO guerrillas. The result was a wanton massacre, including innocent women and children.

When Begin first ordered Israeli troops into Lebanon months earlier, his ardent wish was to put an end once and for all to the PLO threat and to ensure peace on Israel's northern border. Having signed a piece treaty with Egypt in the south four years earlier, his greatest wish was to replicate his success in the north, and to leave a legacy of a lasting peace for his war-weary people.

It was not meant to be. Lebanon, contrary to Israeli intelligence estimates and political analyses, was not as clear cut an issue as getting the British out of Palestine or signing a peace treaty with the Egyptians.

Though the smallest country in the Middle East, Lebanon, as has been made amply clear in recent years, has the most difficult and complicated population of all the countries in the region. Several Muslims sects, mainly Shiite and Sunni, Maronite Christians, Druze, Palestinians, and Syrians are all at war with one another, which is nothing short of a war of survival. Neither Begin, nor Reagan, nor anyone inside or outside the Arab world has been able to cut this Gordian knot and solve this conflict, which still goes on as of this writing and may continue for some time to come.

The murder of hundreds of men, women and children in the Arab refugee camps by the Christian phallangists cast a shadow on Israel, despite the fact that it was a massacre of Arabs by Arabs. There was no escaping the fact that the area was under the control of the IDF.

Rabbi Joseph B. Soloveichik, who has represented the opinion, mood and attitudes especially of Jewry in the United States and has followed closely events in Israel, including the Lebanon war, was shocked by the massacre. On Friday, the eve of Shabbat Shuvah 1982, he called me from Boston and asked me, no, demanded, that I call Prime Minister Begin and ask him in the rabbi's name to appoint a commission of inquiry into this matter forthwith. The rabbi spoke with great emotion, pain and anger.

It was for me not a pleasant mission, but how could I refuse him? I called the prime minister and told him about Rabbi Soloveichik's request, and about the general feeling among Jews and non-Jews.

When the rabbi spoke to me he mentioned that there was great anger in Boston against Israel because of the massacre. Soloveichik had close ties with Harvard University (his son-in-law, Professor Rabbi Yitzhak Tversky, headed the department of Middle East studies). I tried to calm him down, arguing that those who are angry at Israel are leftist intellectuals who in any case are not Israel's sympathizers.

The rabbi did not agree with my observation. He told me that some construction workers who were doing some work at his synagogue were also making angry comments about the event.

I therefore conveyed to the prime minister not only the rabbi's message but also my impression of the general atmosphere. Mr. Begin listened very attentively and responded:

"At this moment this matter is being considered by ministers and jurists. There are some legal hurdles facing the appointment of a commission of inquiry, since some persons have appealed to the High Court of justice and the matter is now *sub judice*. The question is whether the government can act while the court is deliberating the matter. But Rabbi Soloveichik's request is very important, and I will certainly convey it to those who are dealing with this matter."

Two days later, on the morning before the Day of Atonement, Mr. Begin called me and asked me to tell Rabbi Soloveichik that first thing in the morning, on the day after Yom Kippur the cabinet would meet and he would propose the immediate appointment of a commission of inquiry.

I called the rabbi as he was about to go to synagogue for the Kol Nidre service. He thanked me in a trembling voice, and I could sense his deep concern about this matter.

As we said, this realization, particularly after the Sabra and Shatila massacre, broke Begin's heart.

At the cabinet session in which he told the government about his resignation, the ministers tried to persuade him to change his mind. He left the room as the ministers followed him into the corridor and kept asking him to reconsider, he muttered without looking back, "I cannot go on." (See letter to Senator Daniel Patrick Moynihan on this matter, of which he gave me a copy).

In one lifetime Begin saw his people in Europe destroyed, and he helped the survivors effect a national rebirth through an armed struggle, and establish the first Jewish state in two thousand years. He helped nurture the young democracy, playing the painful and thankless role of head of the opposition for some thirty years. He then became prime minister, and performed the miracle of the peace treaty with Egypt. He tried to pull off one more miracle, but it did not quiet work out, and so he felt it was time to go.

It is too early in time to fully assess the effect of the Lebanon War. It was certainly a turning point in the history of the PLO, which quite possibly led to the latest conciliatory posture of Arafat, and may yet lead to the settlement of the Palestinian problem.

Chapter Forty-Seven

Glimpses

Religious leaders who supported Begin

There were quite a number of rabbis and other religious leaders who supported Menachem Begin. To mention only the more preeminent: Rabbi Yitzchok Hutner, the famous head of the Yeshiva Rabbeinu Chaim Berlin and great scholar and author, showed considerable interest and understanding for the practical strivings of Ze'ev Jabotinsky and also of his follower, Menachem Begin. This was related to me by the mediator between them, Irving Unger, a Young Israel leader. Rabbi Hutner mentioned it to Begin at their meeting in the house of Rabbi Moshe Feinstein.

Another outstanding supporter of IZL and its commander was Irving Bunim, the unique religious leader, orator and activist. Mr. Bunim put at the disposal of IZL his influence and connections, including those of Edward Silver, the National Young Israel leader, the father-in-law of his son, Rabbi Amos, who happened to be the District Attorney of Brooklyn.

It is still possible to save Hungarian Jewry

The mass murder of the Hungarian Jews by the Germans took place almost a year and a half after the beginning of the destruction of the Polish Jews. Menachem Begin warned, supplicated, begged to save the Jews in Hungary. In *Be'machteret* (Underground) of February 1, 1943, he wrote:

> Is it still possible to save? Isn't it too late? It is possible~ Jews in Hungary and Bulgaria. . . are beginning to escape the murder and to come to their homeland. Their escape depends, therefore, on our ability to do away with the clamp that closed Eretz Yisrael for the

Jews. This is possible if we will really fight, and we will draw all
the conclusions of Britain's opposition to save the Jews.

I Experienced the Revelation of Leadership

I experienced the revelation of leadership. After we were afflicted
with the worst kind of void in leadership during the German mass
massacre of the Jews in Europe, there emerged from this deepest
abyss an authentic, genuine leader.

Let me quote the real definition of this often abused and misrepresented term, as worded by a man who was himself such a leader,
Ze'ev Jabotinsky:

"True leaders seldom appear. We recognize them by this distinction: they never ask to lead. To follow them, to obey them is not a
question of discipline; when we hearken to them we are swept along
by the song of a great voice—his melody comes from our own longing." (*Memoirs of Our Generation*, by Ze'ev Jabotinsky).

Exactly this feeling overwhelmed me as soon as I heard Begin's
call from the Underground: from the depth of despair and catastrophe
of a kind never suffered by any other people.

Begin's was the voice of a leader who finally emerged after many
years of disastrous disarray and vacuum, of chaos and confusion.

The condemnations by the self-appointed and self-important
"leaders" of the establishment couldn't dim the spark that came from
Begin's calls tp arms, nor weaken his command of the hearts of the
martyred people in the fight for freedom and an independent state.

Self-Sacrifice

Shmuel Schnitzer, former editor-in-chief of the daily *Maariv*, one
of the most outstanding Israeli publicists, has written:

". . . There is another measure of the Zionist leaders. A few of them
. . . reached considerable wealth. What they did for their people didn't
negatively affect their personal interests. One cannot avoid compar-
ing them with the Revisionist leaders, who were poor their entire
lives. All the funds at their disposal were used only for the needs of

their movement" (*Ha'Uma*, Hebrew quarterly, Tel Aviv, summer 1990).

Menachem Begin is the telling example. He contributed his whole income from his books to the worthy causes of his movement, as well as the funds that accompanied his Nobel Prize on 1980. He leads a very modest life without a trace of luxury.

Another trait of begin's leadership: The apparatus and offices of Herut in various countries are plagued by financial and other shortcomings, whereas the vast apparatus of the Zionist World Organization blossoms, provided with considerable means. Why is this so? Are the Heruth members and activists so incapable?

The answer is that Begin and his followers have never forgotten that their party wasn't a goal in itself, but only an instrument to achieve their lofty aims. When this was accomplished, they had no desire to build up and maintain a huge apparatus. A modest operational framework was sufficient for the party.

Menachem Begin is totally dedicated to the people. All his efforts, all his talents, all his thoughts and deeds were concentrated on his people. He is completely devoid of selfish preoccupations and aspirations. And he lacks entirely the trait considered characteristic of public figures: aloofness from the common people, distance from the ordinary crowd.

Instead, Begin treats individuals as close friends no matter on what level of the society ladder they are on.

I know this from first-hand experience. Whenever Begin talks or writes to me, he never fails to ask about my family. On joyous occasions, he expresses hearty congratulations and wishes. At happy occurrences in his family, he shares his happiness with us. I treasure his letters containing news of this kind. I know them to be no mere formalities. They are expressions of a sensitive and caring person's genuine feelings.

Begin's Concern for the Individual

Even in the midst of his intense preoccupation with general concerns, Begin found time for individuals and their needs. I recall an episode which, although trivial, throws light on the kind of person he is.

It was August, 1982, at the beginning of the Lebanon War. I visited the Prime Minister at his office, and afterwards, as I waited outside for a taxi, Begin emerged from the building. I stood hidden behind a column, not wanting him to see me (for some vague reason). But when he was already in his car, Begin noticed me, and all of a sudden, I heard frantic calls in the hall: "Mr. Olmert, Mr. Olmert! The Prime Minister wants you!" Then Olmert, a Knesset Member, came out of the building, and Begin called me and introduced us to each other (not knowing that we had already met). He told Olmert, "Ehud, maybe you could give a ride to Dr. Seidman." "With pleasure," Olmert replied.

In the car, I asked Mr. Olmert to let me out. "Your time as a lawyer is valuable, and I cannot afford it . . . I'll find my own way back to the hotel." But Olmert refused, remarking, "Mr. Begin's wish is my command."

I thought, this is vintage Begin. There he is, preoccupied with the troublesome matters of the government, but he still pays attention to someone in need of a ride—as though this was his only worry.

Chapter Forty-Eight

The Word As Sword

The arms at the disposal of Menachem Begin during the revolt were few and poor. But in addition to guns and bombs, the commander of the IZL was in possession of another weapon, namely, the written word. While hiding in the underground as thousands of soldiers of the occupation army were looking for him, and while the public was advised by the British authorities that 10,000 English Pounds were offered for the "archterrorist," he was unable to resort to the spoken word. But he did manage to issue written messages to the public from his place of hiding. Those words were more powerful than cannons.

They exploded like bombs in the battle against the occupation forces. They burst in the hearts of people who were transformed by them and proceeded to take action.

Even today, long after the battle was won and the struggle has receded into history, these calls continue to reverberate with great power and eloquence. They inspire noble feelings, and will continue to evoke for years justified pride and unshakable faith in the destiny of the eternal people.

His was the voice coming from the abyss of pain and suffering, and from the highest regions of the ideals and values of Judaism.

Even before I heard the authentic voice of Menachem Begin, the attacks against him emanating from the Zionist and the rabbinical establishment revived my hope and faith, as I was experiencing the pain and shame of the most cruel defeat inflicted on our people in all of history, or, for that matter, on any people in the annals of mankind.

When I reached Paris at the end of 1944, I became part of the secret cells of the Irgun supporters. I became privy to messages, leaflets, and other literature of the Irgun. They were, of course, clandestine and anonymous. Even the name Irgun Tzvai Leumi was camouflaged under the pseudonym "Ma'amad."

This literature was my spiritual nourishment. It gave me renewed hope and courage. I translated some of it from Hebrew into Yiddish, Polish and French. It may have lost some of its original beauty and power in translation, but it still aroused and inspired.

Among those who made that literature available to me were such Revisionist Zionists as Shmuel Katz (later Information Minister in Begin's cabinet), Dr. Jacob Rubin, Joseph Klarman and Issac Remba (a friend of mine from Warsaw who later became my editor at *Herut*, Begin's party's newspaper, of which I became the U. S. correspondent). I sensed the influence of Jabotinsky in those writings. The name of the actual author, Menachem Begin, was never mentioned. The closest anyone came to mentioning the author was the title *Mefaked*, commander.

Only later on was I told in strict secrecy who the author was.

The style, the feelings behind the words, the straight line of thinking, the consistency of the deeds and thoughts in all of the writings, bear the imprint of the author. His unshakable faith is apparent in all of them, as well as his absolute devotion to the truth.

Only in 1975, with the publication of Begin's writings during his five years in the underground, titled *Bamachteret*, or Underground (in Hebrew), the full range of his written work during that period came to light.

Today when I read and reread those pronouncements, they evoke in me memories of those fateful years. They still can revive in me, after more than four decades, the sublime feelings I felt back then.

These words are not merely history. They cannot be relegated to the past. They sound alive, fresh, as if they were written today. They have become timeless.

These days, as we are inundated with defeatist and nihilistic writings, mostly by the ideologically bankrupt left who dominate most of the media, it would be a good thing to reissue again at least part of the pronouncements of Menachem Begin during his glorious struggle which led to the creation of the Jewish State.

Chapter Forty-Nine

Lasting Impact

Menachem Begin's life and legacy are of lasting impact. The charisma he radiated, the acts he performed, the ideas he originated and fought for, the changes he brought about—all of these left profound traces. Their consequences reverberate in every sector of the State of Israel and in every segment of world Jewry—and, in a sense, even beyond.

Some of them are visible, some are hidden beneath the surface, some are felt and perceived by sensitive persons. Each one of them and all of them together exert their significant influence on the Jewish people and its face.

If the present Likud government is courageously navigating the ship of state, facing threatening waves of world-wide attacks; if beleaguered Israel is standing strong in its pursuit of a secure peace—there is in all this a continuation of the Begin era.

It is true that there are a number of negative occurrences on the political scene that are at a variance with the teachings and actions of Begin; but those teachings are far from being abandoned. And let us think how much worse things would be if they had never occurred.

From Begin's innumerable achievements, let us choose two: the Israeli-Egyptian Peace Treaty of 1979, and the destruction of the Iraqi nuclear reactor on June 7, 1981.

We will start with the second. Imagine the danger for Israel, and for the world at large, had Begin not made the historic decision in 1981 to bomb the Iraqi nuclear reactor. If not for this fateful deed, Saddam Hussein would today possess nuclear arms, and his threats would be more than empty words. The Western powers, who at the time condemned Israel, are certainly more comfortable today because of Begin's "outrage" of 1981.

And imagine if the threatening posture and preparation for destruction of Israel by the Iraqi dictator would be—God forbid—joined by a bellicose Egypt (not to mention Syria and Jordan)—a scenario that the Israeli-Egyptian Peace Treaty abrogated.

A current political slogan is Israel says, "Only Likud can." Concerning these two events and many others, we may say: "Only Begin could."

Countless individuals and groups in Israel and in the Diaspora have been formed and influenced by Begin's ideas, by his struggle, and by the shining example of his dedication, honesty and self-sacrifice.

Menachem Begin implanted in these people a sound patriotism based on our sacred faith and heritage, and rooted in love of the Jewish people, the Jewish homeland, and in ethical and moral foundations.

Chapter Fifty

Conclusions

How is one to assess the lasting contribution of Menachem Begin to the Jewish people and to the State of Israel?

As we said in the beginning of this book, Begin made a singular contribution to the changing of the Jewish character, from a passive recipient subservient to the will of others, to a nation of fighters, to a people who takes its destiny into its own hands and shape it in its own image. In doing so, Begin has secured for himself a place of preeminence in Jewish history. He is one of those rare leaders who emerge at the darkest hours of that millenial history, and turn the tide of history. In each case, the odds are overwhelming, yet the example of one person makes all the difference. In the history of the State of Israel there were two such leaders: David Ben-Gurion and Menachem Begin.

The late Dr. Azriel Carlebach, one of Israel's most gifted journalists and the first editor-in-chief of Israel's daily *Maariv*, was one of Begin's avowed political adversaries. Yet on May 17, 1948, two days after the proclamation of Israel's independence, Carlebach wrote an article in the *Maariv* under the heading: "To Menachem Begin." He said:

> You, Menachem Begin, liberated us. Your struggle delivered us. Because it was only the language of open rebellion that the British understood. Millions of Jewish men, women and children were murdered, and the world was not moved. Thousands upon thousands of Jews suffered, disappeared in concentration camps, and the world was silent. Pleas, memoranda, diplomatic action did not move hearts of stone. But your language, that of bombs exploding in the King David Hotel and in Acre fortress, that language was understood by the Gentiles. You liberated us!

After twenty centuries of statelessness, the Jewish people had no model of their own to follow in running a sovereign state. It

Theodore Herzl who, nearly a century ago, awoke Jews to states-manship. The Zionist organization Herzl founded became the precursor of Israel's party system and legislature. But Herzl was a late nineteenth-century European romantic, living in a time when Europe was captive of its own dream of utopia, world peace and harmony waiting around the corner. It took a Ze'ev Jabotinsky, who experienced the Kishinev pogroms, to understand the realities of the new twentieth century, to grasp the murderousness of Western civilization, confirmed by World War One, in which Jabotinsky took part, and to give birth to the concept of a Jewish army. It was left to Jabotinsky's leading disciple, Menachem Begin, to make the concept of the fighting Jew a reality.

Contrary to his detractors' belief, Begin never worshipped militarism for its own sake. If his bosom swelled with pride at the sight of Jewish soldiers, it was not because he loved war, but because he knew that the only guarantee for Jewish survival was Jewish defense, and Jewish survival was what he lived for.

And, for that matter, Begin may well go down in history as the Jewish leader who started the peace process with the Arab world by signing a peace treaty with Egypt, the Arab world's leading country. As of this writing, the Middle East continues to be one of the most troubled regions of the world, what with a Lebanon that is threatened with disintegration, and belligerent countries like Iran, Iraq, Syria, Lybia and others plotting war. The Palestinian question is far from resolved. Its complexity cannot be minimized. Mostly through the inaction and deliberate neglect of their Arab brothers and sisters, Palestinian Arabs continue to live in refugee camps throughout the Middle East under hard conditions, and the Palestinian terrorist organizations continue their murderous activities, also among themselves (Abu Nidal, latest purge of his own organization). But in spite of all this, or perhaps because of it, the peace treaty between Israel and Egypt continues to shine through the dark night of the Middle East as a great promise for the future.

Israel is a young state, still in its formation stages. People often lose sight of the fact that Israel is not a France, or a Canada, or a Switzerland. It has not been in existence for generations. Many of its citizens, including those still in their early fifties, remember a time when there was no Israel. As far as countries go, Israel is a small child. Yet this small child has managed to become during its short existence a major player in the world scene, a country whose impact is felt around the world in such areas as medicine, agriculture, high-tech, aviation, weapon systems, music, and so many other fields and specialties of human endeavor that would easily fill up another chapter in this book.

And yet at the same time, Israel is still plagued by several fundamental problems which will take a long time to resolve. Perhaps the most central of those problems is Israel's identity as a nation, as a consolidated people who are not merely a continuation of the Jewish existence in the diaspora during past generations, but a new consolidated sovereign nation with a clear sense of purpose and destiny.

It is precisely in regard to this question that we ought to ask ourselves what has been Begin's legacy during the pre-state period and the first decades of the new state?

In the foregoing chapters we have discussed some aspects of the answer. To begin with, in cultivating the identity of the new Israeli Jew, Begin did not seek—unlike other Zionist leaders—to turn his back on the "Golus Yid," or the Diaspora Jew—the kind of a sorry-looking person who can only be the object of pity and derision. As a young radical Zionist leader in his native Poland, whose entire life was consumed with the dream of a Jewish homeland, Begin continued to be aware of the great spiritual treasures of the Diaspora Jew, of his high moral values, of his great Jewish culture, rich in wisdom and values. He did not turn his back on that Jew, not in Europe, and not later when he finally reached the Promised Land. Throughout his long political career, Begin continued to cultivate his relations with Jews everywhere, setting a personal example of Jewish unity, of Ahavat Yisrael, love for all Jews, of a deep conviction that when Jews are united they can resist any force in the world, while Jewish disunity often results in national tragedy.

Begin realized that the new state was not meant to negate Jewish existence elsewhere, but rather to restore a national and spiritual home for Jews living in their land as well as other lands, not only in the present but also at a future time when Israel will become the home of the majority of Jews, or at least of a very substantial part of world Jewry. He realized that Israel's raison d'être was not to become just another country with citizens called Israelis, but to answer the prayers of many generations of Jews, who never gave up their faith and heritage, and kept believing that some day they will be restored to their ancestral homeland. Thus, he saw himself as the custodian of the ancient heritage, of the promise of Abraham, Isaac and Jacob, an emissary called upon to make the dream of the ages come true.

Jews, though small in numbers, are a highly diverse people. They hail from many countries. They practice their religion in a variety of ways. They espouse a great range of political philosophies. They are not followers but rather leaders. They are by nature suspicious of human authority or leader, no matter how compelling or charismatic, and in general they do not agree on too many things. The great diversity and discord among Jews poses many problems, but it is also their source of strength. This strength has been channelled on many occasions in the past and continues to be channelled to accomplish great things. But in order to do so, one has to recognize Jewish diversity, respect it, and find ways to make it work.

And this is precisely what Menachem Begin has done. The Irgun, the fighting underground, though small in numbers, attracted Jews from all backgrounds—Ashkenazic and Sephardic, secular and religious, humble artisans and creative intellectuals, Jews from all corners of the earth, a veritable microcosm of world Jewry. After the founding of the state, as Begin joined Israeli political life, he proceeded to build his political base in a society almost totally ruled by the socialist Zionist establishment. He erected that base on several solid principles that took into account the diversity of Israeli, read Jewish society.

As was discussed earlier in this book, Israeli democracy as we know it today could not have evolved to the point where it is today without Menachem Begin. During the early years of the state, the young Begin was the only opposition leader who counterbalanced the force of the ruling Labor party. All other parties, whether mainstream Zionists, or religious, or even the smaller left-wing parties, were basically Labor's coalition partners who kept going in and out of the coalition. The only voice on the benches of the opposition that posed a real challenge to Ben-Gurion's government, as evidenced by such episodes as the German reparations, was Begin's. While in the fifties the majority of Israelis did not shower his party with votes, they came to realize in the sixties that Begin was the only power they had by way of a real opposition, and in the seventies brought him to power. Today Labor and Likud are the only two parties with any real chance of ruling, and if this is so it is only thanks to one person, namely, Menachem Begin.

State institutions and private businesses in Israel are closed on the Jewish Sabbath. Jewish holidays are Israel's official holidays.

In the early years of the state the ruling socialist-Zionist establishment had to deal with a relatively small religious population and a dominant secular-national population. The prevalent belief in socialist circles was that religion was on the decline, that in a few short years the vast majorities of Israelis—including the masses of newly-arrived immigrants from the Arab world and from war-devestated Europe—will let socialism replace the old religious values and practices, and Israel would become a secular, predominantly socialist state. This is not quite how it turned out. While forty years ago it was hard to find a Jew wearing the traditional skullcap on the streets of Tel Aviv of Haifa, now it is hard not to find one. Religious Jewry in Israel today is a growing political force, as was evidenced by the last election to the Knesset. The percentage of religious Jews among olim, or new immigrants, is quite high, at times probably exceeding the non-religious.

Begin always fought against discarding the religious values of Judaism. He knew that in rebuilding the new Jewish commonwealth Jews were not turning their backs on the past but rather reshaping it is such a way that Jews could once again live in this world in security and dignity. And this, perhaps, is the most important part of Begin's legacy. Future prime ministers of Israel will look back on Begin's example as Israeli leader and will take notice of his ability to transcend the differences between secular and religious Jew, between Ashkenazi and Sephardi, even between political friend and foe, and think in terms of *Klal Yisrael*, the totality of the Jewish people, a people whose only real source of authority is *Tzur v'goalo*, the Rock and Redeemer of Israel, a people with a purpose in this world, *l'taken Olam b'malchut Shaddai*, to reshape the world according to the Divine imperative of justice and mercy.

Some of Begin's Underground Calls

January 1944—The Declaration of the Revolt by the Irgun Tzvai Leumi

To the Hebrew Nation in Zion!

We have now reached the last stage of this World War. Each nation is currently preoccupied with its own national self-questioning: What was gained and what was lost? Which way to turn in order to attain national goals? Who are one's friends who are the enemies? Who is a true ally and who is a traitor? Who are the ones who are going to wage the decisive battle?

The Jewish nation must also examine its way and draw conclusions for the future, since the last few years have been the most horrible years in our history, and the next few years will be the most decisive years we have ever faced as a people.

Here is the language of facts:

1. In 1939 all the organizations in Israel proclaimed that our people are on the side of England, France and Poland, who had declared war against the aggressor, namely, Hitler's Germany.

2. Germany declared that this world war is a "Jewish war," and that the people of Israel is its number one enemy. Nevertheless, the British Government, with consistent stubbornness, has rejected every suggestion of establishing a Hebrew military force that would wage direct war against German forces.

3. In the land of Israel a truce was reached between the Jews and the Government. The *Yishuv* offered its full help to the Allies in their war against Hitler's tyranny.

4. Over 25 thousand young Jews enlisted in the British Army hoping that England would form a national Hebrew army.

5. The Arabs of Iraq took advantage in 1941 of Britain's precarious situation and with German help attacked its troops; the

Arabs of Syria supported Hitler's emissaries; the Egyptian Fifth Column has exerted an enormous influence; the Arabs of the Land of Israel waited for Rommel the redeemer; and their leader, the Grand Mufti, kept sending orders from Berlin.

6. Jewry remained loyal during the trying years 1940–41. The *Yishuv* served the entire Middle East with its experts and its industry. Its members risked their lives in Syria, Egypt, and Iraq.

7. Germany began to murder the Jews of Europe. Poland became a slaughterhouse; German, Austrian, Dutch and Belgian Jewries were liquidated; the Jews of Lithuania, Latvia and Estonia are dying; the remnants of Polish Jewry are fighting for their lives in the ghettos; Rumanian Jewry is facing annihilation; Bulgarian Jewry is about to be expelled; Hungarian Jewry fears for its life. Sword and famine, plague and poison are decimating our brothers and sisters in Europe. Everywhere in the Jewish Diaspora—blood.

8. Our people have no refuge. All countries are closed to them. Even those who had escaped to Asian Russia from Poland, Romania and the Baltic states, are dying of hunger, cold and disease. No one is helping them, for they are Jews.

9. In light of the horrible slaughter in Europe, the Allies have paid lip service, which is not worth the paper it is written on.

10. The British Government has declared that there is no possibility of rescue, since it would "disturb the war effort." It did not stop at this Satanic observation, but with its own hands wrote bloody chapters in the annals of Hebrew immigration: Patria, Mauritius, Struma.*

11. The White Paper government attacked the Hebrew community. Its agents murdered in the city and in the countryside with impunity; its judges have made false accusations and sought to trample on Jewish dignity throughout the world.

12. The White Paper has remained in effect. It is being carried out despite Arab treachery and Jewish loyalty; despite the mass enlisting in the British Army; despite the truce and the calm in the land of Israel; despite the mass murders of Jews in Europe. And despite the fact, that after the defeat of Hitlerism there is no future for the Jews among the nations of Europe who are consumed with hatred towards Jews.

---

* Patria and Sturma were Jewish refugee ships sunk by Britain, in which hundreds of Jews perished. Some Refugees were exiled to the island of mauritius under inhuman conditions.

The language of facts is both simple and terrible. During the four years of the war we have lost millions of our best sons and daughters; more millions are facing extermination. And the land of Israel is closed to them because it is ruled by the British who are carrying out the White Paper which seeks to destroy our nation's last hope.

Children of Israel, Hebrew youth!

We are now in the last stage of the war. We are facing a historical decision concerning our fate which will affect generations to come.

The truce which was declared at the beginning of the war has been violated by the British rule. The rulers of this land have disregarded our loyalty, our concessions, and our sacrifices. They continue to realize their objective—the liquidation of sovereign Zionism.

Four years have gone by and all the hopes that filled your hearts in 1939 have evaporated without a trace. We have not been granted an international status; a Hebrew army has not been established; the gates of the land of Israel were not opened. The British rule has accepted the shameful betrayal of the Hebrew nation, and it has lost its moral right to exist in the land of Israel.

We shall fearlessly draw all the conclusions. There is no longer a truce between the Hebrew nation and youth and the British administration in the land of Israel which turns our people over to Hitler. This nation is at war with this rule, a war to the end.

This war will require a great many sacrifices, but we shall wage it in the recognition that we are loyal to our people who have been and are being butchered, for we are fighting for them and we are executing their will which they handed to us before they died.

This is our demand:

THE RULE OVER THE LAND OF ISRAEL WILL BE TURNED OVER TO A PROVISIONAL HEBREW GOVERNMENT.

To Our Arab Neighbors

(This flier was distributed among the Arabs in Arabic. Its contents were also given to the general public in Hebrew and English).

Hebrew youth, trained in the martial arts, has begun the fight for the liberation of the homeland. The Irgun Tzvai Leumi with its thousands of soldiers, equipped with the latest weapons, is waging war against the treacherous government, which seeks to put an end to the eternal vision of the great Hebrew nation. This war of liberation, which has only begun to unfold, will continue to increase and spread.

This war is not being waged against you. We do not consider you our enemies. We would like to regard you as good neighbors. There is room for you in the land of Israel, for you and your descendants and for millions of Jews who can live nowhere else except in this land.

The Hebrew government will grant you full equality; the Hebrew and the Arabic languages will be the official languages of the land; there will be no discrimination between a Jew and an Arab in government or public jobs. The Muslim holy places will be under your representatives' supervision.

The Hebrew government will enable your masses to acquire an education, and there will be no illiteracy in the land of the Bible; there will be no epidemics in your villages and towns; the worker's wages will be raised to the European level; your agriculture will be developed; you will build houses instead of tents; water and electricty will reach all your habitations; the Hebrew state will be a common home for all of us, and good neighbor relations will exist between this state and the sovereign Arab states.

The treacherous government is against all of this. It seeks to cause strife between us, to incite you against us and us against you, in order to play the role of the supreme arbiter, in order to leave you here in the middle of the desert and in the darkness of ignorance, and let our people die in the lands of exile. But we do are not letting ourselves be fooled by its words. We have proven it through our actions. We have visited Arab Ramallah, taken over the central radio station despite its proximity to the main police fortress; but we did not harm the local residents. We fought twice in Jaffa, but we only attacked the oppressive ruler without touching the town's residents. We launched attacks in Jerusalem and in

Haifa, but we did not aim our weapons at the Arab inhabitants. This has been and will continue to be our policy.

But you too must be careful not to listen to the inciters. Do not raise your hand against Jews life or property. For, if contrary to your national and personal interest you should raise your hand against us, we will have to cut it off by force of arms. You have found out, as has the entire world, that the power of the new Hebrew youth is great.

It all depends on you and your wisdom. If you choose not to listen to the inciters, there will be peace and friendship between the two nations forever. Together we shall build this holy land; together we shall benefit from its treasures and bounty; together we shall develop its agriculture and industry; together we shall advance with all the free nations of the world towards a life of justice and freedom, happiness and honor.

Our Arab neighbors! We are extending our hand for peace and brotherhood. Do not reject it!

The Irgun Tzvai Leumi in the Land of Israel

Letters from Menachem Begin
to the Author

(Translated from Hebrew)

The Knesset

Member of Knesset

Tel Aviv, 28 Tishre 5724—October 16, 1963

To: Mr. Hillel Seidman
     New York

Dear Friend:

May I express my heartfelt gratitude for your wondrous letter on the occasion of my fiftieth birthday, which I have read with great emotion.

I know what you have gone through during the time when our people were trampled underfoot by the cruel killers. This is why your great appreciation—which you guard in your heart and describe with your pen—for the effort we in the land of Israel, in the underground, have made to bring our people from slavery to freedom, and to ensure that no bloodthirsty enemy may ever again raise his hand on a Jewish child, is so dear to me.

Since we first met after the catastrophe and the national rebirth, a true friendship was formed between us, free of any ulterior motives, but rather grounded in a mutual appreciation of our faith in the redemption of our people and its future. Your friendship is precious to me personally, and all the members of my family share this feeling.

Please convey our best wishes for the New Year to your wife and your family, and may you succeed in everything you undertake to do.

Yours with friendship and appreciation,
M. Begin

227

M. Begin
Minister's Office

Jerusalem, 25 Sivan 5727
July 3, 1967

Mr. Hillel Seidman
New York

Dear Friend:

Many thanks for your encouraging letter. Indeed, I wanted to come
to the United States about two weeks ago, but for several reasons I was
not able to do it. I may travel abroad soon and also visit America. But
these plans are not definite. Neither have they been shelved. In the
meantime, I am doing my best to fulfill my duty here in Israel. Most important: We all must praise and thank our Heavenly Father for the great
salvation that we attained with the help of our fighting sons. There is a
reason to believe that we are also going to pass the political test. With
His help we shall bring our people to a safe shore.

My best to your wife and family.

Respectfully and with good wishes,
M. Begin

The Prime Minister

Jerusalem, 126 Tamuz 5737
July 2, 1977

Mr. Hillel Seidman
New York

Dear Friend:

Your warm and heartfelt Independence Day letter has not yet been
answered. This is due to the fact that in recent months we have been
receiving so many letters which I am not able to answer immediately,
not even letters from dear friends like yourself.

I agree, of course, with the Rabbi from Lubavitch who defines you
as a "good man," and lo and behold, we have been fortunate enough to

have had your good wishes during Independence Day come true. May our wishes be fulfilled for the good, so that we may be able to do good things for our nation and our land.

With faithful blessing,
M. Begin

ALIZA BEGIN

Dear Mr. Seidman:

My deepest thanks for all you have done for Benny [Begin's son, Dr. Zeev Benjamin Begin, now member of the Knesset]. The trip you arranged for him was apparently most successful, to judge from the letters and press clips which we continue to receive.

May you find blessing in all the work you have been doing for so many years for the people and the land of Israel.

Please convey my best to your entire family.

In friendship,
Aliza Begin

Jerusalem, 19 Iyar 5740 [1980]

The Prime Minister

Jerusalem, 17 Shevat 5742
February 10, 1982

To: Rabbi Aharon Soloveichik
    New York

Our Distinguished Rabbi and Teacher:

Please accept my heartiest good wishes for success in your efforts to ensure the welfare and future of the Brisk Yeshivah.

There once was on the road between Warsaw and Moscow a great

Jewish community where thousands of Jews lived. It had illustrious yeshivot and great Torah scholars, headed by Rabbi Chaim Soloveichik, of Blessed memory, who brought glory to Brisk D'Lita, its Jewish residents, and to its place in the annals of Israel. From the standpoint of the Jewish people, Brisk no longer exists, but the memory of the old, poor, small, warm house, rich with the love of Israel and Zion, continues to live in our hearts.

The Brisk Yeshivah will serve as its memorial for the future generations, and your honor lends it the glory of the House of Soloveichik throughout its generations.

Yours, with deep gratitude,

M. Begin

CABLE

State of Israel
Prime Minister, Jerusalem

American Jewish Congress
15 East 84th Street
New York, N.Y.

Jerusalem, May 10, 1983

I extend to my dear friend Dr. Hillel Seidman my very best wishes and congratulations on the publication of his book, *United Nations: Perfidy and Perversion.*

I deem it appropriate that Jerusalem should have been chosen for the occasion to launch the message of this book at the American Jewish Congress, which demonstrate proud Jewish unity and solidarity. For this day declares for all to hear that no perfidy and perversion can succeed in distorting the true history that Yerushalayim is the eternal and indivisible capital of the State of Israel, open and free to all religious and the heart of our nation and people.

From Yerushalayim I greet you all with Chag Sameach.

Menachem Begin

Menachem Begin
Jerusalem

27 Adar B, 5746
April 7, 1986

To: Dr. Hillel Seidman
     Brooklyn

Dear Friend:

Please accept my thanks for your letter which I only received this morning. I was happy to read it, but there is no denying that we are facing some difficulties. We hope to overcome them.

The short paragraph concerning Rabbi Feinstein, ZTL, greatly moved me. The great rabbi, who occupied a special position, has since passed away. Huge throngs from all walks of life in Israel accompanied him to the Mount of Rest in Jerusalem. My his memory be for a blessing.

Please convey my regards to your family. Happy Holidays to you and them.

Respectfully, and with
warmest greetings,

Menachem Begin

The Office of
Menachem Begin

Jerusalem, 2 Av 5742
August 7, 1986

Dr. Hillel Seidman
Brooklyn

Dear Friend:

Many thanks for the letter in which you enclosed your important article. The truth is that the pain of the losses, which we did not wish for and which we have done everything possible to prevent, prevented us for a long time from perceiving the important political results of this operation [the blowing up of the British rule headquarters at the King David Hotel in Jerusalem], in which we too had our losses in the struggle for liberating our land.

Please forgive me for taking the liberty to mention that the discussion about the timing of evacuating the hotel took place between Yitzhak Sadeh [the commander of the Palmach] and Amihai Palgin (Gidi) [operations chief of the Irgun], and the two reached the compromise of allotting half an hour during which the hotel could be evacuated.

Respectfully, and with
warm greetings,

Menachem Begin

Menachem Begin

Jerusalem, 20 Sivan, 5750
June 13, 1990
Reference 5-682-2

Dr. Hillel Seidman:

My thanks for your letter of Monday, Parashat Beha'alotcha, and the good article in which you pay tribute to the work of Mr. Yitzhak Shamir, Israel's Prime Minister.

Your work is very important in reaching Jewish public opinion in the United States.

Please convey my hearty regards to your entire dear family.

Yours in appreciation and friendship,

Menachem Begin

MAILGRAM

05/17/77

M. Begin
Rosenbaum St 1
Telaviv (Israel)

Shehechiyany shehigiyanu ad halom. Mazal Tov. Our hearts are full of joy. Grateful to Hashem for recompensating mesirat nefesh. After I saw greatest churban Ghetto Warsaw I see tonight nechama. The souls of our martyred friends are tonight with you. Reb Aryeh Levin rejoices in Gan Eden.

Nachum Goldman told me today it would not be bad if you win. He will support you with all power.

Hillel Seidman and whole family including Naomi in Jerusalem.

785 East 2 St Brooklyn NY

TELEGRAM

04/04/77

Hillel Seidman
785 East 2 St
Brooklyn NY 11218 USA

Thanks heartwarming cable. Please inform respectfully great Rebbe deeply grateful his interest. Danger probably passed Baruch Hashem. Pesach Eve perhaps leave hospital. Between these difficult days you are always in my fond thoughts.

Love Aliza Menachem Begin

May 17, 1977–May 17, 1979;
Two Years of Historic Changes

Since this memorable day two years ago, May 17, 1977, the day of the Knesset election that elevated Menachem Begin to the helm, tremendous changes occurred in Israel and, as a result, in the Jewish world at large. Most of these are highly visible. Others are almost unnoticed, due to their slow and gradual occurrence.

Two years after the event, in the midterm of the present Israeli administration, it is time to take stock of these changes and to have a look at their impact.

Menachem Begin gave new directions to the course of Jewish history. Not once but thrice.

First, in 1943 by leading the Revolt against the oppressive British mandate government in the then Palestine which waged war and applied a blockade against the remnants of the German slaughter of the European Jews under their occupation, the survivors who strived for a home in their homeland. This heroic struggle of a pitiful small group of Jewish fighters against the then still mighty British Empire, "few against many," led to the abandonment of Eretz Yisrael by the British and the creation of the Jewish State.

Second, on May 17, 1977, by winning the trust of his people through the admirable working of the Israeli democracy which put him on top of the government.

Third, by opening the gates for peace, by starting the process which led to the signing of the Peace Treaty between Israel and Egypt.

In spite of artificial extolling the Egyptian president's admittedly dramatic Jerusalem visit beyond every proportion, it is an established fact that Begin's, not Sadat's, was the first step on this staggering thousands miles journey which culminated in the March 26, 1979 Peace Treaty signbed at the White House. Begin's was the initiative which put in move the chain of events and his was the most tangible contribution to the irreversible peace process.

In addition to this historical breakthrough, the Israeli Prime Minister caused a number of changes in the lives of the people of Israel whose impact is reverberating through the whole Diaspora. Never before was world Jewry so united as in the present time, and united it is around, and because of, Israel.

The solidarity of American Jewry with Israel, always felt and expressed in many ways and forms, became absolute identification. Today world Jewry is not merely the most trusted, reliable ally of Israel, as the saying goes (can you speak of "allies" among the same people?). We are one.

Begin, by his exrtraordinary closeness to Jews everywhere (his "chemistry" acts in relation to every Jew. . .), by his Jewishness which is manifest on every occasion, by his extolling Jewish ideals and values, by his devotion to Jewish tradition and tenets, like Shabbat, Kashruth—strengthened enormously the links of Jews in the Diaspora, including Jews defined as secular ones, to Israel. This is understandable because the bonds of the Jewish people with the Holy Land are essentially rooted in Torah.

Religious LIfe Strengthened

This found practical expression in Israel and America. The substantial financial support for the Yeshivas contributed to make the country a center for Torah learning unequalled in any other country or in any other epoch. The present blossoming of Torah learning in Israel exceeds even the golden era of Yeshivas in Lithuania before the destruction of European Jewry.

The religious parties which, in the former government coalitions were minor partners, are now playing an important role in the State. It was no accident that the Prime Minister entrusted the leadership of the government during his absence for the Treaty signing to a religious minister (Zvulun Hammer, Minister for Education and Culture) or the appointment of another religious member of the Cabinet, the Interior Minister, Dr. Yossef Burg, as head of the Committee for the autonomy negotiation.

The fact that the Agudath Israel is a part of the present government coalition—with the advice and consent, and support of the Moetzeth Gedolei Hatorah, the great Rabbinical authorities in Israel and America—further underscores the attitude of Menachem Begin toward religion and religious Jews. While not all the demands of The Agudah were yet fulfilled, there is considerable progress in this area. During his visits in America the Prime Minister was received very warmly by the Rabbinical world leaders and organizations like the Lubavitcher Rebbe, Rabbi Moshe Feinstein, Rabbi Joseph Dov Soloveitchik, and others. I also recall the meaningful encounter years ago in our house, of Begin with prominent rabbis, religious leaders and educators, and the harmonious mutual understanding which came out of the dialogue at that time.

It is worth recalling a meaningful conversation with Mr. Begin a few years ago when I accompanied him to and from a parlor meeting in the home of the late Oscar Gruss on behalf of the religious schools of Agudath Israel "Chinuch Atzmai," with the participation of Rabbi Joseph Dov Soloveitchik. He praised religious education and deplored the ignorance, and as a result the estrangement, of large segments of youth from Jewishness. His interest and warm attitude toward religious education certainly wasn't a result only of the coalition agreement with Agudath Israel. It was rooted in his own education, knowledge and deep beliefs. When he became prime minister, these beliefs were translated into acts. Never did the Yeshivas get such support from the government like they obtained in the last two years.

While the present growth of the Yeshivas and their standing in the society cannot be attributed to a single factor, and Begin will be the last to take exclusive credit for it, the new government and what they they call "the new style" greatly enhanced the growth.

At this occasion this enromous increase in religious education in Israel may be noted. In 1948, at the founding of the State, there were in the country about 50 yeshivas with around 3,000 students. Presently, there are over 300 schools of higher Talmudic learning wuth more than 32,000 students. Israel became the greatest center of Torah learning. A considerable number of young students are attracted to these schools from countries the world over, and many are staying in Israel. The phenomenon is certainly enhanced by the attitude of the new head of the government. The whole atmosphere changed in the last two years. The fact that at the head of the country stands a man like Begin certainly contributed to this change.

Active Faith Encourages Daring Deeds

Begin's is an active faith, an active confidence in Divine Providence, BITACHON. It is not of the passive kind bordering with fatalism, which is strange to Judaism, but the sort of faith which encourages to daring *deeds*. We pray to the Almighty to bless our work but not to do it for us. . .

He raised Jewish dignity and strengthened Jewish pride, not only through his conduct of the State but also through his conduct of himself, by his deep attachment to the Jewish faith and tradition, to Jewishness. Rooted deeply in sacred Jewish values he is always aware of the context of current happenings within the larger scope of Jewish history, of the ancient and contemporary alike. The ingredients of his acts and the components of his policy are falling in place as part of a comprehensive world outlook.

In order to grasp the significance of these transformations which took place in a relatively short time of the last two years, we have to look back at the sources of his acts and their motives.

"A Brand Plucked From the Fire. . . ."

"A brand plucked from the fire" of the German slaughter of the Jews under their occupation in Europe, Begin came out from the depths below the depths pervaded with the horrendous suffering of his people which he soaked in like a sponge, and which stirred his soul with pain, compassion and anger never since forgotten.

However, he emerged from the abyss not crushed by despair but strengthened by determination. He confronted a cruel world which was divided in its attitude toward the Jews at the time of the German onslaught in two camps; one put them to death, the other refused them help to stay alive.

All the adjustments and adaptations by the Jews to the peoples among whom they dwelt, all their enormous contributions to the countries they inhabited for centuries did not gain them the right to live.

The indescribable catastrophe darkened the horizon but not the perception of Menachem Begin. His mind became even more lucid, his view more clairvoyant. Illusions disappeared but visions were not dimmed.

Begin, who like his great teacher Zeev Jabotinsky, harkened to the awful thunder of the erupting volcano, saw the terrible Jewish condition after the German mass murder. He alerted his people against acquiescence. He believed that to succumb to evil is evil.

The agony and anguish of the generation of the mass killings of the Jews was transformed by him into the cataclysm of the Revolt. His words sounded the clarion for the battle for freedom for the Jewish people and their land. "Shall a clarion be blown in the city and the people shall not tremble?" (Amos III, 6.)

They did. Begin's call aroused the people, molded idealistic youth into courageous phalanxes of self-sacrificing fighters for freedom, for the independence of the Jewish homeland.

On the Move. . .

Thus he reshaped his time, his people and his destiny. *He put Jewish history on the move.* Previously, others decided our destiny. We really did not act, only react—if and when we were able to. Begin reversed this situation. Since then from us came action, from the other side the reaction. Until the British were forced to leave Eretz Yisrael. And later on, since assuming the leadership of the government, his were the acts, his were the decisive steps which activated the peace process. Since the victorious Six Day War in

1867, Israel was somehow in a static position. No dynamic moves came out of Israel's efforts, as hard as the government may have tried.

May 17, 1977 transformed Israel's posture from a static to a *dynamic* one. Already during the election campaign Begin stated that if elected he will initiate a course which will eventually lead to peace. This was dismissed by adversaries as another election promise not to be taken too seriously.

However, Begin, as usual, meant what he said. As soon as he was raised to the helm he steered the ship of state toward achieving this goal, peace. His secret talks with the president of Romania, Ceaucescu, during his visit to Bucharest, led to the latter's mediation between him and President Sadat. The secret encounter of the Israeli Foreign Minister, Moshe Dayan with King Hassan of Morocco, was another effort for achieving peace. And there were other endeavors yet to be disclosed, which led eventually to Sadat's dramatic visit in Jerusalem in November 1977, and finally, to the signing of the Peace Treaty on March 26, 1979.

Another significant change occurred in the spiritual realm. Especially in relation to religious values and tenets. Begin, deeply rooted in traditional Jewishness with which he was imbued in his father's house and in his native town, Brisk, Lithuania–Poland, the famous center of Torah—created a new approach, a new atmosphere in the attitude toward religion. He envigored the Jewish conscientiousness, raised respect for religion and traditional Jewish values.

Some are calling this change somehow condescendingly, a new "style." It is more than "style." It is deep faith and strong conviction. It is the very essence of his innermost being.

It finds expression in his emphasizing spiritual religious factors during his appearances and words at momentous events.

Some leftist writers in Israel (not in the Diaspora) criticize his inclination to ceremonial acts, as they see it. Others, more malicious adversaries, accuse him of theatrical pose. Nothing is farther from the truth! I seldom met a man more sincere, more honest, more authentic than Menachem Begin. He is always himself.

When I used to greet him on his arrivals at Kennedy Airport before he assumed power, he radiated the same solemn dignity as in his official appearances. When I used to visit him in his modest three room apartment at 1 Rosenbaum Street in Tel Aviv, I experienced the same uplift as at his staying in the Blair House during a state visit. The dignity, the solemnity is in him, and not outside.

All this senseless criticism results from the failure to grasp the deeper significance of the unique acts which we witnesses in the last two years, and of the sublime moments we experienced at the historical events.

These moments are worthy of celebrating and preserving. Because to celebrate is to contemplate the *uniqueness* of the event, to revere the singularity of the moment and the profundity of its meaning which transcends the present time.

When we witnessed some of these acts, like the signing of the Peace Treaty, Begin's echoing at this act the Psalm 126 in original Hebrew, we shared in the spiritual uplift, we experienced a sort of personal partnership in these historical acts. Like certain other epochal events in our history, these too, are worthy of celebration by which we feel reverence and participation.

When an extraordinary event meets the singularity of the hour, sometimes it is the *finest hour* we experience, we are duty bound to celebrate in order to grasp the highher significance and to preserve the sharing in the act. We are then uplifted to the feeling of awe which puts us in rapport with higher reality, opens larger horizons and farther visions that range beyond the sphere of our view, into eternity. We have to be alert to marvelous happenings. We have to respond to their grandeur. You don't have to be particularly great in order to live great moments; it is enough that you happen to be there. The Talmud recounts that when the Jews went out of Egypt a maidservant saw more of the Revelation at the parting of the Red Sea than the prophet Yeheskel. How come? Quite simple, she was there. . .

Summing up the two years of the Begin Government of Israel, years of historical events, we may say: we were, we are, there. . . .

The Jewish Press, N.Y. June 1, 1979

I Discovered the Source of Menachem Begin's Strength

In order to know Menachem Begin well, one ought to know his only son, Benny. But it is not easily done. Benny shuns publicity. He avoids the limelight. (I still wonder how he manages never to appear in any picture with his father, or in any picture in the newspapers or TV for that matter, when so many others appear so often in both. . . .) Yet on a few occasions, I had the opportunity to penetrate his "retreat" and catch a glimpse of his hidden values, hidden beneath his natural modesty and self-imposed anonymity.

During my visit to Jerusalem in August, 1979, I was invited for supper to his home. Even Benny's address bore a special connotation and seemed to tell me something. Benny and his family live on a street called *Pirchei Chen*, which translates as Flowers of Charm, in a section aptly named *Yefe Nof*, Beauty of Landscape. (A person blessed with such a charming and beautiful family can afford such an address. . . .)

At the table for supper were the host and his wife, Ruthie, Mrs. Aliza Begin, just back from visiting her husband in the hospital, a doctor, a brother-in-law of Benny's, and myself. in one corner of the room, four of Benny's five (this was before the sixth was born) children (the oldest, Merav, was helping her mother) and Osnat (the daughter of Chasia Milo, Begin's daughter), were playing and occasionally arguing. Benny wanted to chase them into another room so that the adult conversation could continue undisturbed. As interested as I was in what the adults had to say, I begged Benny to let the children stay, and stationed myself at a convenient observation point so as to enjoy an unobstructed view of the kids.

I must admit, my attention was divided between the highly interesting discussion at the table and the not less interesting discussion literally on the floor, in addition to the delightful sight and sound of the children at play. They enchanted me with their beauty, charm and wisdom.

True, Israeli children, in general, cast a spell over me, especially those of Jerusalem. I may prejudiced in their favor, but I cannot pass them by without feasting my eyes on their looks, their walk and their talk. Small wonder that the Midrash devotes a special chapter to the wisdom of Jerusalemite children in ancient times. That praise is still valid in relation to the children in our time.

As I looked at the children, I observed a few of the special traits of each child. Merav, Michal, Yehonadav, Naama and Yonatan, and Chasia's daughter, Osnat. Later on, when their proud grandfather showed me the birthday cards and presents he received from them not long before, I saw those same distinctive features reflected in the various artworks by each child. I thought of Bialik's dictum: "There are no Jewish children—only little Jews." Yes, they are already little Jews, but they radiate the charm of children, combined with premature wisdom.

People will recall the special tenderness in Begin's voice whenever he mentions children in his yearning for an end to war, toiling and actively praying that peace secure children and grandchildren from the fate met by others like them either murdered en masse by the Germans in Europe. You may be sure that when he rises to defend the Jewish state and people, especially in the midst of the current offensive bout to undermine the peace process he initiated, he thinks of these children, and of ways to safeguard them against the dangers hovering over them.

Begin has a special rapport with children (and not only with his own). I remember an episode, a few years ago. Begin was in New York. It was a difficult period for him. When it was time for Begin to fly back home, I accompanied him to Kennedy Airport, as I had done many times in the past, before he became Prime Minister. There, he had prearranged to meet his daughter, Chasia, with her husband and their little girl. (Was it Osnat?) As soon as he saw them, he ran to his granddaughter and lifted her in his arms. At that moment he became a changed man. The signs of worry and sadness disappeared without a trace and were replaced by an unrestrained and, I'm tempted to say, childish joy and happiness. In a mood of enormous elation he repeated over and over again with his granddaughter: "*Nossim habaita, nossim habaita. . .* (We're going home.) I thought then to myself: *This is the real Begin*!

Another scene, which took place in January, 1952, during his protest against the agreement on German reparations. In the wake of a stormy demonstration in front of the Knesset (not against the Knesset!), an intentionally spread rumor had it that Begin was planning a "putsch" to topple the Ben-Gurion government by force and assume the rudder himself.

I happened to be in Tel Aviv the following day. In the vicinity of Rothschild Boulevard, whom did I see? The dangerous, "faschist putschist," leading, not a revolutionary column, but a bunch of tumultuous children, trying hard to keep the unruly group together and in line, without great success. His leadership failed him. It was his fault, too. Instead of barking orders and showing a firm hand, he was unable to suppress his affection for his charges. Instead of a deserved slap, I saw a tender caress on a lovely, little head. Only two or three children were his; the others were strangers' children. But is there such a thing for Begin as a strange child? (I suspect that his fondness for Amy Carter was an element of the "chemistry" between Begin and the President.)

Later I discovered that the neighbors on Rosenblum Street, where he lived, had arranged that a pool of parents take turns getting the children to kindergarten and, on that day, it was Menachem Begin's turn to fulfill his parental function.

As for myself, after having heard Begin's inspired and sometimes fiery speeches, and after I studied his writings and what was written of him, and after my conversations with him, I said to myself once again: this is the true Begin. . . .

So, when at Benny's home, someone raised the question—where does he get the strength to withstand the pressure, to repel the forces against peace and to pursue his aims with such energy?—I thought to have discovered at least one major source of his strength: his children and grandchildren, in addition to his faith, of course.

Later on, during the ride back home, I mentioned this to Mrs. Begin and anticipated the answer I would give her should she ask the obvious question—what was the source of his strength before they were born, during his fight in the underground? I had my answer ready: You. Regrettably, she did not ask. Begin himself acknowledged his debt to her on the memorable night of his victory, may 17, 1977. "I do remember the kindness of thy youth, how thou didst follow me in the wilderness, in a land sown with mines. (So he paraphrased Yeremiyahu II,2.)

In Benny's home, at the table, they were discussing the bitter and often savage attacks in the press against Begin. Quoting Reb Nachman Braslaver who said that his enemies were not attacking *him* but an image of him created by their fantasy, I remarked that this was the case with the Prime Minister as well. Ruthie Begin interjected at this point, that even people friendly to Begin don't really know him. She mentioned that some of the authors of books about Begin who never met him, certainly didn't know him sufficiently, let alone understand him or his policies and ideas. "They don't know Daddy," she concluded. (I was touched by the affectionate way she pronounced Daddy, indicating so much love and admiration.)

When Geula Cohen was mentioned, Benny remarked that when she criticizes his father, it is her right, of course, but when she insults him, calling him a cheat, she destroys herself. "No one will believe her when she says Father is a liar," he said. Pained as he was, understandably, over Geula Cohen's accusations, he was concerned about what she was doing to herself. It is just such nuances that give us a glimpse of the nobility of Benny's private self. For Benny is a remarkable personality in his own right.

When Benny was a student of geology for a few years at a university in Colorado, I asked Rabbi Shlomo Twersky of Denver to invite him for the holidays. Benny and his wife spent the holidays with the Twerskys, and brought along a few other Israeli students to the gracious home and shul of the charismatic, deep-thinking scion of the famous Hassidic dynasty. As the intermediary, Rabbi Twersky "reported" to me on his impression of Benny. "He possesses greatness but it still has to come out," said the rabbi-psychologist. "He did not use or display even a fraction of his potential."

In an encounter with Benny, in my room, during my stay in Jerusalem last August, together with some people from the Academy (Professors Bernard Lander, Jacob J. Hartstein, Marvin Schick and others, as well as Rabbis Pesach Levovitz and Meyer Fund), a sophisticated discussion took place concerning both the internal and external problems facing Israel. Every one of the guests was impressed by the calibre of the young Begin.

Benny is something of an introvert. You have to discover him, force him out of his studied anonymity. Possessed of absolute intellectual integrity, he is also extremely honest in thought, word and deed. His thoughts are profound, his power of analysis remarkable, his eloquence in both Hebrew and English impressive. He expresses his thoughts and opinions in succinct terms, in a way that leaves no ambiguity. Benny avoids ornamental flourishes, inflated rhetoric, and superfluous elaboration. He speaks in matter-of-fact, precise, almost mathematical terms. The highest ideals of Judaism motivate him. All this lends his talks, both private and public, a special significance, grace and force. Benny's is a natural simplicity, an unassuming restraint. His uncompromising truthfulness and unobtrusive decency mirror his father's. But when the exigencies of the elder Begin's high office constrains natural simplicity, the younger Begin's ease and humility come through unhindered.

One needn't be a prophet to foresee that Benny's extraordinary qualities and talents will, in and of themselves, force him out of this restraint and catapult him, perhaps against his plans, into the upper strata of public service and national leadership.

The Jewish Press, N.Y. October 19, 1979

Exchange of Opinions Between Professor Dr. S. M. Lipset and Dr. Hillel Seidman

Dear Editor:

On September 3, you published an article by Dr. Hillel Seidman, which refers to me, among others. Since as a resident of California I do not see your paper regularly, I hope that Dr. Seidman's inaccuracies are not typical of your contents. Among his errors are his statement that "Lipset joined other writers and published an advertisement in the San Francisco Chronicle." The advertisement it referred to is one that I did not sign. If Dr. Seidman can find my name among the signators, I will gladly contribute a thousand dollars to any charity he names. Further, I would note that Seidman identifies me as one of a "troika of Harvard professors." I am a professor at Stanford University, not Harvard.

Dr. Seidman claims that my friend, Nathan Glazer, "supports the PLO." Although I cannot claim to have read everything Glazer has written, I know him well. He has been a lifelong Zionist from the days of the early 40s, when he and I belonged to Avukah, the then student Zionist society. Glazer opposes the PLO as do I. What displeases Dr. Seidman is that we believe Menachem Begin's policies are bad for Israel.

Since Dr. Seidman questions my Jewish and Zionist credentials, may I note that on January 8, 1982, the Senate of the Hebrew University voted me an honorary doctorate. part of their citation reads: "A proud Jew, Professor Lipset has actively identified himself with Jewish causes in the United States and with organizations working on behalf of Israel." I happen to be a national officer of the United Jewish Appeal, the B'nai B'rith Hillel Commission, and the American Professors for Peace in the Middle East. I have also served as a consultant, or on commissions, for the American Jewish Committee, the Anti-Defamation league and the World Jewish Congress. I am a member of more other Jewish and Zionist organizations than you would care to list.

Prof. Seymour Martin Lipset —Stanford U., Stanford, Calif.

Dr. H. Seidman Replies:

I gladly correct, and apologize for, the factual errors in my article "Senator Moynihan Stands by Much Maligned Israel" (*The Jewish Press*, September 3, 1982), concerning Professor Seymour Martin Lipset, an eminent scholar, some of whose books and other writings I have read with pleasure and appreciation.

Regretfully, I cannot say the same about his latest article in *The New York Times*. i would like to believe, in view of Prof. Lipset's forceful denial, that his signature on the San Francisco Chronicle ad was falsified. However, as part of its vicious campaign against Israel, *Newsweek* (July 12, 1982) reprinted excerpts of the ad, placed photographs of Nat Hentoff and Prof. Lipset above it, and inserted the caption: "Hentoff and Lipset, ad in San Francisco Chronicle: Anguished responses to an age-old Jewish dilemma." The article itself states that "They (American Jews) have begun to express their opposition in full-page newspaper ads, at silent vigils and by forming humanitarian relief efforts for the Lebanese victims. Their cause has been highlighted by a number of Jewish intellectuals, including Nathan Glazer, Seymour Martin Lipset and Nat Hentoff." Yet Prof. Lipset did not issue a denial.

As a Zionist, it was Prof. Lipset's duty to ask *Newsweek* for a retraction, so that his name would not be used against Israel—if we may assume that a Zionist against Israel is a *contradictio in adjecto*. We reject the argument that the attacks are directed only against the Israeli government; in this case, they damage the State, whatever the original intentions may have been.

Noblesse oblige. Given the Merits of Prof. Lipset's past activities for the State of Israel, which were duly recognized and rewarded with well deserved honors, Prof. Lipset should have desisted from joining the choir of some American Jewish intellectuals denouncing the Israeli government—at laest at this time and place.

What is this time? And what is this place?

An unscrupulous, hypocritical campaign is raging against Israel and against Jews everywhere. This campaign is waged by a bizarre alliance. Among its partners and collaborators: the Kremlin and the Church; backward, tyrannical regimes such as Lybia and Saudi Arabia and European democracies; the Socialist International with a host of tycoons and capitalist manipulators; and hypocritic preachers of human rights. Among them one also hears the shameless but vociferous voice of Germany, the perpetrators of the most abominable mass murders in the annals of mankind. Feigning compassion, the latter are in the forefront of the uproar.

This lynch mob is disguised in diplomacy, and the media were given free reign to run amuck, threatening the security of the Jewish State and people.

When people define themselves as Zionists but join in the denunciation of Israel (as in the case of Rabbi Arthur Hertzberg), they help, unconsciously or even consciously, the enemies of Israel.

No one denies Prof. Lipset past merits in furthering Zionism, least of all this writer. But his present actions raise the following questions:

Is it possible to be a Zionist and act in a way detrimental to Israel?

How far does the right of criticism go, and is it justified or warranted in all situations, in all circumstances, and in all places at all times?

How does one distinguish between criticizing the government and between causing damage to the country?

In time of stress and danger such as these, when Israel is the target of a worldwide hate rge, aren't some self-imposed restrictions required from Zionists? The present government was democratically elected and is supported by a growing majority; it is identified with the people it leads. Besides, the enemies of the present Israeli government are and will be opposed to any government that refuses to submit to extortion by unjustified pressure. Arafat, the Kremlin, the Vatican, the Arab states, the Arabists in the State Department, and their satellites and manipulators, did not start their nefarious attacks with the advent of the Begin government, or as a result of the Lebanese war.

In a period of national emergency, the hateful, vicious attacks must uield to the higher exigency of the life of the nation, which could be jeopardized when the aforementioned privileges are pushed to their irrational limits. A sense of responsibility for the security of the State should restrict the absolute freedom of expression in order to prevent dangers to the beleaguered country. The most democratic nations, such as Britain, France, and the United States have recognized these limitations and in their legislature and practice.

The Jewish Press, N.Y. November 19, 1982

The Begin Era: Finale or Intermission?

We celebrate Menachem Begin's 71st birthday at the end of the Begin era. For the first time since he became in 1942 the commandant of the Irgun Tzvai Leumi, "Etzel," he is not commanding, fighting, leading, exhorting and inspiring.

But is it really the end of the Begin era?

This is a question which worries countless people of his followers, adherents, admirers and the general public. We refuse to give up the hope for his comeback from his puzzling "retirement." Either way it is certainly not the end of the Begin epoch, but rather a new beginning. It had been assumed that the movement he founded and led, rested on his person, on his leadership alone, but the recent elections proved otherwise. The results demonstrated that his struggle and work, first against the British mandatory regime in Palestine, then at the head of the main parliamentary opposition, and since May 17, 1977, at the helm of the Israeli government, created durable values, powers, ideas, outlooks, world views. They outlive the personal leadership of the creator.

He also *transformed the very sociological fabric and political structure* of the State of Israel. Thus he is entitled to say with the Roman poet Horatius: Exegi monumentum aere perennius (I created a monument overlasting bronze).

It is, therefore, proper to have a look at the man and his works. Inasmuch as no other leader was so misrepresented, maligned and attacked, like Begin. Ever since he became leader of the opposition, a propaganda apparatus was in full gear, defaming him. But the vulgar vilification, the insolent, indecent, inglorious, ignominious incriminations which deluged the Israeli press during the last seven years, and especially during the last election campaign, aimed at Likud and its leader, staggers the imagination. Dr. Herzl Rosenbaum, the editor of the Hebrew daily Yediot Achronot, defined the scurrilous onslaught as "pogrom" saying:

"During the Likud government all the Israeli newspapermen, left, right and in the middle, (with exception) led an unprecedented, unbridled hatred crusade against the Likud. The poison cast upon Begin and then on Shamir by our journalists (spanning the political rainbow) has no equal in our country. Character assassination, cynicism and hatred were intertwined.

The result: zero. The people read it and threw it all in the garbage. Witness: the election results. The people did not accept the theses of the journalists, that preferred the pen-pogrom over the duty to quiet down the devastating polarization" (Yediot Achronot, July 27, 1984).

The Wrong Target

The unbridled accusations are directed against the wrong target. Against the image that these attackers, sick with pathological hatred, created in their perverse fantasy. As Rabbi Nachman of Braslav said:

"Those who attack me are not attacking me. They are attacking someone they created in their fantasy. He deserves it."

The same with Menachem Begin. There is not resemblance whatever between the man and the "image." Nor is the criticism leveled against him relevant to his aims and actions. It is a case of deliberate and malicious creation of "mistaken identity."

It is the result of ignorance, and loathful malice projecting an utterly distorted picture of the man's character, beliefs and deeds.

When an attempt is made to slander a righteous man, he is maligned on the most farfetched groundsL in what he is most irreproachably pure. A telling example of such irony is provided by Moses, of whom the Torah says: "And the man Moses was very humble, more than any man on the face of the earth." (Numbers XII.iii). Yet when Korach attacked Moses, of what did he accuse him? "Why art thou so overbearing against the community of the L-rd?" (Numbers XVI.iii).

Begin is one of the worlds' greatest orators. But the strength of his word is not merely a masterly eloquence but of moral passion and human compassion.

During Begins's years as an underground figher, a well-oiled propaganda machine used all the means at its disposal to depict him as the embodiment of everything evil. This hatred of him frequently reached the depths of obsession.

What Brought Me To Begin?

In a letter by Begin to me (October 16, 1963), he writes:

"I know what you went through in the years when our people were assassinated by the cruel German murderers. Therefore, I cherish the evaluation you are guarding in your heart and expresses with your gifted pen of our efforts in Israel in the underground, in order to bring out our people from slavery into freedom, and to assure that no enemy will be able to raise a hand on a Jewish child.

"Since we met, after the catastrophe and with the emergence of the State, a true friendship developed between us, not dependent on any ulterior motive; its source is in our identical perception of faith in the redemption of our people and in its future."

There was a significant difference between the attitude of Begin's political allies and the deep attachment, and even love, manifest in the people. The more sophisticated political leaders and commentators (unlike the rank and file) often lack true understanding of Menachem Begin's personality and of his ideas and goals.

Everyone "knows" Menachem Begin, but very few understand him. He is famous, perhaps one of the most famous men of the day, yet at the same time, his true character, his essence, greatness, remains almost unknown. His name is on everyone's tongue, but his ideas and ideals are often misunderstood, his very ways and manners misinterpreted, his goals and intentions—distorted. Yet the people do understand Begin. They trust the man, his honest intentions, and his lofty aims.

"You Liberated!"

Begin told me once, at the time of his being Prime Minister, that the most cherished years of his life will always remain the time of his underground fight for the liberation of the Jewish homeland.

No one could, or can, deny the historical merits of the Labor movement, of the chalutzim (pioneers), for the creation of the Jewish State, nor could we underestimate the armed struggle of the Haganah-Palmach.

I for one, look at the history of the emergence of 50 new states after World War II; not a single one achieved independence as a result of speeches, newspaper articles, appeals to justice, negotiations, etc. There was an armed struggle everywhere.

But let me quote an avowed adversary of Etzel, Dr. Ezriel Carlebach, one of the most famous and gifted journalists. On May 17, 1948, two days after the proclamation of Israel's Independence, he wrote in the Tel Aviv Daily, *Maariv*, which he edited, an article inder the heading: "To Menachem Begin."

. . . *You, Menachem Begin, liberated us.* Your struggle delivered us. Because it was only the language of open rebellion that the British understood. Millions of Jewish men, women and children were murdered—and the world was not moved. Thousands upon thousands of Jews suffered, disappeared, in concentration camps—and the world was silent. Pleas, memoranda, diplomatic actions, did not move hearts of stone. But your language, that of bombs exploding in the King David Hotel and in the Acre fortress, that language was understood by the Gentiles.

"*You* liberated us!"

Bernard Baruch Supported Etzel

Let us add that Jews, too, understood this language, even such as Bernard Baruch. An advisor to presidents, a man of powerful influence, Baruch had never displayed even minimal interest in Jewish affairs. Even when millions of his coreligionists were murdered, Baruch did not act. Yet when Ben Hecht approached Baruch on behalf of Etzel with an appeal for arms, Baruch visited Hecht, then ill in the hospital, and personally donated a very substantial sum for Menachem Begin's revolt. The armed fight for Jewish State, for Jewish existence—was grasped by even such assimilated Jews as Ben Hecht and Bernard Baruch.

Myth and Reality

Another proof that the false myth of Begin created malevontly by his enemies is the extreme opposite of the real man; his efforts for peace resulting in Camp David and in the Israeli-Egyptian Peace Treaty of March 26, 1979. The relentless warrior, the extremist fighter pursued the lofty aim of peace with all his soul, and paid an enormous price for achieving his goal.

All the adjustment and adoption by the Jews to the peoples among whom they dwelt for centuries did not gain them the right to live.

The catastrophe darkened the horizon but not the perception of Menachem Begin. His mind became more lucid, more clairvoyant. His thought turned inward. His view of the world grew more penetrating and realistic. Illusions disappeared but visions were not dimmed.

Like his great teacher, Ze'ev Jabotinsky, Begin harkened to the awful thunder of the erupting volcano. He drew the conclusions. He alerted the Jewish people to the new dangers and warned against acquiescence. He believed that to succumb to evil is evil.them

He defied injustice and challenged its power. He threw himself with almost bare fists against the great might of the British Empire which was waging war against the remnants of the mass killings, who were striving for a home in their Jewish homeland.

The anguish and agony of a generation was transformed by him into the cataclysm of Revolt. His words sounded the clarion for the battle of freedom for the Jewish people and their land. "Shall the clarion be blown in the city and the people shalkl not tremble?" (Amos III,6). They did. Begin's call molded idealistic youth into phalanxes of self-sacrificing fighters. Thus he reshaped his time, his people and its destiny.

New Directions

He gave new directions to the course of Jewish history. Not once, but four times. By his *Revolt*. By winning the trust of the Nation which put him *at its helm*. By opening the gates of *peace*. By *emancipating the Sephardi Jews*.

In each of these endeavors, he was on the side of the future. He made the future happen. At the same he was always moved by the spirit of the glorious past, its ideals and visions.

According to Hassidic teaching, Redemption is not a single event. It is a continuation of purposeful deeds. Each may be an act in the drama. Begin's acts are certainly a central part of this drama.

Menachem Zion

The tornado whirlwind of our turbulent epoch hurled him four decades ago to the rudder of the Revolt for Jewish statehood. It brought him through the admirable working of the Israeli democratic process, to the helm, as the new pilot steering the ship of state toward peace.

Begin told me that when the late Chief Rabbi I. Herzog appealed to him (then in underground) for freeing British officers detained by Etzel, he addressed him: "Menachem Zion," "The solace (comforter) of Zion."

At his Shabbat Nachamu birthday our hearts go out to him, and our wishes and prayers go out for him, for his return to good health, and to the helm of our people as Menachem Zion.

The Jewish Press, N.Y. August 17, 1984

Avalanche of New Attacks Against Menachem Begin

An enormous ugly wave of vicious vilification of Menachem Begin is presently deluging Israel, and is about to overflow abroad, and especially in the United States. Until now the attacks on Begin were committed by certain journalists dominating the press in a measure out of proportion to their importance as representatives of the public.

Lately they realized that their nefarious campaign has only an ephemeral influence, if any. Their attacks had at most a momentary effect, lasting no more than the paper where they were published. Their impact on the public, in terms of opinion molding or influencing, were nil, as proved by the results of the elections in 1977, 1981 and 1984.

Their writing ability—a few were in command of genuine talent—did not make up for their lack of credibility.

Therefore, the frustrated implacable enemies of Begin and of what he stands for, decided to venture with their defamatory calumnies into the book market. They camouflaged their abusive, hateful prejudices with pseudo-research and amateurish politico-psychoanalysis, hoping for better resonance and more lasting effects.

In a short span of time no less than five books appeared in Israel and elsewhere whose common denominator is denigration of Menachem Begin, distorting his ideas and acts, and their meaning and impact on the people of Israel and world Jewry.

The most insidious of the volumes is one in Hebrew called, *Begin in Power* by Teddy Preuss (Keter, Jerusalem, 1984) of the Hebrew Socialist daily, *Davar*. Let us note, by the way, that this paper itself is in general relatively more restrained in its criticism of Begin, especially so since the 1984 election campaign. Partly because of the fear of provoking an adverse reaction to the electorate, whose majority respects Begin, to say the least. The malicious slanders and slurs amassed by the author exceed even the widldest

attacks against Begin in the decades when he was the target of furious frenzied hate of the left in Israel and of anti-Semites abroad.

Accumulation of Slanders

Preuss accumulated the most outrageous slanders by a lunatic fringe
committed since decades. Begin-baiting became for him an obsessive fixation. With this cluster of rehashed assaults he is running amock with hate
and defamation.

Every thought and word, every deed and event in Begin's glorious life is
twisted surreptitiously into just the opposite of the reality.

Every value and valor, every goodness and gentleness, every grace and
gallantry of this superb human being (even as the author is forced to admit
some) is misintepreted and misrepresented.

Mr. Preuss doesn't find a single positive trait in Begin's multifaceted
preson and activities. The great leadert of contemporary Jewry, admired and
venerated by so many, is for him the embodiment of evil.

As Rav Nachman of Braslav said: "The ones who attack me are really not
attacking me, only the man whose image they created. And he deserves
it. . . ."

Mr. Preuss, and to a lesser degree other adversaries of teh Heruth leader,
are working furiously on creating "his" image in such a way that it will appear as the extreme contrast of the real man.

Summarizing, Preuss quotes from Ben-Gurion's letter to Moshe Sharett
of May 21, 1963: "I have no doubt that the rule of Begin will bring the
destruction of the State." The author concludes that Ben-Gurion's warning
"is not far from becoming a reality. . . ."

The Attacks Transferred to America

I am told that the author is approaching important publishing houses in
the U.S. and Britain to issue English translations of this book, and similar
books on Begin.

The other volumes in the same vein, although less hateful and nasty (but
no less poisonous) are *Begin* (London, 1984 English) by Eric Silver, a
former Jerusalem correspondent of the *Guardian*, the English daily un-
friendly to Israel, and *Turmoil* by A, Schweitzer (Hebrew. Shocken, Tel
Aviv, 1984), an editor of *Haaretz*, the Hebrew daily in Tel Aviv known for
its very negative attitude toward Begin and his ideology.

Other books in Hebrew dealing with the Lebanon war such as *War of
Deception* by Ze'ev Schiff and Ehud Yaari (Jerusalem, 1984), and *Snowball*
by Shimon Schiffer (Jerusalem, 1984), contain very sharp accusations
against Begin and even more on General Ariel Sharon.

In addition, it was announced in *Maariv* on October 17, 1984 that Leon Wieseltier, the literary editor of *The New Republic*, formerly an Israeli writer (by the way, a Brooklyn-born son of Holocaust survivors), and close to the Peace Now group, is also working on a book on Begin. Some of his pronouncements indicate the tenor of his book: "What damage Begin caused to Israel. . ." "Begin freed att the indomitable forces."

The Unbridled Hate Campaign

Add to these the unbridled hate assaults on Begin during the last few years by writers (mostly of *Yedioth Achronoth*) like Amos Kenon, Chaim Hefer, Aaron Brecher, Silvi Kesheth, Ziva Yariv, Amos Oz and others, and you'll realize what an avalanche of malicious defamations is polluting the atmosphere and poisoning the political climate, just when a quieting down of passions and conflicts is presently taking place in Israel.

Against the New Style of Unity

It is even more upsetting and astonishing that this happens at a time when the leaders of both Labor and Likud embarked on a policy of unity, of mutual understanding and harmonious cooperation in the Government of National Unity. The new Prime Minister, Shimon Peres, spoke convincingly of the New Style of moderation and collaboration, and his deputy Itzhak Shamir contributes his share to this change in the political climate. At present the bitterness has evaporated and instead there are emerging friendly relations, and even a kind of "chemistry" between former adversaries and present partners in common efforts.

The new offensive against Begin is therefore more puzzling and more distressing.

What Is the Purpose?

Begin is at present no longer active. He distanced himself completely from political life; he isolated himself. What, then, prompted these writers to wage an implacable war against him? What moved them to such savage verbal assaults bordering on character assassination?

In short range this may be a result of inertia, of going on with the routine of decades which turned into a compulsory habit of which they are unable or unwilling to free themselves.

Their Aim: Distort Begin's Place In History

However, the intensity and frequency of these assaults indicate that there is something more to this. They are obviously aiming at perverting Begin's role in the State of Israel, and his place in history.

Through this, they intend to destroy the enormous impact of his ideas and acts, of his struggle and leadership which formed and transformed the people of Israel, and inspired and influenced Jews the world over and, by the way, to destroy the Likud.

The public should be made aware, warned and alerted to it.

The Jewish Press, N.Y. December 2, 1984

Benny, Vidi, Vici...

The emergence of Dr. Ze'ev Binyamin Begin
on the political scene of the State of Israel

Benny, Vidi, Vici! (I saw, I won), one may attrribute Caesar's famous announcement to Dr. Ze'ev Binyamin Begin, after the latter's recent appearance.

Dr. Binyamin Begin, who insists on being called Benny, was the guest of honor and the principal speaker on December 19, 1985 in Tel-Aviv, at mass celebration of the 60th anniversary of the founding by Ze'ev Jabotinsky of the Revisionist Movement which became Herut.

His emergence in the current political debate in Israel, his lucid comprehensive address evoked lively interest and praise in many quarters. He struck a new and refreshing note when he warned: "Beware of mystics! You don't notice them. They are smartly dressed, well established, seated in comfortable offices and produce memorandums. However, whoever believes that King Hussein, wants or is able to, transfer territories of *Eretz Yisrael* to the Jews is a mystic! Our Israel is based on two things: our historical right to *Eretz Yisrael*, and our power to implement it. There is no chance for peace without Jewish sovereignty on Yehuda and Shomron. On this we have to insist openly and vigorously without hesitation and defeatism.

"Some are solemnizing the green line, the imaginable border between Yehuda and Shomron and the other parts of Israel. They are talking against strength. This is powerlessness. This goes against Jewish history, against the Jewish moral foundations."

Yaacov Meridor, former minister and Chief of the Irgun Tzvai Leumi, who passed the command in 1943 to Menachem Begin, solemnly proclaimed after Dr. Begin's speech: "We pass the command to the new generation!"

I Congratulated Menachem Begin

The response was enthusiastic. I called Menachem Begin afterwards to congratulate him on his son "going public." The older Mr. Begin wasn't unhappy with the event. . . As a matter of fact, I had seldom found him in such an upbeat mood.

Dr. Begin's view is a new way of presenting Israel's cause and case to the world, and to the Israelis themselves.

While Dr. Begin is a member of Herut he is not a partisan stalwart, and certainly not an organization man. His way of thinking is not of a politician, but of a statesman. Not surprisingly not unlike his father.

Maybe some of the bickering factions in his party are either hopeful that he could be enlisted in their ranks, or afraid of his joining the opponents' camp. Knowing the man, I am predicting that both sides are bound to be disappointed.

His thinking is just not partisan and certainly not sectarian. This is an outcome of both his character and of his education—at home and school.

New Way of Presenting The Cause and Case of Israel

Dr. Begin does not defend Israel; he merely states its case. He does it in a matter-of-fact manner, without apology but also without arrogance. His is not on the defensive nor does he attack. He describes the situation factually, quietly, expertly. There is a solemn serenity in his presentation, yet it is vivid with the dynamic events described and it sparkles with subtle humor.

Benny does not attempt to argue, interpret or explain. He simply renders a true picture of the realities and the resulting conclusions are reached on the basis of common sense and of the veracity of the man and his words.

Another singularity of Benny's is his avoidance of verbosity which is the trademark of most speakers and the affliction of their listeners. Being perfectly in command of English, he excels at stripping his presentations of all trimmings and embellishments, reducing them to essentials.

Thus it would be no exaggeration to claim that a star spokesman for Israel was born—except that he is not keen on "starring". . . But his sense of responsibility and dedication to his people and country may yet force him to relinquish part of his treasured privacy—at least for a while—to enter the forum of serious debate so as to elucidate the problems facing the embattled, beleaguered State of Israel.

The Jewish Press, N.Y. January 17, 1986

40 Years After the Bombing of the King David Hotel In Jerusalem By Etzel

Historical events rarely result from a single act. They are usually the outcome of many factors which combine in complicated processes to produce results. One can understand, then, the frequent disputes and differences of opinions as to which of the multiple causes or components of a certain event was the decisive one. The Rabbis settled the question thus: In Talmudic Law, the responsibility for commiting certain transgressions rests with the one who "struck the final blow of the hammer" (Makeh BePatish).

We are not looking back now at the millenia of Jewish history where the dream of a Jewish State, in whatever form, was constantly alive. We are focusing on the events immediately preceding the emergence of the State of Israel. With the perspective of forty years of research and hindsight, from the evidence of the events which ensued, we must come to the following inevitable and undisputable conclusion:

The decisive factor in the creation of the State of Israel was the armed struggle by the Irgun Tzvai Leumi (Etzel) against the British Mandate Government in Palestine, a struggle which reached its peak on July 22, 1946, with the bombing of the English Administrative Headquarters at the King David Hotel.

If I were asked to pinpoint the exact moment at which the State of Israel became possible, if not inevitable, I would say: July 22, 1946, at 12:37 p.m. when the explosion crushed the southwest wing of the King David Hotel, burying the seat of the British Mandate Government in rubble.

Rabbi Aryeh Levine, the *Tzaddik* of Jerusalem, repeatedly comforted imprisoned Etzel members with these words: "G-d's help comes in the blink of an eye." Some historical reversals, even very major ones, take only a short while. The Viennese Jewish writer Stephen Zweig titled one of his books *The Star Hours of Humanity (Die Sternenstunden der Menschheit)*. In the struggle for the Jewish State, 12:37 p.m., July 22, 1946 was the "star hour" or more precisely the "star moment" of our destiny.

On July 22, 1986, at 6:37 a.m. New York time, 12:37 p.m. Israel time, I telephoned the man who had been the Commander of Etzel on July 22, 1946 to congratulate him on the 40th anniversary of that fiery flash. Mr. Menachem Begin was glad that someone overseas had recalled the event. Yet this date should have been engraved in the memories of all Jewish people as the anniversary of one of the most crucial events in our history. It happened this way: Amichai (Giddi) Paglin, the main planner and organizer of the deed, had seven milk cans stuffed with high-power TNT delivered to the basement kitchen of the hotel in a truck. At 12:37, the milk containers were detonated. The huge explosion shook the city. The entire southwest wing crumbled, one story crashing into the next in a roar of collapsing masonry and woodwork.

Over the deafening noise of the crumbling walls, ceilings and floors could be heard the screams of the trapped and injured. With a final tremendous crash the whole Secretariat General was turned into a pile of rubble, 91 people were killed, 41 wounded, among them British, Jews and Arabs. British rule in Palestine, dominated by the brutal anti-Semitic Foreign Secretary, Ernest Bevin, and the vicious regime of Prime Minister Clement Attlee, virtually collapsed with the collapse of its headquarters.

With the publication of documents and research concerning this period, certain factors have come to light. Now we know, for instance, that brutal anti-Semitism governed British policy in Palestine. We also know the decisive impact of the hotel bombing on the decision of London to quit Palestine. On July 28, six days after the bombing, Winston Churchill, then the opposition leader, asked the House of Commons: "What more has to happen that we should get out of the mess the Attlee policy caused?"

Another important issue which has since been completely clarified is the Etzel's efforts and measures to avoid casualties. Today there is no doubt that Etzel issued a triple warning a half hour before the assault, allowing enough time to evacuate the hotel. One warning was telephoned to the hotel, a second to the Jerusalem daily Palestine Post, and a third to the nearby French Consulate. But Sir John Shaw, the Secretary General of the Government to whom the warnings were immediately conveyed, rejected the evacuation with these words: "I am here to give orders to the Jews and not to take orders from them."

Begin, who was, of course, glued to the radio listening to the reports of the bombing was deeply shocked and grieved to hear of the casualties. He thought, with horror, that they were the result of some oversight or neglect by his people in issuing the warnings. Chaim Landau, who was with Begin at the time, disconnected the radio receiver and told Begin that the radio had stopped working, in his worry at Begin's extreme, almost physical pain because of the victims.

Even later when the Etzel members had convinced Begin that the casualties were not their fault, and that they had sent the warnings on time, Begin still could not regain peace of mind. In fact he never recovered from his gloom at the loss of human lives in the bombing. We, who can share his distress over these deaths, should nevertheless not permit our grief to obscure the enormous significance of the deed and to recognize it as the determining force generating the later developments which eventually led to the emergence of the Jewish State.

When I called Begin exactly forty years after the bombing, I couldn't help but express my regret that the import of his climactic event in the struggle for the liberation of *Eretz Yisrael* wasn't sufficiently understood and acknowledged.

Begin agreed. He spoke again of the pain caused by the loss of lives, which Etzel did everything possible to avoid, a pain which obscured his own appreciation of the act.

Today, forty years later, even the most sensitive awareness of the sanctity of human life cannot obscure our perception that the men who bombed the King David Hotel and their leader struck that decisive blow of the hammer at the British rule in Palestine. Let us finally give these people the praise due to them.

The Jewish Press, N.Y. September 19, 1986

The Begin Era Did Not End

At the 74th birthday of Menachem Begin, *Erev Shabbath Nachmu*, (born August 1913), and ten years after he came to power as head of the Government of Israel, May 17, 1977, it is proper to look back at his years at the helm of the Jewish State.

In the present turmoil of noisy discussions and disputes, conflicts and confrontations, Begin's stewardship tends to be dimmed and its significance obscured, either by human forgetfulness or on purpose—by his adversaries and detractors.

It is therefore necessary, for the sake of historical truth, and for learning a lesson, to direct our gaze at the Begin era which basically did not yet end; its imprint on the country is of lasting durability.

In five areas Menachem Begin changed the course of Jewish history. One before the emergence of the State and four afterwards. Let us recall them here in very brief summary.

The Revolutionary Revolt

Jews in the Diaspora were the object of history, and not its subject. Other peoples interests, wills, goals, dominated our life. We had to submit to them. We had to adjust ourselves to them. We had to react whenever we were able to.

Menachem Begin, by his armed revolt against the British Mandate government in Palestine, (which waged a cruel war against the martyred Jewish remnants of the German mass killngs) for the first time since the loss of independence of the Jewish State, fought the enemy. He fought not with statements and articles, not with one-sided "negotiations" which were in fact dictates by Ernest Bevin, or with futile appeals to consciousness, to humanitarian sensitivity of the English rulers, but with bombs and bullets.

For the first time Jews literally fought the enemy. Courageously, heroically—and victoriously.

The British were forced out by the Irgun Tzvai Leumi (Etzel) of the Mandate they misused against the Jews and their homeland.

Of course, there were also other forces which fought them. It is far from us to diminish their historical glory, but Begin's was the decisive role.

Begin told me once, at the time of his being Prime Minister, that the most cherished years of his life will always remain the time of his underground fight for the liberation of the Jewish homeland.

No one should, or can, deny the historical merits of the Labor movement, of the chalutzim (pioneers), for the creation of the Jewish State, nor could we underestimate the armed struggle of the Haganah and the Palmach.

I, for one, look at the history of the emergence of 50 new states after World War II; not a single one achieved independence as a result of speeches, newspaper articles, appeals to justice, negotiations, etc. There were armed struggles everywhere.

Peace With Egypt

Begin,who was decried as a war monger, achieved peace with Egypt. True, there are shortcomings in the implementation, but better a flawed peace that a perfect war.

Emancipation Of Sephardic Jewry

One of the great, indeed, historical achievements of Menachem Begin, was the emancipation fo the Sephardic Jews.

However, this feat of his was so distorted and twisted by hostile journalists, writers and politicians, that it was turned into another trumped up charge against him. Instead of the praise he deserved he was blamed for the antagonism between the Ashkenazi and Sephardi Jews.

When the latter thronged to Begin during the Knesset elections in 1977, 1981, 1984, as a way of protest against their treatment by the ruling Labor party, Begin was accused of "polarizing" the two groups, of "inflaming the mob" as the leftist contemptuously called "those Jews." But the truth is that this Jew from Brisk in Poland felt very close to the Jews of Morocco and Iraq, of Yemen and Algeria, in fact to every Jew. The closeness was mutual. The downtrodden Sephardic Jews saw in Begin a friend, a defender and leader. They flocked to him at the Knesset elections in 1977, 1981, 1984.

Begin respected and recognized their beliefs and traditions, and their way of life, their rich culture and their human dignity. He contributed enormously to their emancipation and elevation. He was also influenced, like in many other things, by Ze'ev Jabotinsky, who was the only Zionist leader of his stature to visit the Jews of Arab countries, such as Morocco, Algeria, Tunisia, Syria, Iraq, Lebanon, etc.

Jabotinsky showed interest also in the descendants of the exiles of Spain of 1492. He studied Judeo-Spanish, also called Ladino, so that he could converse with them in this dialect.

With the formation of the fighting group Irgun Tzvai Leumi, significant numbers of Sephardic Jews joined its ranks and distinguished themselves in the armed struggle.

Strengthened Religious Life

Menachem Begin, imbued with relgious spirit, with vast knowledge and deep understanding of Judaism, found a common language with religious Jewry in Israel and outside. It wasn't merely a political alliance, but a spiritual identification. Therefore a lasting one, with a significant imprint on the State. The present growth of Torah and of Torah Jewry in Israel is to a considerable measure a result of his blessed influence.

Invigorated Democracy

With his victory in the Knesset elections in 1977, Begin, maligned by his adversaries as a "fascist," strengthened and perhaps saved democracy in Israel. The long rule of the ruling party, Mapai, threatened to degenerate into a one-party regime. The achieving of power by Likud established a two-party (or multi-party) system similar to the regimes of the great Western Democracies of U.S.A., Britain, France, etc.

In view of the domination of the long ruling leftist party of all the areas of life in the country, this was no small achievement.

Begin mow lives in isolation. I am privileged to talk to him by phone and correspond with him. He is as vigorous and watchful as before. I am not going to speculate on the reasons of his seclusion. It reminds me of the great religious leaders who practiced *Hitbodeduth* (seclusion in Hebrew), which we have to recognize and respect.

Menachem Begin transformed the very sociological fabric and political structure of the State of Israel. Thus he is entitled to say with the Roman poet Horatius: Exegi monumentum aere perennius—"I created a monument everlasting."

The Jewish Press, N.Y. August 14, 1987

"No More War," Those Were Not Empty Words

Ten years since Sadat's visit to Jerusalem
on November 19, 1977.

The greatest achievement of Menachem Begin was that during the ten years since Anwar Sadat's visit to Jerusalem on November 19, 1977 not a single Jewish soldier fell on the Egyptian-Israeli border.

Historians, newspapermen, statesmen and politicians will define the event as an epochal breakthrough, a beginning of a new era.

But knowing Menachem Begin, his deep concern for every child or youth, in fact, for the life of every human being, I am convinced that, today, when he looks back at the past ten years, the fact that there was not one war casualty in the period of 1977–1987 on the Egyptian-Israeli border, will be considered by him as the dominant accomplishment of his peace efforts, perhaps of his premiership.

There were many persons, facts and factors, events and circumstances, which contributed cumulatively to the Egyptian-Israeli Peace Treaty of March 1979. The determinant generator of the long and tortuous process that led to this historic milestone was Menachem Begin.

It was Begin's courageous initiative that persuaded the Romanian President Ceaucescu during a visit to Romania, and the King of Morocco (through Dayan), to induce Sadat to consider an understanding with Israel. Begin moved boldly and swiftly to respond to the Egyptian's rhetoric flourish (most considered it as no more than that) in his speech in the Parliament on November 9, 1977, to go to Israel in order to promote peace.

When Sadat's offer reached Israel, most people, including seasoned politicians and experts, were skeptical and suspicious. Moshe Dayan, the Foreign Minister, and Ezer Weitzman, the Defense Minister, who later took the unassuming role as "the sole Champion of peace," were disdainful of Sadat's bombastic, flashy oratory. Motti Gur, the Chief of Staff of the Israeli Army, warned against a dangerous betrayal.

But their suspicions were quelled by Begin's quick, bold and clear positive response: "Begin finally shed all doubt and skepticism and wholeheartedly favored the visit," wrote Dayan. "He realized its value as a first step in the march to peace and as an act of historic importance." (*Moshe Dayan: Breakthrough*, p. 76.)

Begin took a firm hold of Sadat's offer which others dismissed as not serious, not binding, and even frivolous and incongruous.

"Begin rose to the towering height of the occasion," writes Prof. Cruise O'Brien in his excellent book *The Siege* (Simon & Schuster, NY 1986, p. 574).

We may add: and he never descended from this height in spite of many pitfalls and attacks. Whether offering to relinquish the Sinai to Egypt, or resisting any attempt to deprive Israel of vital territories and security guarantees, he stood, unflinching, at the peace process.

This stubborn stance earned him vituperation and denigration from many quarters, including Jewish ones. But with the same courage he sacrificed for the sake of peace, Sinai and its valuable military air-bases and settlements (Yamit). he successfully withstood the most powerful pressures.

He was the powerful prime mover of the chain of events which eventually led to the momentous act of signing the Peace Treaty between Israel and Egypt.

Of course, there were and there still are difficulties, disillusionment, disappointment and suspicion, and may yet be some in the future. But, in spite of all this, one overwhelming fact must not be obscured: since the pronouncement "No More War," there was no more war between Egypt and Israel—these were not empty words!

When all the turmoil of these past years is weighed against the pain of bereaved parents of fallen soldiers, the frictions and disappointments pale by comparison. Sinai, and all the disenchantments that afflicted the tenuous relations between the two countries, are a small price to pay for the fact that there were no more casualties. It is incomparably more worthwhile to abandon some territories than give up lives.

As in many other instances, the role of Begin was distorted, falsified and diminished. Most praise was heaped on his Egyptian partner. True, Sadat performed the dramatic feat by his visit to Jerusalem. But Begin's were the long prosaic efforts, the painful sacrifices, all less flamboyant but no less daring.

There, too, we witnessed something paradoxical. The man decried as terrorist, as a war monger, as extremist, showed himself to be the man of peace, ready for great sacrifices to achieve peace. Dayan said before that "better Sharm el Sheikh without peace than peace without Sharm el Sheikh."

Shimon Peres said recently that if he would have been prime Minister at the time he would have kept the air-forces bases and the settlements. Perhaps. But then there would have been no Peace Treaty. Besides, why is he now inclined to territorial concessions in exchange for peace?

Many benefits were derived from the peace with Egypt. Some are related to the war in Lebanon, for example. Now let us imagine if there had been no peace with Egypt, the front would have then been two-pronged—from the north and from the south; and Jordan with Iraq might have joined it. How many casualties would the Israeli Army have suffered?

On this 10th anniversary of the Sadat visit let us recall the Saturday night of November 19, 1977 in Israel, when it seemed that half of Israel, and the whole leadership, was at the airport, and the other half was glued to television screens, as were untold Jews the world over. Following that came the Camp David accords celebration on September 17, 1978 in the White House, and eventually the climactic signing of the Treaty of Peace between Egypt and Israel at the White House on March 26, 1979.

Begin, after leaving the government and the public scene is looked upon as a man of many facets and faces. But there is no split personality in his character. His whole life was devoted to the defense of his people. If diplomacy is another way of war, according to Clausewitz, it cannot be deprived of its prime and essential task—to avoid war. When the British Mandate administration in Palestine and the London government waged a vicious war, a pitiless onslaught against the remainder of the slaughtered Jewish people in Europe, denying them a home in their homeland, Begin fought a courageous, heroic war against the English occupiers of Palestine.

But when he was elected to head the government of Israel, achieving peace was his top priority. And when he glimpsed an opportunity to realize this most cherished dream, he seized the moment with all his strength, and achieved the peace treaty with the greatest and most powerful Arab country, and as a result, since then, not one Israeli soldier lost his life on the southern border.

Today Menachem Begin can look back upon this Egyptian treaty as his greatest accomplishment while heading the government of Israel.

The Jewish Press, N.Y. November 20, 1987

On the Occasion of Menachem Begin's 75th Birthday

Suppressing the Truth About the IZL

The WZO-Jewish Agency dispensed many favors and large sums for propaganda. They built an enormous apparatus that spewed vicious defamation to discredit IZL. A well-oiled machine of hired scribes inundated the kept press with defamatory falsehoods about these idealistic, heroic fighters locked in a bloody battle with the oppressor.

A number of Anglo-Jewish papers were subsidized by the WZO and Jewish Agency. There was a particular relationship between the Jewish press media and the establishment—based mostly on interests. These organs were used to attack the IZL in most vicious vituperations. "Fascist" was only one of the frequent epithets used to malign the freedom-fighters.

Rewriting History

Mapai, which dominated the Zionist movement for a long period, has historical merits for creation of the Jewish state, for which they deserve full credit.

However, the vast propaganda machine of the movement also endeavored, and to a large extent succeeded, to rewrite history from its narrow partisan outlook.

Thus it has taken 40 years of rewriting history to pervert the truth and distort the facts. A good percentage of the historians were propagandists dependent on the left-wing establishment, which dominated all sectors of the political, social, economic and cultural life of the country, including the halls of academe.

Many political scientists (not a few of whom were more politicians than scientists) were fanatically antagonistic to the IZL.

Recently, however, a scholarly book was authored on the question of what compelled the British to leave Palestine. This is answered thoroughly and convincingly by Dr. Yosef Nedava in his Hebrew work, *What Caused the British to Leave Eretz Yisrael?*

The manuscript was kindly made available to me by Mr. Yechiel Kadishai, Menachem Begin's closest friend and aide. Having encountered so many misrepresentations of the subject, I found Nedava's book to be like a breath of fresh air, since it breathes the truth—the undiluted historical truth.

Dr. Nedava makes use of new sources and archival material that have only recently become available., in order to explain why the British Empire, still at the height of its power in 1947, surprisingly abandoned its crucial position in the Middle East. Dr. Nedava reaches the incontestable conclusion: The British were forced out of *Eretz Yisrael* by the Irgun, led by Menachem Begin.

This eminent historian avoids any trace of polemics in his research. He does not foist his opinions on the reader nor does he assume the role of judge in the court of history.

Instead, he investigates and presents the case like the lawyer he is (JD, University of London), drawing upon an impressive list of witnesses to substantiate his findings: Winston Churchill, Franklin D. Roosevelt, Cordell Hull, Ernest Bevin, Clement Atlee, Lord Moyne, and Lord Cunningham—the last British High Commissioner in Palestine.

On May 16, 1948, Dr. Azriel Carlebach, then editor of the *Maariv*, wrote an editorial under the heading, Menachem Begin, *Ata Schichrarta!* (Menachem Begin, you liberated.)

Forty years later a wealth of documents, among them the mentioned book by Dr. Nedava, establish the irrefutable truth that it was the Irgun Zvai Leumi, led by Menachem Begin which forced the British out of Palestine, making possible the emergence of the State of Israel.

The Jewish Press, N.Y. August 19, 1988

Renewed Attacks On Menachem Begin

There appears to be no end in sight to the stream of distortions of the person of Menachem Begin and his role in our contemporary history. But while until now this unsavory work has been carried out by hired propagandists and unprincipled publicists, echoing each other's hackneyed falsifications, lately, a new breed of Begin "experts" has emerged: distortionists under the masks of "scholars," pseudo-historians and so-called political scientists who parade the usual credentials of university lecturers, researchers and other marginal appendages of the academic underworld.

One, Sasson Sofer, for example, published a voluminous work in this vein under the deceptively objective title, Menachem Begin: An Anatomy of Leadership (Basil Blackwell, Oxford, 1988). The author accumulates and assembles, with a diligence more suited to worthier causes, an abundance of falsifications and vilifications, culled from the tabloid newspapers and the calumnnitory and libelous leaflets and pamphlets o the party hacks and apparatchiks of the Jewish Agency-Zionist Organization and other professional slanderers and shameless muckrakers serving the leftist establishment.

Mr. Sofer clothes these mean insinuations and outrageous utterances in an "academic" babble designed to deceive the unsuspecting reader into believing that he is revealing the results of serious scholarship rather than merely reshuffling the usual phrases and juggling the same senseless and baseless maligning.

All these obfuscations and distortions have one essential aim: to deny and defuse the enormous beneficial impact of Menachem Begin's personality and leadership.

This historical truth has simply been considered unacceptable; thus mountains of printed trash continue to be produced in an effort to bury and erase the undeniable facts.

Sofer's naming of his pastiche "Anatomy of Leadership," is, like the work itself, subversively misleading. The proper title should be "Anatomy of an Academic Fraud." The book opens with an outright

libel. In the preface Sofer accuses Begin of ordering the bombing of the
Iraqi nuclear reactor (designed to produce atom bombs to be used against
Israel) for the sole purpose of winning votes in the upcoming parliamen-
tary elections! Sofer writes:

June 7, 1981. Prime Minister Begin sent Israel's airforce to bomb Iraq's
nuclear reactor. Within a few months he had won an election in which he
had appeared to face a certain defeat (p. VII).

Even in the rough-and-tumble Israeli elections no one of consequence
had dared to impute to Begin such a monstrous deed—to endanger the Israeli airforce with such a perilous mission, fraught with far-reaching mortal
risks—as a campaign trick!

This *magnum opus* is a product of a great number of professors and
commentators who contributed to the research work, which was lavishly
subsidized by the Leonard Davis Institute for International Relations and
the Research Fund of the Faculty at the Hebrew University!

There is no doubt in my mind that not a few of the individuals and institutions involved in this work deliberately and consciously intended to support and abet Mr. Sofer's endeavors to blacken the activities and
accomplishments of Menachem Begin in the emergence of the Jewish State,
and to pervert the public perception of his decisive and lasting historical
role. But certainly there must be others who are embarrassed and even
ashamed of their part in a work about whose purpose they may have been
misled.

We wouldn't grace this deceitful publication with our attention if it
weren't for the sad fact that it is far from a singular phenomenon, Sofer
is only one marcher among the dismal parade of biased leftist writers
posing as "historians" and "political scientists." Their "scholarly"
camouflage cannot hide their essential similarity to the woefully familiar
publicists and propagandists of the old and new left. They misuse their
titles and chairs to validate their rewriting of history in the manner of the
Kremlin. More specifically, they persist in attempting to rewrite the history of the Irgun Zvai Leumi, the Lechi and their leaders.

As they realize that the influence of Menachem Begin's ideas and
achievements did not vanish with his voluntarily leaving the political scene,
these decades-long hateful adversaries are continuing to labor to erase the
indelible stamp that this leader left on our people, changing the course of
history.

We must not allow this to happen.

The Jewish Press, N.Y. December 30, 1988

Ten Years Later

On March 26, 1979, the peace treaty between Israel and Egypt was signed at the White House. Today, from the perspective of ten years later, let us have a look at this momentous event.

Historical happenings are like high mountains. As long as we stand near them, as we dwell under their shadows, we cannot see their tremendous height. Only from afar are we able to perceive their true greatness. Thus, only now, ten years after, are we able to grasp the enormous significance of this historical occurrence.

This treaty, the only one so far between Israel and an Arab state, has been an enormous achievement. True, we know its shortcomings. We know disillusionments and deceptions. The treaty and its accompanying commentaries talked a lot about "normalization" of relations between the two countries. Most of these hopes have not borne fruit. Economic relations, two-way tourism, cooperation in many areas have not become a reality.

However, there is one outstanding fact which overshadows all the others. During the past ten years, not a single Israeli soldier has fallen on the Egyptian-Israeli border.

Knowing Menachem Begin's deep sensitivity to human life; aware of his overriding concern during his heroic fight against the British oppressors, for the safety of the fighters and of his efforts to avoid unnecessary casualties on the British side as well, I am sure that this factor plays a decisive role in his appreciation of the peace treaty's importance.

During these ten years, there have been clashes, bloodshed and skirmishes between Israel and its Arab neighbors. In the north, there was the Lebanon war. Imagine what would have happened if at the same time there would have been a conflagration of hostilities on all fronts, in particular at Israel's southern border, with the biggest and most powerful Arab state, Egypt, and Iraq, Syria and Jordan joining the battle.

On September 17, 1988, the 10th anniversary of the Camp David Agreement, I called Menachem Begin and congratulated him on his achievement. "This was," I said, "one of your finest hours."

Usually, in my calls to Begin, I avoid political remarks. I respect his self-imposed "reserve." But this time I took the liberty of sharing with him a thought on the subject. Where did I take this liberty? From Rashi. The Torah says: "many (of the Jews) may die (if they ascend Mt. Sinai)." Rashi comments, "G-d said: 'Even if one dies, I consider it like many.' " (*Exodus* XIX, 22)

Accordingly, Begin's sensitivity to life and his ardent efforts to end bloodshed, as expressed in his role a\in the Camp David Agreement, made it one of Menachem Begin's finest hours.

I am going to call Begin again next Sunday, March 26 and repeat my evaluation of this glorious act as one of his greatest achievements.

There were, and still are, many ways to rob Begin of the credit for this accomplishment. In addition to the unbridled enmity toward him by propagandists of the leftist establishment, there is another motive. Begin was described by his detractors as a war monger, a dangerous fanatic inciting hatred and bloodshed. Now, as soon as he reached the helm of the government, his first and most tremendous effort was to achieve peace with Israel's Arab neighbors, even at the cost of considerable sacrifices—of relinquishing vast territories with the strategic and economic values, such as the military air bases in the Sinai, the Rhodes oil wells, and some Jewish settlements.

This gave lie to most of the distortions and falsehoods about Begin.

Partisan "historians" and "political scientists" (most are more politicians than scientists. . .) tried to diminish and distort Begin's place in the peace process. They have attributed the main role to Anwar Sadat, describing Sadat's visit to Jerusalem as his own stroke of genius.

Nothing could be farther from the truth. This extraordinary visit was the result of a scrupulously thought-out plan conceived by the Israeli Prime Minister and executed meticulously under his careful supervision. Begin had to overcome enormous difficulties and opposition, including that of the Labor leadership, ostensibly committed to peace efforts.

One episode will illustrate this strange development. In the Knesset debate on the Camp David Agreement, the leader of the Labor Party, Shimon Peres, severely criticized the agreement. In his opinion, the evacuation of the Sinai Settlements could have been avoided; the agreement, he warned, would lead eventually to a Palestine state. Nevertheless, Labor voted for the government resolution. It could not do otherwise, as loathsome as Begin's triumph was for them.

All the Knesset members voted—the only time this has ever happened!— 84 in favor, 19 against, and 17 abstaining.

An illustration. At Camp David, Begin did not make the decision to accept the treaty. Rather, he committed himself to put it before the Knesset.

President Carter, mindful of Begin's hard bargaining, convinced of his "inflexibility," was afraid that in submitting the resolution the Knesset, Begin would present in such a way that would influence Knesset members negatively. Thus, Carter asked him to be neutral in his presentation to the Knesset, not to speak at the debate.

What happened was this: as steadfast as Begin was in his convictions and positions at Camp David, once it was agreed upon he threw the full weight of his authority—then at its peak—behind the agreement.

True, no Prime Minister rules alone, and certainly not one of Begin's ilk.

The roles of the Foreign Minister, Moshe Dayan, and the Defense Minister, Ezer Weitzman, were significant. And so the intensive work of the gifted and dedicated aides, such as Meir Rosenne, the chief Legal Advisor, Yechiel Kadishai, the Prime Minister's devoted secretary, Eliyakim Rubenstein, Judge Aron Barak, as well as Naftali Lavie, Dayan's spokesman, and others. But the driving force behind all these efforts was Menachem Begin.

Today, on the 10th anniversary of the Peace Treaty, Israel is surrounded by a sea of openly hostile coalitions and hypocritical "peace seekers"; the Western European democracies, the Scandanavian governments of Count Folke Bernadotte's "school," as well as the Kremlin and its satellites, and the Third World countries—all these abetted and aided by biased one-sided attitudes of the media.

From this perspective and from the distance of a decade, we have to celebrate this event as a tremendous achievement of the State of Israel, and one of Menachem Begin's finest hours.

The Jewish Press, N.Y. March 31, 1989

During his visit to New York over a year after he had assumed the office of Prime Minister of Israel, Menachem Begin reassured Jewish Leaders in America that he would never allow any division of Jerusalem. He is shown here embracing the author, Dr. Hillel Seidman, at the Regency Hotel. Looking on is Hugh Carey, Governor of New York.

Britain, You Have A Choice Between Being Cyrus Or Titus!

A moving address by Dr. Hillel Seidman at a caucus of the members of the House of Commons in Westminster, December 12, 1945 (from the press).

BRITAIN to-day has a choice of roles in her attitude towards Jews—to be a Cyrus or a Titus, said Dr. Hillel Seidman, a delegate from Paris to the Agudah Conference, addressing a private meeting of Members of Parliament and others, called by Miss Eleanor Rathbone, last week.

Dr. Seidman, a well-known historian and one of the few survivors of the Warsaw ghetto, who has made a tour of the camps in Germany, declared that the Jews in these camps were suffering from shortage of food, lack of heating and perhaps most of all—disillusionment.

"When the Jews were liberated seven months ago, weakened and emaciated as they were, they were sustained by hope. Their eyes were turned to Great Britain who they believed would redeem her promises and would enable them to find a home in Palestine. But Britain's actions had gone far to extinguish their belief in her."

Dr. Seidman declared that only in the British zone were the Jews not given separate accommodation, and what was more they were housed together with Poles. It was also the only zone to which it was forbidden to bring extra food from outside—lest the Germans should go short.

Discussing conditions in Poland he pointed out that the majority of the Poles had remained anti-semites and the good-will of the Government was no compensation to the Jews now being attacked and forced to go to Germany as a temporary refuge. Even Communists coming from Poland were proclaiming their desire to go to Palestine.

27/12/45

"HABOKER" DAILY NEWSPAPER   TEL-AVIV   עתון יומי   תל־אביב

«כורש או טיטוס – בחרו!»

הלל זיידמן באספת צירי בית־הנבחרים

– בדואר־אויר, מלונדון –

–ביזמת צירת ביה״נ הבריטי מיס אליאנור רטבון, נערכה באחד מאולמי
ביה״נ ישיבת צירים אנגלים שבקשו לשמע על המצב במחנות הפליטים בגרמניה.
סופר "הבוקר" מר הלל זיידמן, אשר חזר זה לא מכבר מסיור ממושך במחנות
בגרמניה היה (כפי שכבר נמסר סלגרפיה) המרצה בשאלה זו. בעתונות האנגלית
נמסרו פרטים על ההרצאה וצוין כי סייר במחנות כסופר "הבוקר" הארצישראלי.
יש שהכתירו את דבריו בפסוקו: "כורש או טיטוס — בחרו!"-

275

Words Timely and For Generations To Come

Preface to the publication of the address by Menachem Begin in the
Knesset, February 9, 1970 (translated and published
by Rabbi Noah Chodos, Esq.).

In this address, which we present to the reader, Menachem Begin rose to his finest hour at the very same time when people of high standing showed deterioration and nearsightedness in degrading what is holy to our people.

At the time when the ugly wave of "progressives," leftists, Canaanites, and others who dropped all reins pose the threat of swamping us; at a time when some come up "spewing obscenity and saying without hesitation that the Jewish Halacha is racist: that it reminds them of Nazism"; at a time when Jews brought out a blood libel, the libel concocted by our very selves (there), at that very time Minister Menachem Begin jumped into the breach, his loud voice booming from the rostrum of the Knesset, into the ears of his detractors: "Woe to the ears that hear this!"

In the face of a general attack on our foundations he spoke words based on our foundations, and he fortified and buttressed these foundations.

The man who unstintingly proffered his life in the struggle with a foreign, hostile and plotting government in our land, the man who became one of the decisive factors in the creation of the State of Israel' who prevented a civil war at one time and stood as the pivotal column in the cause of national dignity and national unity at another time—both such times fateful in our history—the man who now stands like a wall defying defeatism and retreat—that very man also rose like a wall against those who proposed to tear down from the inside the walls of our besieged fortress.

When the song of praise of the Halacha was not heard from the lips of the leader of the official Orthodox Party, but the man who stands for oneness and unity, all conflicts between the religious and worldly blocks, leading to a dangerous split, immediately stopped.

At a time when others set the fires of hate to the sacred values of our Nation and to those who man the guard, at a time of siege, Menachem Begin rose to defend and to bring relief. In reading the address presented here, we feel his burning faith and his deep sadness at the plight of the downgrading of everything that is hallowed and sacred to us; and yet, despite this burning fire, he nourished his with wisdom and a knowledge of the sources, and he presented them with moderation.

Dr. Hillel Seidman

New York, New York, Eve of Passover in the year 5730
April 20, 1970

The Author Helped Revisionists in the Warsaw Ghetto

Excerpt of the book The Warsaw Fortress by Haim Lazar (Hebrew), Tel-Aviv, 1943, p. 85:

In one of the days of 1940, we gathered in the office of Dr. Hillel Seidman. Present also were Dr. Michael Strikowsky and Dr. Lipman Propes. Dr. Strikowsky said: "We must start a defense against the Germans."

[The abovementioned were leaders of the Revisionists and resistance.]

A Historical Document

Foreword to the publication of the address by Prime Minister Menachem Begin at the Nobel Peace Prize ceremony, Oslo, December 10, 1978.

This memorable address of one of the great orators of our time reflects main currents of the present Jewish condition—and beyond. Yet the uniqueness of this pronouncement was ironically somewhere eclipsed by the very events of which this speech was one of the most significant. This oration seems to share the lot of another historical speech, the Gettysburg Address, which too, failed in its time to gain immediate recognition.

It is my deep conviction that the full meaning of the happenings which led to the signing of the Peace Treaty between Israel and Egypt, on March 26, 1979, at the White House can be best perceived by careful reading, and delving beneath the surface, of these stirring words spoken by Prime Minister Menachem Begin in accepting the Nobel Prize for Peace in Solo, Norway, on December 10, 1978.

This address, Like Lincoln's, is destined to become a classic. Therefore, it must be valued as a text worthy of study by young and old, as a source of inspiration and perception. Indeed, it has been recommended by major Jewish educational organizations that it be taught and studies in schools as a historical document by a man who made history, and in order to comprehend history.

Through these words, his character so much maligned and his intentions so often misinterpreted come out in their innermost truth and glory. He was motivated not by a desire of power but by power of desire, desire for freedom and for peace.

He proved that he is worthy of the prize. His was, as by now firmly established, the proverbial first step on the staggering thousand-mile journey on the tortuous road which led to the signing of the Treaty, and trustfully, making it a reality.

"A brand plucked from the fire" of the German mass slaughter of the Jews in Europe, Begin came out from the depth below the depth not crushed by despair but strengthened by determination. He emerged from the epoch; when the Jews' right simply to live was denied. The world was then divided in its attitude toward Jews, in two camps. One put them to death; the other refused them help to stay alive.

All the adjustment and adaptation by the Jews to the peoples among whom they dwelt for centuries did not gain them the right to live.

The catastrophe darkened the horizon, but not the perception, of Menachem Begin. His mind became even more lucid, more clairvoyant. His thought turned inward. His view of the world grew more penetrating and—realistic. Illusions disappeared but visions were not dimmed.

Like his great teacher Ze'ev Jabotinsky, Begin harkened to the awful thunder of the erupting volcano. He drew the conclusions. He alerted the Jewish people to the new dangers and warned against acquiescence. He believed that to succumb to evil *is* evil.

He defied injustice and challenged its power. He threw himself with almost bare fists against the still great might of the British Empire waging war against the remnants of the mass killings who were striving for a home for their Jewish Homeland.

The anguish and agony of a generation was transformed by him into the cataclysm of Revolt. His words sounded the clarion for the battle for freedom for the Jewish people and their land. "Shall the clarion be blown in the city and the people shall not tremble?" (Amos III, 6). They did. Begin's call molded idealistic youth into phalanxes of self-sacrificing fighters. Thus he reshaped his time, his people and his destiny.

He gave new directions to the course of Jewish history. By winning the trust of the Nation which put him at its helm. By opening the gates of peace.

In each of these endeavors he was on the side of the future. He made the future happen. At the same time he was always moved by the spirit of the glorious past, its ideals and visions.

This great speech of the last of the epoch orators giants may be considered a blueprint for his sacred mission of peace. Certain single steps or gestures of his may be slighted by his many critics but in the overall entirety, of his mission and in the aftermath of its results and repercussions, the pieces fall into place as part of a wee-conceived architectural plan.

It is the final goal that counts. According to Hassidic teaching, Redemption is not a single event. It is a continuation of purposeful deeds. Each may be an act in the drama.

The tornado whirlwind of our turbulent epoch hurled Menachem Begin four decades ago to the rudder of the Revolt for Jewish statehood. It brought him, through the admirable working of the Israeli democratic process, to the helm as the new pilot steering the ship of State toward peace. His Oslo oration reflects the drama he generated.

These graceful cadences not only charm with splendor and grandeur but, even more, with the integrity and the authenticity of a man who hates war and longs for peace. Let me finish with an excerpt of a letter addressed to me on February 26, 1979 by the Chief Rabbi of Great Britain, Harav Immanuel Jakobovits on the Oslo speech:

This is indeed a notable document, worthy of the historic occasion prompting its delivery. Blending the aspirations for universal peace rooted in our Prophetic heritage with the current striving for peace rooted in the Holy Land, and suffused by an idealism of truly Biblical fervor, the speech certainly merits close study and wide circulation. It gives noble expressions to profoundly Jewish sentiments of hope and faith in the ultimate triumph of peace as our highest ideal, whilst also stressing the struggle needed to turn this ideal into reality.

In constantly praying for the Peace of Jerusalem, millions sustain Mr. Begin's efforts to bring decades of bloodshed and hostility to an end and to the beginning of a new era of tranquility. once he achieves this, he will enter Jewish history as one of its most singular luminaries, combining the achievements of David with the peace of Solomon. May that be his ultimate award, transcending all others.

This publication was made possible by Mr. Shragai Cohen, a close longtime friend of Mr. Begin, and by Mr. Sol Weinreich of the Noble offset Printers, New York, who followed a precedent: he printed free another speech by Mr. Begin, "Jew—Nation and Religion," of February 9, 1970, in the Knesset.

Hillel Seidman
May 2, 1979
Israel's Independence Day

Some Thoughts About This Book

by Mordecai Schreiber

Like Dr. Seidman, I too am not a member of Begin's political movement. I was born and educated in Haifa, known as the "red city," because it was always dominated by socialist Zionism and by the Histadrut, the leading labor union in Israel. My father was associated with the Histadrut and the Haganah from the day he came to Palestine from his native Poland in 1931. He did not, however, vote labor, but rather General Zionists, to the "bourgeois" middle-of-the-road Zionist party. He taught me how to think independently. Though a secular Zionist, he had a deep respect for the Jewish religion. Though a member of the Haganah, he admired Begin and the Irgun. I suppose that unlike many of his friends and coworkers, he was not blinded by partisan politics—a common trend during the pre-state and early-state days—but was both a national and traditional Jew.

As a child growing up in Haifa, I remember seeing in 1949 (shortly after the establishment of the state) a group of Ha'Noar Ha'Oved (labor youth movement) young men assaulting a "ken," or small club house of Betar (Begin's youth organization) near my home on Arlozoroff Street, and completely destroying the modest furnishings of that one-room club. I also recall seeing Irgun teenagers in 1946 (a year before the birth of Israel) darting out of dark alleys into the main street of Haifa, Herzl Street, quickly pasting Irgun anti-British posters on the walls, and disappearing into the night. Invariably, labor vigilantes would show up and tear those fresh printed, wet posters off the wall.

And I recall, as a child, seeing the ragtag boats with Holocaust survivors arriving in Haifa harbor, and being sent back by the British to detention camps in Cyprus and even in Germany. And as a child, I recall my rage, expressed by a poet who was immensely popular at that time, named Natan Alterman, whose poems I would memorize ("When Our Children Wept in the Shadow of Gallows," "The Unvanquished Armada," and so on). And I recall that even in Laborite Haifa the words "Irgun" and "Begin" sounded like magic. Each time a boatload of refugees was sent back a bomb went off in my neighborhood, a British military vehicle went up in the air, and one day, around noon, the British oil refineries in Haifa were blown up, turning day into night, and people kept whispering rumors about a mysterious man who could not be found, who masterminded those operations, named Begin. The other mysterious figure, Avraham "Yair" Stern, founder of LEHI, had already been assassinated by the British.

For many years I have felt that Begin and his movement have been victims of unfair and biased treatment by the Zionist and Israeli establishment. I realize that I was born and raised in violent times, and much was done and said in the heat of great passions. Yet even now, as the State of Israel is approaching middle-age, a spate of books keeps appearing in Israel and elsewhere which continues to distort the image and career of Begin and his brand of Zionism. These books, written by prestigious professors and well-known journalists, are so full of distortions, half-truths, and malicious fallacies, that they poison the atmosphere and create a potential danger of misinforming those who, younger than myself, did not witness the aftermath of the Holocaust and the creation of the State of Israel, and are easy mark for this falsification of history.

This is why, when I was approached in the summer of 1989 by Dr. Hillel Seidman with the proposition of collaborating on a book about the legacy of Menachem Begin, I did not think twice—despite my heavy schedule—and agreed to put aside urgent projects and concentrate on this historical task.

I have known Dr. Seidman for many years. He is perhaps the "last of the Mohicans" of the political and intellectual leadership of the greatest Jewish community of the twentieth century—the Jewish community of Warsaw. He is not only a Holocaust survivor, but also a survivor of a glorious chapter in Jewish history— Jewish Warsaw of the twenties and thirties, the heart of the Jewish world at that time.

Few people in the world have known Menachem Begin for as long and as well as Dr. Seidman. Over the years, Seidman has written numerous articles in the Jewish press in Europe, Israel and the United States, in Polish, Yiddish, Hebrew and English explaining Begin and his cause, and giving the lie to his many critics.

THE CITY OF NEW YORK
OFFICE OF THE MAYOR
NEW YORK, N.Y. 10007

June 9, 1971

Dr. Hillel Seidman
1743 50th Street
Brooklyn, New York

Dear Dr. Seidman:

My best personal wishes to you on the occasion of your
election as President of the Beth Jacob Schools. This new
distinction is another chapter in a lifetime of dedicated
service to the Jewish people and the welfare of mankind
throughout the world.

The Beth Jacob Schools are outstanding educational
institutions that have contributed much to the preparation
of thousands of Jewish girls for lives of dedicated adherence
to the traditions of a great people. The growth of the Beth
Jacob Schools is symbolic of the vitality of New York Jews.
It is also an expression of commitment to New York City.

I know that you have the good wishes of all New Yorkers
as you undertake this new and challenging responsibility.
With best personal wishes.

Sincerely,

John V. Lindsay
MAYOR

Award to Dr. Hillel Seidman by Yeshiva University at the commencement exercises, June 4, 1984.

It is my privilege to present this year's award to Dr. Hillel Seidman, noted scholar, author, essayist, contributor to outstanding journals in our country and Israel, and an active proud and loyal Jew. The pen has been his sword, and he has defended the honor of our people with strength and pride, from the Ghetto of Warsaw to Turtle Bay. His most recent volume, among some 20 he has authored, in

English, "United Nations: Perfidy and Perversion," depicts in his distinctive and insightful style the pollution of honor and hate which befouls the atmosphere of international relations. It is a sad commentary on our times that it is a companion piece to his ,169Diary of the Warsaw Ghetto," published in Yiddish and Hebrew, an important documentary history of the Holocaust.

Dr. Seidman was born in Poland, studied at yeshivot, at the Institute for Judaic Studies and at the University of Warsaw, where he received his doctorate in history. He literally and figuratively remains the תלמיד חכם, the eternal student of the wise, whose own wisdom and knowledge is reflected in his weekly commentary on the Sedra, which is both learned and inspiring.

His commitment to the future of our faith, community and people is reflected in his support of Jewish education through the written word, and as president of the Board of the Beth Jacob Schools in New York and chairman of the American Committee of the Beth Jacob Seminary in Israel. He is an activist—for Israel, the people and the land—and for Yiddishkeit.

As with the sage Hillel, Dr. Hillel Seidman shuns honors.

נגיד שמא, אבד שמה

"He who seeks renown loses his name," but we are honored to have sought him out, and to honor him with the 1984 Mordecai Ben David Award, presented with our best wishes for a continued fruitful career.

Rabbi Israel Miller
Senior Vice-President,
Yeshiva University

May 18, 1972

Dear Dr. Seidman:

Word has reached me of your support for
the measures I announced on May 8 to bring
the fighting in Vietnam to an end, and I
want to tell you how much I appreciate
your encouragement.

As we all know, this has been the longest,
most difficult conflict in our nation's
history. All of us look forward to a
lasting, honorable peace. That day is
near -- and can surely be brought even
closer by two means. First, the enemy
must return our prisoners of war and
join in an internationally supervised
ceasefire. Second, a demonstration of
national unity will make unmistakably
clear to the world our commitment to
South Vietnam, our determination to
protect American servicemen there, and
our resolve to secure the release of
our prisoners.

Your comments play an important part in
this effort, and I am grateful for your
willingness to speak out.

With my best wishes,

Sincerely,

Richard Nixon

Daniel P. Moynihan
New York

United States Senate
Washington, D.C.

January 9, 1989

Dear Dr. Seidman,

   History shall record the invaluable role
you have played in so many of this century's
great moral causes. Your prescience and
tenacity in the matter of Kurt Waldheim have
earned you the abiding admiration of all Americans
who cherish human freedom and human dignity. I am
proud to be your friend and have long treasured
your sage counsel and unstinting support.

   May the Bestower of all Blessings grant you
many more vigorous years of advocacy and
accomplishment.

                    Sincerely,

                    Daniel Patrick Moynihan

Dr. Hillel Seidman
745 East 2nd Street
Brooklyn, New York 11218